Digital Justice

Digital Justice

Technology and the Internet of Disputes

ETHAN KATSH

ORNA RABINOVICH-EINY

Foreword by
Richard Susskind

OXFORD
UNIVERSITY PRESS

OXFORD
UNIVERSITY PRESS

Oxford University Press is a department of the University of Oxford. It furthers the University's objective of excellence in research, scholarship, and education by publishing worldwide. Oxford is a registered trademark of Oxford University Press in the UK and certain other countries.

Published in the United States of America by Oxford University Press
198 Madison Avenue, New York, NY 10016, United States of America.

Library of Congress Cataloging-in-Publication Data
Names: Katsh, M. Ethan, author. | Rabinovich-Einy, Orna, author.
Title: Digital justice : technology and the internet of disputes / Ethan Katsh and
    Orna Rabinovich-Einy ; foreword by Richard Susskind.
Description: New York : Oxford University Press, 2017. | Includes bibliographical
    references and index.
Identifiers: LCCN 2016051090 | ISBN 9780190464585 ((hardback) : alk. paper) |
    ISBN 9780190675677 ((pbk.) : alk. paper)
Subjects: LCSH: Law—Data processing. | Information technology—Law and
    legislation. | Technology and law. | Internet—Law and legislation. |
    Computer networks—Law and legislation. | Torts.
Classification: LCC K564.C6 .K38 2017 | DDC 347/.0902854678—dc23 LC record available at
https://lccn.loc.gov/2016051090

To Bev

To my parents, Efrat and Itamar Rabinovich

CONTENTS

ACKNOWLEDGMENTS

We are most grateful to the community of international Fellows of the National Center for Technology and Dispute Resolution (NCTDR), whose in-person and online conversations have contributed greatly to many of the ideas put forward in this book. They include Jeffrey Aresty (United States), David Bilinsky (Canada), Pablo Cortés (Great Britain), Benjamin Davis (United States), Dave deBronkart (United States), Alberto Elisavetsky (Argentina), Frank Fowlie (Canada), Sanjana Hattutowa (Sri Lanka), Ayo Kusamotu (Nigeria), David Larson (United States), Anyu (Andy) Lee (China), Zbynek Loebl (Czech Republic), Ian Macduff (New Zealand), Chittu Nagarajan (India), Ijeoma Ononogbu (Nigeria/Great Britain), Chris Peterson (United States), Daniel Rainey (United States), Vikki Rogers (United States), Fernando Esteban de la Rosa (Spain) Graham Ross (Great Britain), Colin Rule (United States), Irene Sigismondi (Italy), Gabriela Szlak (Latin America), Jin Ho Verdonschot (Netherlands), Aura Esther Vilalta (Spain), Mohamed S. Abdel Wahab (Egypt), and, most important, Co-director Leah Wing.

We are particularly thankful to those who read the whole manuscript or one or more chapters. These include Sagit Mor, Niva Elkin-Koren, Faina Milman-Sivan, Tal Zarsky, Arianne Renan-Barzilay, Yair Sagy, Talia Fisher, Michael Birnhack, Assaf Jacob, Itai Brun, and Chris Peterson. We received feedback from attendees at the Colloquium on Law, Society & Technology at the Haifa Law Faculty, the Law and Information Technology Workshop at the Tel Aviv University Law Faculty, the Works in Progress in ADR conference hosted at Cardozo Law School, and presentations made at the International Online Dispute Resolution conferences hosted at The Hague Institute for Innovations in Law (HiiL), the University of International Business and Economics in Beijing, and Hastings, Stanford, Pace, and University of Montreal Law Schools. Many thanks to the following who granted us the opportunity for interviews: Shannon Salter and Darin Thompson, Maurits Barendrecht, J. J. Prescott, M.J. Cartwright, Colin

Rule, and Zbynek Loebl; and for ongoing advice from Carrie Menkel-Meadow, Nancy Welsh, Michal Alberstein and Moti Mironi, all of whose input was significant in the development of our thinking on novel justice systems.

Our research efforts have benefited from assistance provided by Daniel Rainey and Harry Hoglander of the National Mediation Board, Jeff Aresty of the Internet Bar Organization and Peacetones, Prashila Dullabh of NORC, Jodi Daniels and her colleagues at the Office of National Coordinator of the U.S. Department of Health and Human Services, Norm Sondheimer, Lee Osterweil and Lori Grant, our colleagues at the University of Massachusetts on several National Science Foundation grants, opportunities provided by the Fulbright Program and the United States–Israel Educational Foundation, and the universities of Haifa and Massachusetts. We appreciate our association with Karim Benyekhlef, Fabien Gélinas, and the University of Montreal Law School Cyberjustice Project, the opportunity to observe firsthand the ODR internet start-ups Modria, Youstice, and SquareTrade, and the HiiL *Rechtwijzer* and British Columbia Civil Resolution Tribunal projects. We are most grateful to the faculty, fellows, and staff of the Berkman Klein Center for Internet and Society at Harvard University for a year spent as a Research Affiliate in 2014–2015.

Special gratitude to Nico Pfund, Alex Flach and Alden Domizio at Oxford University Press for their support and encouragement and to Irene Natan, Justin Rostoff, Hanne Tidman-Winarsky, and Rachel Ran for the research and editorial assistance they provided. Our gratitude to Richard Susskind for his intellectual support as well as for contributing the Foreward to this book. Lastly, our appreciation of our families, Beverly, Rebecca, Gabriel, Gideon, Jordan, Abby, Sarah, and Ari and Uri, Ella, Roy, Ido, and Iris for inspiring us.

FOREWORD

Modern court systems in both civil and common law jurisdictions can be traced directly to bodies that came into being roughly one thousand years ago. While much has changed in the intervening millennium, many of today's court processes and sometimes even the buildings themselves have not been altered greatly since the nineteenth century.

It is an uncomfortable truth that court systems around the world are creaking—they are too costly and slow, and they are unintelligible for the great majority of non-lawyers. More, these paper-based institutions appear increasingly outmoded in a society in which so much daily activity is enabled by the internet and advanced technology. Conceived in the Dark Ages and reformed in the nineteenth century, these court systems became unfit for many purposes in the late twentieth century. Now they seem destined, if unchanged, to be inappropriate for most disputes of the twenty-first. While it was seditious to make such allegations in the 1980s, many policymakers, judges, and lawyers around the world are now alive to the shortcomings of our courts. And there seems to be a growing worldwide appetite for comprehensive overhaul.

There have, of course, been calls for reform in the past. For decades now, supporters of ADR (alternative dispute resolution) have promoted non-court-based methods for resolving disputes, such as mediation, conciliation, and early neutral evaluation. But ADR has delivered mixed results and its long-term impact looks unlikely to be fundamental. In contrast, those who advocate ODR (online dispute resolution) look set to have greater traction. Indeed, there are signs that work in this field will reshape tomorrow's court systems.

It is timely, therefore, that *Digital Justice*, by Ethan Katsh and Orna Rabinovich-Einy, now appears on our shelves and tablets. The authors are ideally placed to have taken on the job of writing what is an accessible and yet definitive account of ODR. Ethan is an all-time star in the world of academic legal technology, and an undoubted pioneer in ODR. In joining forces with Orna, an authority on both ADR and ODR, they make a formidable team. They are also *mensches*—it is gratifying when nice people produce outstanding books.

In the words of the authors, the book shows "not only how technology generates disputes of all types—some serious, some just annoying—but how technology can be employed to resolve and prevent them." The first part of the book focuses on the history and development of online dispute resolution (it is remarkable, as they observe, that the first ODR conference was held as long ago as 1996), while the second highlights five areas that are argued to be in particular need of ODR—e-commerce, healthcare, social media, employment, and the courts. They conclude that online dispute resolution and prevention activities can be extended to enhance access to justice, both online and offline.

Crucial insights are peppered across the pages. The authors show, for example, why traditional dispute resolution and ADR do not work in the digital era. They place great emphasis on processes that help prevent disputes as well as resolve them. They note that disputes arise in 3–5 percent of online transactions, totaling over seven hundred million e-commerce disputes in 2015 alone. They anticipate a future in which increasingly capable machines will use large bodies of data to enable or suggest solutions to parties and, more distantly, when human intervention in disputes will be substituted by algorithms.

Digital Justice comes to us at a pivotal moment in the evolution of court systems. Not long ago, ODR was the preoccupation of but a small group of visionaries and academics. In many countries, debate about online courts is suddenly in the mainstream. For England and Wales, to take one example, the U.K. government has recently confirmed that the modernization and digitization of our courts will be financially supported to the tune of more than £700 million. Much of this investment is to be in online courts. And the senior judiciary is highly supportive.

Nonetheless, in the broader context of the history of law, the spirit of ODR remains bold. Judges without courtrooms, justice without lawyers, court as a service and not a place—these are radical aspirations. It is no surprise, then, that ODR has its detractors. Tellingly, many of the naysayers are lawyers who raise objections in the name of justice and in the interests of their clients. ODR, it is claimed, will deliver a second-class form of justice for those of limited means; it will not provide a fair trial; it will alienate the digitally deprived; it is driven by an unhealthy preoccupation with cost reduction; and it is really an attempt to exclude lawyers. These are important challenges, but they are advanced too often by lawyers who have not taken the time to road test the technology and study its actual impact so far. All critics should read this book. Many of their understandable fears will be allayed.

Meanwhile, we should be wary of wholesale rejection of ODR. Claims of inaccess to justice, it transpires, are often smoke screens for self-preservation on the part of lawyers (consciously or unconsciously). Nostalgically, they hanker after the Rolls Royce service that today's finest court systems can doubtless deliver. But that is a service that is now affordable only for a very few, and everyone else is left to walk. We need an accessible and reasonably priced system for all, and I have found a no more promising option for that future than that offered by various types of ODR. Lawyers should surely be the pioneers in upgrading justice rather than standing in the way of processes that, as Ethan and Orna so compellingly show, are great improvements on what we have today.

I wish this work the very great success that it deserves.

Professor Richard Susskind
President, Society for Computers and Law
IT Adviser to the Lord Chief Justice of England and Wales

Introduction

It is hard to imagine a machine handling a complaint.
—Comment in James Gleick, *What Just Happened: A Chronicle from the Information Frontier*

In January 2007, Dave deBronkart was diagnosed with stage IV kidney cancer, a condition which, at the time, had a median survival rate of twenty-four weeks. He immediately underwent surgery and became a participant in a clinical drug trial. DeBronkart, who was employed in the computer industry, also became a determined "e-patient,"[1] using any and all online resources that might help his treatment and help him cope with his condition. It worked. DeBronkart became a technology-focused cancer survivor, an active blogger on an e-patient website,[2] and, a year later, co-chair of the Society for Participatory Medicine.[3]

The hospital that provided his medical care—Beth Israel Deaconess Medical Center in Boston—had been a pioneer in providing patients with online access to their medical records.[4] In early 2009, deBronkart took advantage of a new feature that allowed him to upload his medical data into an electronic health-record system called Google Health.[5] The Beth Israel system was not linked electronically to other area hospital systems. If, for example, he had needed to see a doctor at Massachusetts General Hospital a few miles away, deBronkart would have had to print out his file and carry it over. The attraction of Google Health was that it allowed deBronkart to keep all his medical data, from any system or physician, in one place, accessible anywhere.

Almost immediately after deBronkart's data was copied into the Google Health system, the Google site reported to him that his cancer had spread to his spine, that he had chronic lung disease, and many other illnesses and conditions.[6] A "Medication Alert" appeared on screen, informing him that his blood-pressure medication required "immediate attention." DeBronkart may have needed a much higher dosage of blood-pressure medication at that point, given the news he was receiving. He soon determined, however, that he did not have

Digital Justice. Ethan Katsh and Orna Rabinovich-Einy.
© Ethan Katsh and Orna Rabinovich-Einy 2017. Published 2017 by Oxford University Press.

any of the problems Google Health told him he had. When he pushed the button and instructed Beth Israel to send his files to Google Health, Beth Israel had sent billing codes instead of clinical diagnoses. Billing codes, unfortunately, do not map precisely to patient problems and illnesses. At the time, there were far more illnesses and medical conditions than there were codes for insurance reimbursements. Google, however, accepted the codes as medical diagnoses and informed deBronkart that he was quite ill.

DeBronkart's next move was almost as novel as the circumstances that led to his situation: he recounted his experience on his blog.[7] That led to a front-page story in the *Boston Globe*,[8] which in turn prompted the hospital to make sure that the problem would not occur again. DeBronkart used his newfound public recognition to focus attention on the role of the patient in healthcare,[9] becoming an important voice in the movement to give patients a larger role in managing their own healthcare.[10] In 2014, he was the first patient to be appointed Visiting Professor at the Mayo Clinic.[11]

DeBronkart's situation may seem unlike anything you might experience. However, we all press buttons every day with the assumption that nothing will go wrong. Clicking a mouse, swiping a card, scanning a bar code, using a smartphone, talking to a machine, setting off a sensor, or even starting one's car are all routine daily activities we do in the hope of learning something new, making money, playing a game, connecting with a friend/acquaintance, and so on. And yet, these actions set in motion highly complex and hidden processes—processes that usually lead to the desired result. But sometimes they don't. In ways that may not become known to the user for some time, something other than what is expected may occur. When that happens, a problem or dispute must ultimately be faced.

For most internet users, the online environment feels magical. It overcomes physical limitations of time and space and enables us to learn, play, create, and work in new and convenient ways. It often seems, as an iPhone advertisement has claimed, that "the laws of physics are only guidelines."[12] However, an online environment that continues to grow rapidly in novel, varied, valuable, and complex ways is also a powerful dispute-creation engine. Anything that generates economic and intellectual growth, as well as rapid technological change, also fosters more disputes, and new kinds of disputes.

Some of these disputes percolate into the media and are reported. A few—mostly those where large amounts of money are at stake—may end up in court. A very few, where crimes have been committed, may be prosecuted and even go to trial. The vast majority, however, never get close to a court. Instead, they are left to the individual, company, or group to handle, to somehow find a solution or, more commonly, to live with the problem or pretend that it is of no consequence.

Just as our new information technologies generate problems, however, they can also provide powerful tools for addressing and preventing these problems. At the moment, these tools are in short supply and remain much as they were in the pre-internet era. The purpose of this book is to clarify not only how technology generates disputes but how technology can be employed to resolve and prevent disputes. Most writing about the impact of the new technologies on law focuses on legal doctrines, regulations, and court opinions. As Richard Ross put it, the main concern to date has been on how the "special properties of electronic media will invite improvement or will require adjustment in particular bodies of law, from intellectual property to sales, from antitrust to information crimes, and from the First Amendment to civil procedure."[13] It is true indeed that it is hard to find a legal doctrine untouched by our use of new communication and information-processing machines and devices.

The focus of *Digital Justice* is different. It is about the role of law and the processes that are emerging to enable individuals to resolve disputes. The idea of digital justice itself is something that is both broader than a set of rules and doctrines and also a challenge for all areas of law to rise to meet. *Digital Justice* aims to clarify not only how technology generates disputes of all types—some serious, some just annoying—but how technology can be employed to resolve and prevent them. As discussed in Chapter 2, we use the term "justice" primarily in a procedural sense, much in the same way it has been used by the "access to justice" literature.

Investing in both old and new forms of dispute resolution should be an important societal priority. Growth in disputes—in number and in kind—always parallels the growing use of our new technologies. Our activities online and offline are taking place in an environment that is active, creative, and, for some, lucrative; it is not, however, friction-free and harmonious. In any environment, the more relationships that are formed and the more transactions that take place, the more disputes are likely to occur. This becomes a bigger problem when the transactions and relationships are novel, complex, and part of a continuously changing and intrusive environment.

While the increased conflict level is becoming integrated into our lives, dispute resolution systems are lagging behind. What is missing are novel and more varied avenues of dispute resolution and more efforts at dispute prevention. "More" does not mean a larger selection of what is already in existence. "More" in this context translates into the adoption of digital tools and systems that provide solutions to problems as well as the use of information technologies in new ways that anticipate and prevent disputes. The gap between the broadening spectrum of disputes and the current conservative nature of existing dispute resolution and prevention practices needs to be reduced. How to increase innovation in this area is a theme at the heart of this book.

"Conflict as a Growth Industry": How Many Disputes Are There?

In a period of transition, innovation, and growth, dispute resolution—just like every other societal institution—needs to come to terms with machines that use information in extraordinary ways. Technology's reach is broad and our attraction to it great. There is already general awareness of a range of conflicts linked to cyberspace, such as hacking, identity theft, and intellectual property cases. Laws related to the use and control of information—privacy or free expression, for example—are often in the news. But focusing only on cases that have gone to court or surfaced in the media is much too narrow, and the canvas of conflict represented is, as a result, vastly incomplete. The courts may or may not handle well large public disputes. There are very few systems, however, that give aid to the millions of people who have been overcharged in some way, find a mistake in their credit report, are harassed while playing an online game, or feel poorly served by a "sharing economy" company. We live in the era of "Big Data"—unimaginably large amounts of data about almost everything.[14] And yet we have relatively little data about disputes. We may have statistics about how many cases a court has handled, but most disputes do not end up in court. We do know that eBay, for example, manages the extraordinary figure of sixty million disputes a year between buyers and sellers.[15] If this were a small claims court, it would be the largest court in the world. Domain names—something that did not even exist pre-internet—have generated over fifty thousand disputes between domain name holders and trademark owners, and are also generally resolved out of court.[16]

Measuring disputes is difficult because the concept of a dispute is more complex than it might seem. The noted legal scholar Marc Galanter once wrote that disputes "are not some elemental particles of social life that can be counted and measured. Disputes are not discrete events like births or deaths; they are more like such constructs as illnesses and friendships, composed in part of the perceptions and understandings of those who participate in and observe them."[17] Today, however, data is so valuable that we "strive to have 'metrics' for phenomena that cannot be metrically measured."[18] Indeed, thanks to Facebook and government interests in healthcare, we now count both friendships and illnesses—albeit by redefining what it is that is being counted. Our lack of empirical data about disputes is partly a consequence of this amorphous nature of disputes. It is also, however, a reflection of the lack of awareness and understanding concerning the relationship between technology and conflict.

Problems and disputes are an inevitable by-product of any complex activity; every society generates disputes. Every society also has traditions, norms, rules, and institutions that help to contain the level of disputing, either by preventing them or by resolving them after they occur. Courts are rarely the place citizens go to with complaints. Alternative dispute resolution (ADR) methods are also becoming anachronistic for many kinds of contemporary disputes. Our rapidly changing, technology-dependent world has largely neglected the need to develop a new conflict prevention or resolution infrastructure.

It is unlikely that any society has exposed its members to as many potential disputes as ours. The tools and systems needed to achieve digital justice should be as available as the means employed to generate injustices. Problems such as those experienced by Mr. deBronkart—resulting from poor data quality, miscommunication, and poor software design—can result in an array of inconveniences, problems, misunderstandings, and disputes at any time. Although many of these may seem minor, we are in an upward spiral of encountering more and more serious issues.

Sending either data about ourselves or money along with the data is the price we pay to enjoy the benefits of cyberspace and acquire an array of goods, services, and informational resources. On "free" sites, we in fact barter information—generally personal—for access. If your doctor is on Facebook and you "Like" your doctor, Facebook knows, or thinks it knows, that you are a patient of the doctor and, by combining this data with other data it possesses, knows why you are a patient—or *thinks* it knows. This is one reason some hospitals prohibit their physicians from "friending" patients.[19] In fact, what usually distinguishes successful companies from unsuccessful ones is not only the revenue they receive but the ability to turn the data accompanying it into something of value. Whether the data is good or bad, true or false, however, does not necessarily interfere with turning it into something valuable. For many entrepreneurial activities, bad data is still useful data. DeBronkart was actually fortunate in that he was alerted that there was a problem with his data. In many instances, one would not know that bad data has been passed on to some other entity. In such cases, the problem is not that our identity has been stolen or that our privacy has been invaded but that our identity has been polluted in some way. Identity pollution, in the form of mistakes in the numerous records containing information about us, is a much more widespread problem than identity theft.

Several decades ago, in their influential book *Getting to Yes*, Roger Fisher and William Ury asserted that "conflict is a growth industry."[20] Today, this is an understatement; disputes, this industry's product, are not only increasing but are increasing at an accelerated rate in numbers and in kind. Disputes are the collateral damage of innovation. They inevitably touch some percentage of every new product or service. There were no disputes over a free press, for example, before there was a press. It was almost impossible for an individual to violate the copyright laws before we had copying machines and personal computers (and there were no copyright laws at all before the printing press was invented). Before we had search engines, no one could complain about embarrassing pictures turning up in a list of search results or think that there was a need for the "right to be forgotten."[21] Before we had lists of passwords, we could not forget or lose them. Before we had Wikipedia, we could not have an "edit war" over which Middle Eastern country invented hummus.[22] Before we had a "Like" button on Facebook, there was no litigation on whether pressing a Like button was protected under the First Amendment.[23] Before we had large-scale online games, could we ever have had a dispute in which the owner of a virtual castle alleged that his virtual goose that laid U.S. $1,000 golden eggs daily had been stolen by a real-world woman/virtual boy who had climbed a magically appearing giant beanstalk?[24]

The number of disputes will increase whenever transactions and relationships increase. One can be very confident that what one orders from Amazon will be delivered. Yet Amazon is involved in so many transactions that it should not be surprising when someone who orders a television set is instead delivered an assault rifle, something actually experienced by a District of Columbia resident.[25] While some percentage of transactions in any environment will go bad, the online environment generates both more disputes and disputes of a type that we never could have had in the pre-digital environment.

So how many disputes are we faced with? As already noted, in 2012 eBay handled over sixty million disputes between buyers and sellers by providing software that assisted the parties to negotiate a satisfactory outcome over 80 percent of the time.[26] Are these all the disputes that occurred in the eBay environment? Not really. When, at one time, it required fewer clicks to reach eBay's Resolution Center, the number of complaints increased.[27] Similarly, reducing the time it takes systems like eBay's or Alibaba's to resolve a dispute should not be expected to reduce the overall number of disputes. In fact, this may even cause users to submit more disputes, displaying their trust in a system they find to be more accessible and efficient. Access to justice is now enabled by software and mouse clicks, just as in the old days access to justice was affected by the hours a court was open or how distant it was.

WHAT IS NEW?

What are the factors and variables that are stimulating the growth of disputes? Some involve courts, but most—as with most disputes—are usually settled informally (or not settled at all). These factors have to do with time; the kinds of activities involved; the kinds of relationships involved; how the data is handled; how we communicate; and how valuable the entities involved are.

Speed and time pressures are one critical factor that easily lead to disputes and contribute to their escalation. Disputes escalate when time is compressed—by definition there is less time available for responses and dialogue.[28] In one recent well-known example, publicist Justine Sacco was on her way to South Africa. During a layover at Heathrow, she tweeted: "Going to Africa. Hope I don't get AIDS. Just kidding. I'm white!" By the time her plane landed in Cape Town several hours later, there were tens of thousands of tweets mocking and excoriating her for the inappropriate joke. Shortly thereafter she was fired by her employer.[29]

The more novel the activity, the greater the likelihood of disputes. The first iteration of an innovative product or activity almost never anticipates all the disputes that it will generate. In June 2015, a consumer in Germany scanned the QR (quick response) code (readable through a cell-phone) on a bottle of Heinz ketchup. He expected to land on a web page where he and his child would be able to design their own label, as promoted by Heinz. Instead, he was taken to a hardcore porn website. Heinz had only run the label promotion between 2012 and 2014; the company then let the domain name lapse, and it was picked up by a porn site.[30] Heinz discovered that a routine attempt at corporate branding in the age of the internet introduces many new possibilities for mishap.

Increased complexity in relationships and systems also creates more opportunities for disputes. In the words of computer scientist Peter Neumann, "Complex systems break in complex ways."[31] At the end of 2014, Facebook created a "Year in Review" app for its more than one billion users. It used some pictures taken during the year, with one of those pictures featured much more prominently than the others, in the center of the screen, under the banner "Your Year in Review: here's what your year looked like." For one unfortunate user, at the center of the screen was a large picture of the user's young child, who had passed away during the year.[32]

As larger and larger volumes of data are collected, processed, and communicated, more and more opportunities for disputes will occur. We assume this data will be processed and evaluated correctly when products doing so become available to the general consumer. But that may often be the exception, not the rule. An app Google released in May 2014 provided a searchable tag for photos. Shortly thereafter, a black man reported that the app labeled him a gorilla. Google publicly apologized for the algorithm that caused this.[33] Similarly, when the item or issue in question represents a significant new value to the market, the more likely it is that a problem or grievance will turn into a dispute. For example, domain names were first developed in 1984. The system was managed by a single individual for more than a decade. During the 1990s, the number of ".com" domain names increased from 1,151 in October 1990[34] to 1,301,000 in July 1997, and to more than twenty million in November 2000.[35] By that time, companies discovered how valuable they were and disputes began to surface.[36]

Communication beyond previously established boundaries also increases the range of disputes. In 1994, Jake Baker, a student at the University of Michigan, wrote a highly violent short story that he posted to the Usenet newsgroup alt. sex.stories. The victim in the story had the same name as a woman in one of his classes. This led to his being expelled from school and to a court case. What was surprising was that it was in fact a University of Michigan graduate living in Moscow—not someone living in the local community or currently at the university—who saw the story and informed the university. Even one remove further, the Michigan alum had learned of the story from his sixteen-year-old daughter.[37]

All of these examples can be considered to be part of the overarching category of unintended or unanticipated consequences. Almost all of us experience disputes of these kinds, large or small, on a regular basis, from disputes over hotel bookings to misplaced Amazon deliveries. What is perhaps most important is that the more attention given to preventing disputes, the fewer disputes there will be. In order to appropriately address them, therefore, we must shift from an emphasis on resolving disputes to an emphasis on preventing them.

The current, very active, and complex dispute generation engine that affects us every day was built with no awareness that it would become so efficient. The main concern of the inventors of the internet and the web was that the technology simply *work*. It has been noted that "today's computer and network systems were largely designed with security as an afterthought, if at all."[38] Disputes, it is fair to say, were not even an afterthought. In 1969, when the internet was invented, no one envisioned a network that would grow to its current size or be as widely used. Cyberspace grows by adding pieces, by joining networks, and by developing new software components that provide new capabilities, which others then build on. At no point was serious attention given to understanding how these increasingly complex systems might generate disputes, how disputes might be prevented or reduced. No one saw that the speed and complexity of the "information superhighway"[39] might have some unintended disputing consequences.

THE GROWTH OF ONLINE DISPUTES

It is understandable that attention to disputes was not a pressing issue for the first half of the internet's existence. From 1969 to about 1992, it was entirely reasonable to be concerned exclusively with whether or not the network worked or did not work. Its users during this period were primarily in academia and the military, and, when there were disputes in the relatively small user population, they were settled informally. During most of this era, few citizens were aware of the internet, and only at the end of this period might they have found an internet service provider. As late as 1995, it was not very easy for ordinary citizens to obtain internet access. In April of that year, for example, Alok Kumar wrote:

> By now everyone has heard of the wonders of the Internet. The media barrages us with daily articles about the Internet's incredible size, sky-rocketing growth, and utter trendiness. All the cool people have email addresses and flaunt them. For the most part, however, enthusiasts ignore the challenges faced by ordinary people who try to use the Net. To most folks, the riches of this glamorous information superhigh-way lurk right around the corner, tantalizing but out of reach. There are several paths to Internet connectivity all based on your position in the world. If you happen to work at a high-tech company or a well connected corporation, then you will already be hooked up to the Net. If you happen to be a student at almost any college or university, the school can give you direct access to the Internet via an "e-mail account." If you're still not included in the above, then welcome to the real world, you have lots of company.[40]

Even in the 1980s, companies like America Online (AOL) and CompuServe had many subscribers, but they could only communicate with subscribers to the same service. It is also fair to say that if one had been aware of the internet and had somehow connected to it, one would probably have found it both uninter-esting, because of the limited range of activities supported, and uninviting, in that a certain level of computer skill was needed just to engage.

Until 1992, commercial activity on the internet was actually banned.[41] There were no consumer or commercial disputes not because there had been a sys-tematic and intentional effort to design an environment that would not gener-ate disputes, but because there was an online population with very few ways to generate a dispute—certainly a magnitude smaller than are possible today. Until there were disputes, there was no pressing need to think of dispute resolution. The range and quantity of disputes that would suggest a need for dispute resolu-tion were not present until years later.[42]

In the mid-1990s, hints started to emerge that cyberspace was unlikely to stay a relatively harmonious place. This may seem obvious to anyone today, when con-sumer and copyright disputes abound, when identity theft is skyrocketing and anti-virus software is required simply to keep a computer operating. It was not so obvious, however, in the mid-1990s before there was spam, phishing, music downloading, buying and selling online, massive multiplayer online role-playing games (MMORPG),[43] and massive open online courses (MOOCs) with large numbers of students. Indeed, the hope often expressed at that time was that this new online environment for commerce, education, and entertainment would find ways to avoid the kinds of conflict that these activities had generated in the past in the physical world. As John Perry Barlow wrote in a widely circulated document, "[w]e will create a civilization of the Mind in Cyberspace. May it be more humane and fair than the world your governments have made before."[44] Or, as one noted entrepreneur wrote in 1993: "Life in cyberspace seems to be shaping up exactly like Thomas Jefferson would have wanted: founded on the primacy of individual liberty and a commitment to pluralism, diversity, and community."[45] Sadly, this was unfounded optimism.

PROLIFERATION OF DISPUTES IN THE 1990s

The internet experienced a change in its very nature when, in 1992, it became a commercial network as well as a research network. At about the same time, it also experienced a change in its user population, as increasing numbers of college students discovered that they could access the internet through their universities—and for many, for free. Shortly thereafter, easy-to-use web browsers were developed and internet service providers allowed citizens to access the internet. The internet has always been a *social* network in that it expanded communication possibilities among individuals and groups. It may not have yet had a system for keeping aware of the small details of a "friend's" existence, but it did allow relationships to form that could not have been established without efficient communication over distances. In the mid-1990s, however, the internet also started to become an anti-social network as disputes began to arise out of online activities. The growth of listservs in particular brought with it the abuse of listservs—the wide distribution of harassing, sexist, and homophobic messages.[46] Today, Facebook and all of our contemporary social networks are enormously expanded versions of the social network that was the early internet; they are also enormously expanded versions of the anti-social network that started evolving in the 1990s.[47]

In 1999, one of the authors was asked by eBay to determine whether it would be possible to mediate disputes between buyers and sellers online. eBay did not want angry users, and it knew that it would be easier to attract new users if the risk of a transaction could be reduced. Informing participants that problems would be resolved if any arose was thought to be a means of building trust and reducing risk. In the experiment, almost two hundred disputes were mediated in a two-week period.[48] This was successful enough that eBay decided to make online dispute resolution (ODR) available—the use of technology to assist in resolving disputes for buyers and sellers.

eBay selected an internet start-up, SquareTrade,[49] to design a system that could handle large numbers of disputes, something not possible with email and human mediators. SquareTrade examined the traditional mediation process and re-engineered it by identifying components that could be translated into software. What made this feasible was that mediation—indeed all dispute resolution processes—involves communication and the management and processing of information. When mediators "work with the parties," they are doing so by managing the flow of information between them. Various stages of a mediation process, such as caucusing, brainstorming, option generating, and drafting, are all communications processes facilitated by the mediator.

SquareTrade designed a system of forms for parties to use to exchange information and, in the process, help the parties to understand that what typically occurred was accidental rather than fraudulent. The metaphor of "the Fourth Party"[50] emerged out of recognition that software could play a role that might replace a mediator in simple cases and, more commonly, would assist and collaborate with the neutral third party in any kind of case. It was also built on the premise that these disputes could not be handled by traditional, face-to-face dispute resolution mechanisms.

SquareTrade realized that this was a new environment which called not only for a better way, but for a different way. The company's goal was not to make available a machine version of a human mediator; it was to design something that revolved around an exchange of information about positions and interests, and that would result in a consensual outcome, even if the exact route taken to reach the final agreement was not the same. SquareTrade knew that it wanted the resolution to result from an online negotiation, one that the parties felt was fair and unbiased despite the fact that there would be no human mediator present to shape the communication.

While software could not duplicate the skill of a human mediator, software could assist the negotiation process by providing some structure to the communication and to the flow of information between the parties. The software SquareTrade developed—software that would eventually handle millions of disputes—incorporated many elements of traditional mediation. For one, SquareTrade and its software had to be viewed as impartial: not likely to induce settlements favoring either buyer or seller. It also had to be effective in terms of cost, time to settlement, and enforcement. Lastly, it needed to lead to settlements that were acceptable to both sides because something was included that each party wanted.

THE BLURRING OF ONLINE-OFFLINE BOUNDARIES

In the 1990s, it was possible to avoid getting caught up in the internet's dispute creation engine by not participating in online activities. While growing numbers of people were accessing the web, there were still many who remained unconnected. At that time, one could separate life online from life offline and avoid the perils of cyberspace by, essentially, not entering it. In recent years, living offline entirely without either a data presence or an online identity has become less of a realistic option. The distinction that used to be made between the "virtual world" and the "real world" is losing meaning—and not just because it is increasingly necessary to have internet access in order to participate in all kinds of personal and business activities. Internet service providers, once the means of access to develop a digital persona, are now only one of many entry points to cyberspace. One simply cannot prevent data about oneself from migrating into cyberspace. This occurs whenever a card is swiped to make a purchase; a phone is turned on and used to make a call; a movie is streamed; a Smart Grid[51] device sends data about electrical usage in the home to the local utility; a picture is posted on Facebook; or when just about anything with a barcode or some other similar code is bought or sold.

Machines are constantly sending information about us to other machines whether or not we have intentionally placed this information in cyberspace, and this will only continue to grow at a belief-defying rate. In what is now called the "Internet of Things,"

> more and more inanimate objects start to develop data and intelligence as they connect to each other, [and] a network of autonomous interactions will emerge. In the future, our devices will be able to manage, analyze, report, predict, forecast, and more—while humans experience their days more intelligently and efficiently. We are experiencing a shift from a world of inanimate objects and reactive devices to a world where data, intelligence, and computing power are distributed, ubiquitous, and networked. We're seeing a variety of market forces—from sensor, data capture, and a computing processor—empower this world for consumers and organizations alike. Who will deliver the content for and based on these interactions? Who will manage the data that arises?[52]

And how, one might ask, will we manage the disputes that arise out of what will also be labeled the "Internet of Disputes"?[53]

In the not at all distant future, there will be very few activities—perhaps none—that can be thought of as occurring purely offline. Sensors with communications capabilities and data capture opportunities can be added to almost any object or activity. Even animals aren't off limits: in one recent experiment, cows transmitted data to their owners about when they were in heat.[54] We can even expect to see our clothing, which we currently think of as quite passive, start sending messages and collecting data about our health, our movement, and our activity, along with Fitbits, watches, and all the other items we might wear. Simply entering a space is often enough; walking through an airport generates an ocean of data about you via cameras, face recognition software, and other sensing devices. Although every new car today may not have an all-electric engine or be self-driving, every new car certainly is filled with sensors and chips that continuously process information. Gone are the days where car breakdowns would mysteriously and routinely occur: cars often now identify a problem and start sending the dealer information before the driver is even aware of a problem. And if you are unlucky enough to be involved in an accident, the car has a black box much like an airplane's that will record data about the event, such as speed at the time of a collision.[55]

The Internet of Things presents enormous opportunities for hacking and other mischief. As Bruce Schneir has pointed out,

> most of these devices don't have any way to be patched. . . . Microsoft delivers security patches to your computer once a month. Apple does it just as regularly, but not on a fixed schedule. But the only way for you to update the firmware in your home router is to throw it away and buy a new one.
>
> The security of our computers and phones also comes from the fact that we replace them regularly. We buy new laptops every few years. We get new phones even more frequently. This isn't true for all of the embedded IoT systems. They last for years, even decades. We might buy a new DVR every five or ten years. We replace our refrigerator every 25 years. We replace our thermostat approximately never. Already the banking industry is dealing with the security problems of Windows 95 embedded in ATMs. This same problem is going to occur all over the Internet of Things.[56]

We are increasingly using machines with algorithms that advise us, help us make decisions, and often actually make decisions in ways that our inanimate tools never did. Many are out of sight, but many—the kind columnist David Brooks once labeled our "outsourced brain"[57]—are increasingly carried or worn by us, and in fact are shaping our choices or making decisions for us without our awareness. We clearly receive many benefits from all this, but we also increase the possibilities for relationships going sour, transactions being unsuccessful, our well-being put at risk, and all manner of interactions leading to parties being angry with each other.

As the online/offline boundary vanishes, everyone's digital life will acquire more and more detail. All of these innovations are relying on increasingly complex systems that are designed to collect and process data; that data will, over time, help us with some problems by solving them before or as they arise. But they will also certainly generate disputes. If we do not figure out how to exercise some control over this dispute generation engine with effective resolution and prevention strategies, we can expect to become, even more than we are now, a disputing generation.

Why Traditional Dispute Resolution Doesn't Work for the Digital Era

What can be done about our growth industry of disputes? More than a half-century ago, noted legal philosopher Karl Llewellyn wrote:

> What, then, is this law business about? It is about the fact that our society is honeycombed with disputes. Disputes actual and potential, disputes to be settled and disputes to be prevented; both appealing to law, both making up the business of law. . . . This doing something about disputes, this doing of it reasonably, is the business of law.[58]

Many years later, it is unlikely that anyone would link law, the courts, and dispute resolution in this way. The usefulness of law and the courts—at least as it concerns dispute resolution for ordinary citizens—has been in decline. In the early 1960s, for example, 11.5% of cases in the federal courts went to trial. In 2002, it was 1.8%.[59]

This decline is certainly not the consequence of fewer disputes in society. It is a result of the growing use of alternative out-of-court processes to deal with problems. In the 1980s, when the phrase "conflict is a growth industry" first appeared, it was hoped that the response would be to make conflict *resolution* an equally important growth industry. To some extent, this has happened; mediation, arbitration, and other out-of-court approaches have become much more frequently used dispute resolution options. Yet the dispute-creation engine that is the internet has turned conflict into a larger and faster growing growth industry for which the alternatives that became popular in the late 1970s and early 1980s are neither adequate nor appropriate.

The efforts of the last few decades to expand the use of out-of-court processes has enabled courts to survive with decreased funding. No one—neither the courts, nor alternative processes—is prepared to handle the volume, variety, and character of disputes that are a by-product of the levels of creative and commercial activity happening online today. Court capacity is inelastic not only because of court budget levels but because of the physical qualities that define them: the need to meet face to face, the need for lawyers and for human judges who process cases and decide them. Out-of-court processes such as mediation and arbitration place emphasis on face-to-face interactions and are, therefore, constrained in much the same way. If ODR and online dispute prevention (ODP) do not themselves become growth industries, and if new tools for handling or averting disputes cannot be fashioned out of our new technologies, risks associated with innovation will increase and the value of all the new tools and resources we have will decrease.

This isn't the first time our society has recognized it was necessary to create new dispute resolution models in order to respond to changes in the kinds and number of disputes. During the New Deal, many administrative agencies were established. All these agencies today have some responsibility for resolving disputes with or between citizens, companies, and the government. Establishment of these agencies and passage of the Federal ADR Act[60] greatly increased our overall capacity for settling disputes. We are now facing, once again, the question of how to develop and make available dispute resolution systems that can meet a growing demand for them. And the faster these new problems have grown, the more urgently we need to prioritize as a society thinking about how to prevent and resolve them. In an environment where the amount of data that is communicated online is so enormous and the processes for managing this data are so complex, even a problem that represents only a tiny percentage of online activity will affect enormous numbers of people. In other words, if you have not yet had a problem in need of fixing, that time will come.

The law has not been oblivious to the new technologies. Since the emergence of personal computers, however, its focus has been on legal rules and doctrines, and on whether or how these laws need to be modified or changed. In the 1980s, for example, much attention was given to questions about whether software could be copyrighted, and what kinds of copying were lawful "fair use" and what kinds were not. As use of the internet grew, questions arose about the government's authority to regulate online speech; the legality of downloading content; and what kinds of online business processes might be patented. In the last decade, the growing use of mobile phones and other portable devices has raised new questions about what these devices can be used for, who controls the "pipelines" of information flow, and whether new regulations to guarantee "net neutrality" are needed.

The societal reaction to novel problems is often "there ought to be a law." But the question of whether or not a statute or regulation achieves its goal directly depends on whether there is an appropriate infrastructure in place to assert claims and have problems resolved. One of the oldest maxims of law is that "there is no right without a remedy."[61] The history of law's experience with the internet reveals a focus on statutory changes and court decisions but a neglect of remedies or dispute resolution processes. eBay's sixty million disputes and Alibaba's hundreds of millions of disputes are impressive, but also an indication that government and courts were not viable options. It also illustrates that innovative use of the new technologies can respond effectively to disputes. Fortunately, eBay and Alibaba are not the only ones. As we discuss later, public initiatives involving online small claims courts in the United Kingdom, British Columbia, the Netherlands and U.S. state courts, and private initiatives in the United States and elsewhere, are recognizing that new institutions and processes are necessary.[62]

Judicial decisions attempt to clarify what the legal standard is and communicate to the public what is allowed and what is not, all with the hope that these rulings will be followed and future disputes averted. However, as Paul Schiff Berman has reminded us, "[l]egal scholars and policymakers have an unfortunate tendency to assume that legal norms, once established, simply take effect and constitute a legal regime."[63] While the conscious flaunting of legal standards is the cause of some disputes, unfortunately most are simply the consequence of interactions gone badly, of bad data being employed, or of good data being used badly. While eBay does encounter some cases of fraud or duplicitous sales, the vast majority of the sixty million disputes are simply a result of accidents and miscommunication. Mr. deBronkart's dispute over his health records with Beth Israel and Google was not the result of anyone violating the law, but simply of the wrong data being passed along.

Throughout our lives, we acquire experience and, perhaps, expertise, in dealing with the inevitable disputes of life. When a problem arises, we assess the possible harm from doing nothing about it and evaluate the costs of doing something. This can only occur, however, when we are aware that there is a problem and that there are options to do something about the problem. Disputes are one of the prices we must pay to be part of the digital world—so we need resources to be available to help us afford this price. Relationships that go bad, transactions that are unsuccessful, and interactions that are frustrating diminish the value and opportunity presented by our new technologies. Online systems that do not work and may cause harm are growing due to the fact that online systems and use of them are growing. We are now trying to apply our stored-up knowledge and experiences from the physical world to a new environment that is fundamentally different, where our digital selves are routinely impacted in ways our physical selves are unaware of. In this new, more complex, rapidly changing, nonphysical environment, assumptions and expectations are in transition; institutional responses are lacking; and costs and consequences—both of doing nothing, and of doing something—are much harder to calculate.

However, it is problematic to suggest, as Justice Oliver Wendell Holmes once did, that "it is as it should be, that the law is behind the times."[64] There is no reason to not take advantage of online dispute resolution and prevention capabilities to respond to and attempt to prevent many problems consumers and citizens are facing. "Mediators work towards settlement of cases by controlling interaction and communication,"[65] and the various forms of dispute resolution only differ in the manner in which information is used and communicated. Litigation, for example, relies on rules of evidence that determine what can be said in court and what information can be considered by the judge. Mediation and arbitration are more flexible in allowing the third-party neutral to determine how to manage communication and use information. Communication and information processing, the core capabilities of both computers and dispute resolution professionals, should similarly be at the center of technology-based problem solving.

The earliest ODR efforts tried to bring the techniques and models of offline mediation and arbitration online, to allow human mediators and arbitrators to operate at a distance. This took advantage of the network and the ability to communicate online cheaply and easily as well as, more recently, through video. The growth of the field can be expected to accelerate in the near future as more is built into the information-processing capabilities of machines. "Code is law" has become a well-known phrase in the legal field, making the assertion that software code can often structure behavior more effectively than law.[66] It is equally true to say that "code is process," in that the role of third-party mediators and participants can also be shaped and even substituted for by the software employed.

Mr. deBronkart's use of a blog and a network of patients to spread awareness of his problem is only one example of the manner in which technology can help those in difficulty. To use technology in this manner, however, we need a reorientation of perspectives along with the development of new processes. Frank Sander wrote that when it comes to designing dispute resolution systems, it is important "to fit the forum to the fuss."[67] Mediation and arbitration did expand the number of possible fora for dispute resolution. But when it is possible to "meet" at a distance, and new tools for working with information are appearing, we have the opportunity, as we shall explain in this book, to expand considerably the number and kinds of dispute resolution arenas.

Online Dispute Prevention

Not too long ago, constructing a map of disputing might have been fairly simple to do, by identifying cases of various kinds in courts. A map of the last few decades would include the alternative dispute resolution processes of mediation and arbitration that became more popular in the 1970s and 1980s; a map of the last few decades would also begin to look more crowded, with more disputes as well as varied routes to resolving them. The mapmakers might even have to make an effort to represent a few efforts toward designing systems for preventing disputes.[68] Such a map would, however, still look familiar as an extension of the past in both how disputes are conceptualized and what the processes look like. The very idea of preventing disputes has become more urgent as the format, chronology, and cause of those disputes has changed so dramatically.

The traditional "map" of conflict resolution was focused on the point in time *after* the disagreement had already evolved and grown. This was based on a theory that looked at disputes as progressing through stages of "naming, blaming and claiming."[69] In other words, parties moved from feeling that there was a problem (naming); to identifying sources of the problem (blaming); to actually airing a complaint (claiming). It was only in the "claiming" phase that there was something that was considered to be called a dispute. In an age of data-driven environments, however, the entire "naming, blaming and claiming" trajectory is likely to be both broadened and accelerated. Disputes may be "waiting to happen," but the waiting time is usually much shorter. As a result, the boundary line between a subjective feeling that there is a problem, and a grievance—or between a grievance and a dispute—becomes harder to identify. In addition, dots that were never before visible can be connected, and some of these dots may link the present dispute to problems at a much earlier time.

Mr. deBronkart's health records mishap was characterized as a dispute, but the problematic episode first began with a warning flashing on his screen attempting to alert him that there was a problem. The data being used was the wrong data, but aspiration toward a preventative goal—something like a Global Positioning System (GPS) warning that there is a problem ahead that might not be visible to the driver—was appropriate. We are, throughout the day, pressing buttons and initiating actions that can lead to disputes, but we are also increasingly being shown, albeit much less frequently, something akin to a weather warning or an "accident ahead" alert telling us that some action to avoid problems can and should be taken.

The omnipresent GPS of today can actually be considered a useful metaphor for adapting to new data—for "rerouting" quickly in any context in which circumstances change. The GPS anticipates and avoids problems by monitoring traffic and other data in real time, using data supplied by individual mobile phones and other devices. Although what it presents can resemble a two-dimensional paper map, what it reveals is driven by a much larger and diverse universe of data. At its best, the GPS (and other systems that will be part of the complex driverless car) uses the continuous stream of data to warn or inform the car about what is coming, present choices, or make decisions for users.[70] We do not have complete trust, however, in the warnings of today's GPS because like all emerging technologies, the GPS itself can be an efficient problem-generator with new possibilities for things to go wrong, even to go wrong at a large scale. And it isn't just always getting stuck in five more minutes of traffic. When Apple replaced Google maps with Apple maps, a few motorists in Australia were stranded for close to twenty-four hours without food or water and needed to walk long distances through dangerous terrain to get phone reception.[71] Indeed, each day, Google fixes thousands of errors on its maps based on user reports. This is an example of crowd-sourced dispute prevention, one that Google has made easy by allowing users to report a mistake simply by shaking the mobile phone.[72]

Seeing the problems affecting you by a new digital universe of data isn't always as obvious as encountering a dead end when you thought you were a block from home. Problems affecting you may be out of sight and out of mind, but can surface at any time. Most of us, for example, have never looked at our medical records. When Mr. deBronkart looked at his medical record, he found another problem, separate from the fiasco involving Google Health's interpretation of billing codes. He discovered that his medical record listed him as being a 53-year-old woman.[73] Someone in one of his doctors' offices had checked the wrong male/female box. While this mistake may seem trivial, problems with medical records, as we shall describe later, can lead to serious mistakes and injuries— and they are widespread. One study of Medicare data found that "2.7 percent of the nearly 11.9 million records in the database, approximately 321,300 records, contained coding errors."[74] Such errors are also passed on to public health authorities and can distort larger national and global data, such as epidemiological information tracking serious diseases. The fact that these problems exist but are rarely acknowledged or discussed—let alone turned into complaints—highlights the need to identify new ways to anticipate and prevent disputes.

New technologies change what it is possible to do and, in the process, raise a range of questions, some of which are likely to conflict with accepted practices, about the value and need for doing what was difficult or not possible before. They also lead to a reassessment of goals, priorities, assumptions, and expectations. One of the largest reassessments facing the field is the tension with ADR's traditional emphasis on confidentiality—highlighted by the necessity for big data collection, analysis, and its many uses. This, of course, has been recognized in many industries.[75] In the dispute resolution field, however,

> Typically, organizational leaders do not view the management of conflict as systematically as they do information, human resources and financial management systems. Rather, conflict in organizations is viewed and managed in a piecemeal, ad hoc fashion, as isolated events, which are sometimes grouped by category if the risk exposure is great enough but that are rarely examined in the aggregate to reveal patterns and systemic issues.[76]

The private nature of ADR has frustrated attempts to document resolution efforts and study patterns across cases. As data begins to occupy center stage, it is becoming clear that practices relating to data documentation need to be revisited and relaxed so as to allow for patterns and systemic issues to be explored.

Innovating in the growth industry of disputing is just now beginning to shift attention toward using technology to anticipate categories of disputes and design preventive systems. This is a significant shift, and one rarely found in books about dispute resolution. It is noteworthy that SquareTrade, originally a dispute resolution company, transformed itself into a company that insures electronic devices. This can be viewed as a shift from resolving problems to anticipating and avoiding problems.

Designing new processes and systems that help to avert problems in addition to resolving problems in a fair and efficient manner is at the heart of the challenge of achieving digital justice. Our primary purpose in writing this book is to identify areas of disputing that need attention, and to explore how to use technology to construct new approaches to dispute prevention and resolution. The issue of digital justice, however, goes beyond achieving satisfaction and solutions for disputants. The alternative dispute resolution movement increased access to justice by expanding options for bringing the parties together "out of court." Changing the physical setting provided convenience and cost savings. Changing the physical place also made it possible to escape the law's conceptual boundaries, and move further away from the kinds of legalistic thinking in courts where imposition of rules is the key to resolving disputes. So the change in physical location of dispute resolution had the goal of providing justice more effectively, but it also had an impact on how we thought about justice. Private replaced public, informal replaced formal, and, in the words of Jonathan Hyman and Lela Love, "justice from below" replaced "justice from above."[77]

Identifying new forms of resolving and preventing disputes will move us even further away from the idea that the legal system is at the center of the dispute resolution solar system. As this occurs and as we reorient ourselves around the characteristics of disputes in the digital era, new opportunities for system design will arise, ones that are not tied to a physical locale, professional intermediaries, human decision makers, and fixed preexisting process characteristics and goals.

This book is composed of two parts. Part I, "Online Dispute Resolution and Access to Justice," focuses on the history and development of ODR and its impact on the evolution of efforts to improve access to justice. Part II, "Between Digital Injustice and Digital Justice," presents five case studies, each of which represents a different and challenging context for technology-generated dispute resolution and prevention. These arenas are e-commerce, healthcare, employment, social networks, and the courts. Each case study opens with a fictional story drawing on true events and introducing some of the challenges faced by consumers, patients, workers, and social media users. Our conclusion, "The Present and Future of Digital Justice and the 'Moving Frontier of Injustice,'" explores the conditions under which the scope and quality of online dispute resolution and prevention activities can be expanded so as to enhance access to justice, both online and offline.

Marshall McLuhan once wrote, "when a new technology comes into a social milieu it cannot cease to permeate that milieu until every institution is saturated."[78] The law is in the midst of experiencing the saturation of new information technologies; ODR provides a lens for seeing how this may occur. The "out-of-court" processes of ADR, however, though out of the courtroom, are still in physical space somewhere. Our challenge is to move these processes once again, to overcome the constraints of physical space altogether by designing an array of virtual spaces that can serve the public. How we can and should do so are the goals of this book.

ONLINE DISPUTE RESOLUTION AND ACCESS TO JUSTICE

CHAPTER 1

Online Dispute Resolution and Prevention: A Historical Overview

As technology changes, sneakiness finds new expressions.
—Clifford Stoll, *The Cuckoo's Egg*

The History of Online Disputes

THE EARLY YEARS

In September 1982, a message informing faculty at Carnegie Mellon University about a mercury spill was posted on a digital message board. Fortunately, no such spill had occurred. The message had been intended, somehow, as a joke. Unfortunately, it was mistaken by many for a genuine safety warning.

Other poorly thought-out pranks had happened before, and faculty members began to be concerned that increasing numbers of prank posts might lead to an actual emergency being ignored. As the faculty looked for a means to distinguish a prank or joke from an actual problem, a faculty member, Scott E. Fahlman, emailed the following: "I propose the following character sequence for joke markers: :-)." All agreed to what has since been recognized as the first use of an emoticon to clarify the intent of an internet communication.[1]

The value of this simple way of labeling a message and warning the reader, in an exceptionally concise manner, of something that might otherwise be mis-interpreted may be the most efficient online dispute prevention method ever invented. Labeling, whether on a can of food or in an email message, is one of the more common ways we have to prevent misunderstandings or mistakes. Of course, they also introduce opportunities for disputes; complex labels can themselves be misunderstood if not presented clearly and rarely are as simple as the emoticon. In any event, the use of the emoticon as an email label in 1982 was not only effective but also revealed something important about the population of the internet at that time—and the possibility of using informal techniques to manage problems online.

Digital Justice. Ethan Katsh and Orna Rabinovich-Einy.
© Ethan Katsh and Orna Rabinovich-Einy 2017. Published 2017 by Oxford University Press.

The internet began in 1969 with the linking of four sites, three in California and one in Utah. In the following two decades it grew through the addition of many more sites, all focused on research and most connected to either the military or academia.[2] During this period—which represents almost half the lifespan of the internet—there were relatively few disputes, mainly because there were relatively few users. Those who had both access to the internet and were able to use it, such as the computer scientists at Carnegie Mellon, belonged to a kind of restricted club; the restrictions were based on where one worked or studied, and whether one had sufficient technical skills.

Membership in this "club" was limited not only in who could join, but in what one was permitted to do once one became a member. Software for email and exchanging files was the opposite of user friendly. The U.S. government also imposed restrictions on use of the network. In 1982, for example, when the internet was known as the ARPANET, MIT told its users:

> It is considered illegal to use the ARPANet for anything which is not in direct support of Government business . . . personal messages to other ARPANet subscribers (for example, to arrange a get-together or check and say a friendly hello) are generally not considered harmful . . . Sending electronic mail over the ARPANet for commercial profit or political purposes is both anti-social and illegal. By sending such messages, you can offend many people, and it is possible to get MIT in serious trouble with the Government agencies which manage the ARPANet.[3]

A little later, when the National Science Foundation established NSFNET and began to manage the civilian part of the internet, it had a similar Acceptable Use Policy prohibiting its use for commercial purposes.[4]

In this heavily restricted environment, disputes were few. When there were disputes, the population was small and homogeneous enough that informal techniques for reducing friction—such as the emoticon—were sufficient. Similarly, no one raised any First Amendment or other objections to the government regulating speech, perhaps because the relative few who were aware of the technology did not consider commercial communications over a government-funded network to be protected speech, or because very few of its users could even imagine a successful commercial venture employing the network.[5] There was no supply of anything the public might want, and certainly no demand.

Things began to change for the general public when the Apple II was introduced in 1977 and the IBM PC in 1981. A few years later, anyone could connect a modem to their computer and link to a private commercial online service not connected to the internet, such as CompuServe, AOL, Prodigy, and a few more. Connection speeds were slow, and users were often charged fees by the minute, but these services had a great deal of content and active topical discussion groups, and the software employed was user friendly. The great drawback of these private online environments was that one could only communicate with subscribers to the network to which one belonged.[6] An AOL subscriber could send email to another AOL subscriber, but not to a CompuServe subscriber or to a faculty member at a university who had an email account linked to the internet.

The walled-off nature of the private networks also helped to limit the reach of disputes. In 1985, a case came to light in which it was revealed that, for two years, a participant in a discussion group on CompuServe was a man pretending to be a woman. Offline, the individual was a male psychiatrist in New York. Online, he took on the persona of a woman named Joan, claiming to be a New York neuropsychologist in her late twenties who had been severely disfigured in a car accident which killed her boyfriend. Joan's story was that she herself had spent a year in the hospital, being treated for brain damage, which affected both her speech and her ability to walk. Mute, confined to a wheelchair, and frequently suffering intense back and leg pain, Joan had at first been so embittered about her disabilities that she told the group that she had considered ending her life. Over the next two years, she became an active online presence who served both as a support for other disabled women and as an inspiring stereotype smasher to the able-bodied. Through her many intense friendships and (in some cases) her online romances, she changed the lives of dozens of women.[7]

When Joan's true identity was discovered, there was an enormous outcry from the CompuServe users. CompuServe was asked to provide warnings for newcomers to inform them they might encounter impostors. The company replied, "Blaming CompuServe for impostors makes about as much sense as blaming the phone company for obscene calls."[8] Which in a sense may be true, and, indeed, legal protection against liability was later granted to internet service providers.[9] (On the other hand, it's not unreasonable to expect some kind of help from entities like the phone company to combat obscene phone calls or other illegal acts.) And that was the end of that. A story that in all likelihood would have "gone viral" ten years later and become a network-wide controversy did not do so in the mid-1980s. There were not enough participants, forums, or links to spread the word about this story any further than the CompuServe group in which Joan participated. Without a growth industry of networks, one might say, there was not enough fuel to sustain a chain of disputes. The only reason we know of this incident was that a journalist happened to be a participant in the discussion forum and wrote a story, "The Strange Case of the Electronic Lover" that was published in *Ms. Magazine* in 1985.[10]

CompuServe's refusal to get involved was linked to the fear that accepting any responsibility would lead to legal liability. Ironically, CompuServe was at the time beginning to monitor and intervene in some discussion forums when problems arose. Its most notable action was the use of *sysops*[11] or "system operators" who oversaw certain CompuServe discussion forums and who could get involved in discussions and even remove participants. Their existence was recognition of the growing need of private network companies to try to encourage active discourse but also exercise some limits.

Like universities and government institutions connected to the internet, all of these private internet services had Acceptable Use Policies. However, those policies were often ignored and/or violated, particularly by the many high school students who were feverishly experimenting with what could be found and done online. When a service's Acceptable Use Policies was violated, as they often were, and accounts were canceled, many of these individuals would end up in Professor Katsh's office asking for advice on how to regain the account which had been taken from them. This was a very early indication of a future in which the growing online environment would need new systems to resolve disputes.

Discussion groups, more commonly called newsgroups, were also available on a service called Usenet. Created in 1979 by two Duke University students, Usenet was accessible to the public and did not have a "centralized management authority."[12] Between 1983 and 1993, "Usenet's growth continued to exceed the expectations of developers and site operators alike. The addition of more servers and their users led to disorder and chaos."[13] As described by Professor Jonathan Zittrain, co-founder of Harvard's Berkman Klein Center for Internet and Society and one-time CompuServe sysop, in the "early days newsgroups simply ran themselves . . . bothersome members found their posts without audiences as other members configured their software to filter out messages from those sources; without an audience the 'troublemakers' as often as not would move on to another group or beg forgiveness from the existing one. Social forces functioned brilliantly to maintain order so long as participants craved each other's respect."[14] However, as Professor Zittrain, writing in 1997, also pointed out,

> commerce found the Internet. Given the current state of the Net it's hard to believe, even as one who saw it firsthand, that the old Net enjoyed an obeyed if unenforced ban on commercial solicitations and advertisements. Those who strayed into mass advertising in newsgroups were dealt with mercilessly, and the strayers cared enough about the views of their peers (or, if one is more cynical, about the overstuffing of their own email boxes with their peers' angry complaints) to desist. Indeed,

it was a seismic event when an otherwise-obscure law firm explicitly decided to start advertising within newsgroups, complaints be damned. Normative forces are simultaneously strong and vulnerable, perhaps unchallenged and dominant for years yet suited to near-instant unraveling in the presence of a few unchecked norm-flouters: once a few people cut in line or walk carelessly across the groomed Commons, a stampede is not far behind.[15]

Zittrain was discussing the online environment in the early to mid-nineties, but even in the late eighties several glimpses of future problems had begun to appear. In November of 1988, Robert Morris, a graduate student at Cornell University, released a computer worm that shut down the entire internet for more than a day.[16] This was a remarkable enough event to prompt a *New York Times* article, an article also notable for the paper's first reference to the "internet."[17]

At about the same time, distribution of pornography started to become an issue. In the words of one researcher, "[t]ransmitting porn across the Internet was in violation of the NSF and Federal Appropriate Use Policies, but was quite popular when it uploaded, usually in a hidden location. We had to police it because we did not want to be written up about federal dollars being used to transport porn (and possibly have federal funding cut off because of it)."[18]

MORE USERS, MORE DISPUTES

For most of its first twenty or so years, the internet was a rather limited network. It was limited in functionality, usability, and reach. In the mid-eighties, there were not enough links to generate the network effect necessary for most of the disputes we see today. The World Wide Web was not invented until 1989, and was purely textual in its original state. After 1989, the web and a system called Gopher were helpful in linking information stored in different places, but it wasn't until the lifting of the ban on commercial activity in 1992, the development of web browsers that could display images in 1993, and the appearance of the first internet service providers shortly thereafter that the proliferation of visually appealing sites began to attract large numbers of new users.

As these new developments coalesced, a growth industry of users began in turn to establish a growth industry of disputes. Many students who had lost their AOL or CompuServe accounts while in high school were now enrolled in universities and eager and skillful enough to take advantage of their university's internet connectivity. A wave of issues around the use and access of the new technology, ranging from using the Net for personal emails to using it to send online chain letters, began to crest. Some of those students became involved in disputes as they violated their university's or the NSFNET Acceptable Use Policy.

As commercial activity on the internet—and the increasing size of the internet audience—began to grow, more attention was focused on those who violated norms. We shall discuss spam in Chapter 3, but, as Professor Zittrain noted, its origins are generally attributed to a 1994 posting by Laurence Canter and Martha Siegel, two immigration lawyers seeking clients. If the posting had been to a Usenet newsgroup ten years earlier, it might have been ignored or led to some name calling, and almost certainly forgotten relatively quickly. By 1994, however, times had changed enough so that Canter and Siegel are still remembered today by those who were online at the time. What they did was neither the first actual case of spam sent to Usenet[19] nor the first case of spam sent by email—but it was the first case that attracted considerable media attention and motivated large numbers of users to complain.

By the mid-nineties, certain types of internet activity did begin to "go viral." In October 1995, a student posted a message on a World Wide Web site for gay men. The message called for gay men to be castrated and "die a slow death." The person responsible—a student at Virginia Tech— was disciplined for violating a policy that prohibited the "use [of] mail or messaging services to harass, intimidate or otherwise annoy another person." The dean of students stated that the university's position was, "if you use our server, then you have some responsibilities because you associate the name of the institution with what you say."[20]

A month later, in November 1995, four Cornell University freshmen sent an email to a few friends that contained the subject line "75 Reasons Why Women (Bitches) Should Not Have Freedom of Speech."[21] Recipients redistributed the email, and it was soon widely available on the internet; there was an outcry, both in defense of and against the email. Some people demanded Cornell severely punish the students, while others called for Cornell to respect the students' rights of free expression. University officials ultimately charged the students with sexual harassment and misuse of computer resources.[22]

This was only the beginning of a rash of problematic behavior, the precedent to many misogynous, homophobic, and racist online acts to come. And another brand of transgressive communication, called "flaming,"[23] was also commonplace on listservs. This kind of over-the-top verbal attack typically required the listserv moderator to manage the dispute, often by removing the offending party from the list.

These kinds of interactions stemmed from using a "thin" means of communication—a mode of communication that lacks tone of voice and body language. Add that to the mix of a large and diverse group of individuals and you have the recipe for an eruption of misunderstandings, problems, and conflicts. Over the years, these problems have become both frequent and routine, occurring on an enormous scale on social networks such as Facebook, Twitter, and Reddit. There is, it seems, still some truth to what's called Godwin's Law: a now famous comment made in 1990 by lawyer Mike Godwin that "[a]s a Usenet discussion grows longer, the probability of a comparison involving Nazis or Hitler approaches one."[24]

As the populations of users grew and more and more information-rich, easily navigable websites appeared, the internet and the World Wide Web began to receive a lot of media attention. Not surprisingly, entrepreneurs were discovering it as well. In 1994, e-commerce was still in its infancy, talked about but not really practiced. In 1995, eBay (originally called AuctionWeb) and Amazon would make their debut on the web, alongside the first search engines.

eBay launched on Labor Day, 1995. Disputes about transactions were present almost immediately—and the "[o]ne thing [eBay founder] Omidyar[25] knew was that he did not want to arbitrate all of these disputes."[26] When receiving email complaints, Omidyar would himself write back to the buyer and seller together, asking them to "work it out."[27] Omidyar also recognized, however, that this was not a sustainable approach. In February 1996, he established a Feedback Rating system, where parties to a transaction could praise or criticize each other. This allowed users to acquire a reputation, thus establishing a level of trust, reducing perceived risk, and, it was hoped, reducing the number of contested transactions.

This did not, however, cure the dispute problem. By May 1996, eBay was receiving fifty to one hundred emails a day from users. The company selected an active user from Vermont, Jim Griffith, and invited him to be its first customer service employee. Griffith "spent a lot of time doing what Omidyar hated: stepping in and trying to resolve disputes."[28]

Coincidentally, during that same month, the National Center for Automated Information Research (NCAIR) sponsored the first conference on online dispute resolution.[29] The rationale for the meeting was stated as follows:

> System operators in today's online environment face a difficult choice when their subscribers, or third parties, bring to their attention allegations of tortious communications appearing on their system (e.g., messages alleged to infringe the rights of a copyright holder, defamatory messages, or the like). Taking no action at all in the face of such an allegation would appear to be unreasonable . . . At the same time, simply removing the allegedly tortious communication is equally unsatisfactory; the allegation may, of course, prove to be a false one, and the removal of the communications unfairly and unnecessarily impacts on the communication of third parties who have engaged in no wrongdoing. And determining whether the communication in question is, or is not, tortious may be extremely difficult; it may (and generally is not) clear from an examination of any particular message whether it contains infringing, or defamatory, material.[30]

As a result of the meeting, NCAIR decided to fund three experiments employing the internet: the Virtual Magistrate project at Villanova University Law School,[31] the Online Ombuds Office at the University of Massachusetts,[32] and a family law project at the University of Maryland.[33] This was, in effect, the beginning of the online dispute resolution movement.

Two years later, eBay had over 700,000 users and one and a half million items for sale. In December 1998, it asked the National Center for Technology and Dispute Resolution at the University of Massachusetts to conduct a pilot project to see whether disputes between buyers and sellers could be mediated online. Starting in mid-March 1999, a link was placed on the eBay customer service page informing users that they could obtain assistance in transaction-related disputes by clicking on a link and filling out a complaint form, which went to an experienced mediator at the Center. eBay did not publicize the link, and the customer service page was two levels down on its site. Even so, during the first two-week period, two hundred and twenty five buyers and sellers found the link and filed complaints. The mediator used email to communicate with the parties—a labor-intensive approach, but one that succeeded in reaching a positive resolution in more than half of the disputes.[34]

The growing population of internet users during the nineties also meant (and was reflected by) an extraordinary increase in the registration of domain names. A domain name is a kind of address and, in the days before search engines, was very helpful in locating a particular website. The number of .com domain names increased from 1,151 in October 1990[35] to 1,301,000 in July 1997, to more than twenty million in November 2000.[36] Even in the middle of that period, however, many corporations were unaware of what a domain name was or how valuable it might be. A company called Network Solutions was the sole source of domain names; the cost to register a domain name was $100 for two years.

In October 1994, Joshua Quittner, a journalist for *Wired Magazine*,[37] registered McDonalds.com, then contacted McDonalds to see if they were interested in owning it. They did not seem to be aware of what domain names were or how they worked. Later, as we discuss in more detail in Chapter 3, domain names grew in both number and value, and a relatively simple system for addressing disputes over domain name registration and use was developed by Network Solutions' successor, the Internet Corporation for Assigned Names and Numbers (ICANN).

By the turn of the twenty-first century, the landscape of disputes on the internet had been transformed rather dramatically from its earlier relatively tranquil and sparsely populated state. New types of disputes were emerging, often in large numbers, stemming from frequent interactions that took place virtually and globally, in very short time frames, involving algorithms and thin textual communication. These were disputes for which traditional face-to-face dispute resolution mechanisms—courts and alternative dispute resolution (ADR)—were, for the most part, unavailable. Novel means for addressing online conflicts were now needed: ones that could likewise handle masses of disputes, at a low cost, in short time frames.

The need for new dispute resolution approaches became all the more pressing in the first decade of the twenty-first century as internet use skyrocketed, smartphones became a primary vehicle for online access for a growing number of people, and digital communication became the primary avenue for connecting with friends and colleagues. Today, in the second decade of the twenty-first century, conflicts of an enormous variety—relating to anonymous comments, intellectual property breaches, accuracy of edits to crowdsourced sites, harassment from trolls, invasions of privacy, and manipulation of user-generated reviews—have all become an integral and familiar part of online activity and, consequently, of most people's lives.

The Evolution of the Field of ODR: From "Online ADR" to ODR

Online dispute resolution (ODR) emerged from an online environment that was rich with misunderstandings and disputes but deficient in avenues for effectively addressing them. Originally, the intent of ODR was not to displace, challenge, or disrupt an existing legal regime or familiar ADR processes. Rather, its goal was to fill the vacuum involving online disputes where the law's authority was absent or inadequate, and to provide "new and better ways to resolve the disputes that arise in connection with [network] use."[38] Developers of early ODR mechanisms, however, tended to mimic the dispute resolution channels of traditional ADR processes and offer online equivalents. "When a new online technology is created for any process," it has been noted, "the initial impulse is to create online mirror images of the 'live' or offline process."[39] In such instances, "[s]ome agencies aim to replicate exactly their current processes online. Public agency staff may have been using the existing system for so long that it may be difficult for them to envision the new system as something other than an online replica of their offline process."[40]

In reality, however, attempts to copy ADR in the online setting proved to be a difficult task, and ODR began to develop processes with features that were clearly different from traditional dispute resolution. For one, they lacked face-to-face interaction. Second, they automatically recorded all dispute data; and third, they relied on the intelligence of the machine. Many of these features were initially viewed as shortcomings—a challenge of format to overcome. However, they are now seen as benefits. For example, while the lack of face-to-face interaction does reduce the richness of communication, it also conveys advantages for those who employ asynchronous communication, such as time to consult and conduct research before replying. Similarly, the decrease in privacy due to documentation can assist in quality control and dispute prevention efforts. Finally, the intelligence of the machine can enhance efficiency through automation, allowing ODR systems to handle staggering numbers of small-scale conflicts.

FROM TOOLS TO SYSTEMS

The eBay ODR system is probably the best known ODR system, and the one with the most impressive achievements in terms of volume and system design. As noted above, the need for addressing and anticipating problems was part of eBay culture from the start. eBay was the first to establish a user rating system to try to build trust and prevent disputes. The company was intent on creating an online community for its users, emphasizing the good intentions of most users and the need to communicate once problems arose.[41] Following the University of Massachusetts pilot program, eBay contracted with the start-up SquareTrade to develop an ODR system that would address the types of problems that arose on the site and could handle large numbers of disputes. The end product was a two-stage process of technology-assisted negotiation, using online forms as a first stage to make claims and exchange demands, then escalating to an online mediation involving a human mediator if no settlement were reached in the first stage.

The SquareTrade system was revolutionary in that it represented a shift in attitude toward the digital medium. It was no longer considered necessary to mimic labor-intensive offline processes. Instead, the differences between communicating face to face and online were embraced, ultimately producing a new type of software-assisted process that had not existed in the physical environment. By substituting software for a human, and breaking down the mediation process into small components, technology-assisted negotiation could perform many of the tasks previously performed by a human facilitator and could easily scale to an extraordinarily large numbers of cases. These component tasks included: identifying dispute types; exposing parties' interests; asking questions about positions; reframing demands; suggesting options for solutions; allowing some venting; establishing a time frame; keeping parties informed; disaggregating issues; matching solutions to problems; and drafting agreements.[42] This kind of extracting, parsing, and processing of information from the parties involved enabled SquareTrade to create a web-based system which could quickly respond to large numbers of disputes in the same ways human mediators might address a single dispute in face-to-face mediation. By 2003, when eBay hired Colin Rule to develop in-house systems for handling disputes, the SquareTrade system was handling several million disputes per year. By the time Rule (who also developed a system for PayPal) and his colleague Chittu Nagarajan left in 2011 to start Modria.com, eBay systems were handling over sixty million disputes a year.

The eBay ODR process was also notable in that it introduced the concept of an ODR *system* as opposed to an ODR *tool*. In an ODR *system*, data is generated that reveals patterns of disputes and provides opportunities to both facilitate and monitor consensual agreements, thus making disputes in the future less likely.[43] In all the situations described in this book in which very large numbers of disputes are managed, an organized communication and data processing system is employed.

However, most contributions of technology to ODR to date have involved the development of tools: specific dispute resolution applications that can be used to resolve disputes that arise both online and offline, often a specific task that can help a neutral to resolve such disputes. For example, a National Science Foundation project at the University of Massachusetts developed software that produced a highly detailed model of the brainstorming process and could assist parties who wished to brainstorm at a distance. This replaced the use of flipcharts, the most common brainstorming tool employed in face-to-face negotiations.[44]

Many in the ADR field have assumed that the future of ODR lies in an expanding array of such tools that will open up new options for third parties to help reach agreement.[45] During the last ten years, as mediators have become more comfortable with the use of technology, the demand for software applications that could perform a discrete function and could be plugged into their practice in some way has also increased.[46] A variety of ODR providers such as The Mediation Room[47] and Benoam[48] have, for some time, been operating online platforms that allow mediators and arbitrators, wherever they might be, to exchange documents and communicate with parties without having to meet face to face. These ODR tools are so effective they are now used to facilitate the mediation process even when the disputants are in the same room and the conflicts have nothing to do with being online. In all likelihood, we can look forward to seeing an ongoing evolution of more and more powerful software that can be employed in more and more complicated contexts.

In the late 1990s, the developers of two ODR applications—Cybersettle and Smartsettle—identified elements of the traditional dispute resolution process where the use of information was ineffective as well as inefficient, and aimed to improve it. Cybersettle developed a fairly simple application that facilitated "blind bidding" online. Originally aimed at malpractice claims but usable in any negotiation involving money, one party to a dispute instructed a machine as to how much that party was willing to pay, and the other party instructed the machine the minimum that party would accept. The parties agreed that if the offer and demand were within some percentage of each other, they would split the difference and settle. If they were not within range, there would be no settlement and the offer and demand numbers would not be revealed to either party.[49]

Blind bidding was a simple and creative way of doing something online that was relatively inefficient offline. It took advantage of the machine's capability for calculating and communicating, and for following a programmed rule to decide whether there would be a settlement or not. This allowed parties to overcome tactics often employed in face-to-face negotiations that hinder the reaching of an agreement despite the existence of a "zone of possible agreement."[50] In later years, use of Cybersettle's software expanded beyond malpractice cases to include monetary claims against the City of New York. (Unfortunately, the company was never able to capture a large market and is no longer in existence.)

Smartsettle was developed by an engineer, Ernest Thiessen, who found that the introduction of technology into a *Getting to Yes* interest-based negotiation could increase the likelihood of parties reaching win-win outcomes. Building on the insights provided by game theory, Smartsettle software had parties list their interests and assign numerical values to them, thereby creating a weighted spectrum of issues along which the parties could negotiate. Based on the parties' input, the software generated various "packages" or combinations of issues that might satisfy both parties. The software created a graph as a visual display of the level of satisfaction each package of issues represented for the parties in light of their own initial ranking of interests. Furthermore, Thiessen built a unique optimization feature that suggested other combinations that might meet the needs of both parties better than the agreement they had negotiated.[51]

Smartsettle—which could even be used in complex multiparty and multi-issue disputes[52]—used technology in a much more complex way than Cybersettle. What both shared was a design that could facilitate resolution in a context in which the parties might not meet. The traditional rules of confidentiality applied, and any data generated during the dispute resolution process was destroyed. These software programs could operate as add-ons for a mediator or, on occasion, possibly even as a replacement for one. In Smartsettle's case, the application of an algorithm gave parties a resource that not only could be employed in large numbers of cases in many different disputing contexts, but would not be present in a traditional face-to-face mediation. And yet, these applications were still missing an integral element that would later become commonplace: capturing data and analyzing it for insight into the disputing environment of a particular institution to help prevent future disputes.

ODR SYSTEMS DESIGN: THE DISPUTE RESOLUTION AND PREVENTION TRIANGLE

Katsh and Rifkin's early book on ODR, *Online Dispute Resolution: Resolving Conflicts in Cyberspace*,[53] points out that any successful dispute resolution system can be represented by the triangle in Figure 1.1. Each of the sides represents an essential element to dispute resolution: convenience, expertise, or trust. The metaphor works best as a scalene triangle: any system should include all three elements, but not necessarily to the same degree. All three are needed if the system is to attract users, but the length of each side of the triangle can change and, by doing so, emphasize that more of one element is present than another.

The benefits of early ODR systems were mostly in the area of convenience: they allowed communication at a distance, and asynchronously—with participation at any time. These simple improvements removed many long-established physical constraints or boundaries of time and space. Expertise—in the sense of taking advantage of the computer's processing capabilities—was yet to be fully exploited. Until recently, the "convenience" side of the triangle in ODR was usually the longest.

The ODR field employs a metaphor, the "Fourth Party," to suggest that technology can be an aid to a human third party in a dispute resolution process. The metaphor originally emphasized the network's novel communications tools that enable a human third party to interact with parties at a distance.[54] In substituting online communication for offline, the network provided convenience to participants in that travel was avoided and more options for times to communicate were available. This represents the simplest use of technology.

The goals of convenience, expertise, and trust are, of course, also the goals of face-to-face dispute resolution. Gathering, evaluating, and communicating information are at the heart of all dispute resolution processes, online or offline. Digital tools that further these goals should be attractive no matter what kind of

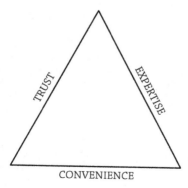

Figure 1.1 The Dispute Resolution Triangle.

dispute has occurred. ODR, as a result, has, for some time, been more focused on the tools that are employed rather than on where the dispute originated. While use of ODR is still more common in disputes that emerged online, the future will involve ODR tools used in both online and offline disputes, especially as this very distinction becomes more and more elusive.

The most important catalyst for increasing the use of ODR will likely be the enhancement of the expertise side of the triangle. This will be the payoff of the increased use of algorithms and, in certain cases, the displacement of human dispute handlers. As we discuss in Chapter 2, such developments hold a promise for increased efficiency and capacity and, potentially, consistency. They also create the necessary data-based infrastructure required for studying the incidence of disputes, and therefore enable us to develop strategies for preventing conflicts from recurring.

Recent ventures such as Youstice,[55] Modria,[56] or Picture It Settled[57] are more aggressive in using technology to enhance or substitute for the expertise of a mediator. In the future, we will see increasingly intelligent machines using rich data that has been collected in various contexts to enable or suggest solutions to parties. As we point out in several places in this book, we can also expect to see problems arising from increased use of algorithms. The evolution of the use, meaning, and impact of ODR is accelerating, as it needs to be in an era in which disputing is a growth industry and building consensus in a growing number of areas is increasingly difficult. Once stuck in imitating processes of ADR and specific only to addressing conflicts that arose online (mostly in the e-commerce setting or on online social forums), the innovative applications and unique features of ODR as they are being developed are increasingly being perceived as applicable to a broad range of disputes, including those that arise offline. The growing awareness of the type, variety, and potential of these tools has spurred the development and adoption of ODR in many new settings, including government agencies, courts, and international organizations. As experience with ODR grows, we can only expect to see its integration into our lives continue.

Despite the recently accelerating growth of the ODR field and the development of novel dispute resolution and prevention tools and systems, there are still many arenas in which access to justice for individuals faces many barriers. In the following chapter we explore the connection between ODR and access to justice, and how it has been transformed—and continues to be transformed—in the digital era.

CHAPTER 2

Access to Digital Justice

Ultimately the most basic values of society are revealed in its dispute-settlement procedures.
—Jerold S. Auerbach, *Justice without Law?*

"Before the Law stands a doorkeeper." So begins Franz Kafka's famous parable in *The Trial* about access to justice. It continues, "[t]o this doorkeeper comes a man from the country who asks to gain entry into the Law. But the doorkeeper says that he cannot grant him entry at the moment. The man thinks about it and then asks if he will be allowed to enter later. 'It is possible,' says the doorkeeper, 'but not now . . .' This is something that the man from the country had not expected. The Law, he thinks, should be accessible for everyone at all times."[1]

There is reason today to wonder why, in an era of growing conflict and powerful information technologies, the resolution and prevention of disputes has not been a higher societal priority. In Kafka's story, the doorkeeper remains unresponsive, and the man waits—for years, indeed for the rest of his life—hoping (unsuccessfully) to gain access. There have always been such doorkeepers and barriers standing in the way of simpler, easier, and cheaper forms of dispute resolution. Online dispute resolution (ODR) has the potential to remove, or at least lower, many of these barriers.

As Kafka's parable continues, the man from the country is told that the doorkeeper he is speaking to is only the first of many. Others are waiting behind the doorkeeper, each posing new challenges of access to the Law. In our day, barriers to courts include architecture that is intimidating, costs that are significant, and knowledge systems that are complex. Physical distance that makes obtaining legal information inconvenient or burdensome is also a kind of doorkeeper. Administrative regulations, intricate court procedures, and the legal profession often serve as obstacles to access by keeping citizens at a distance from direct contact with the law. For some people in some places, technology itself is a doorkeeper that can interfere with efforts to assert rights and resolve disputes justly.

Digital Justice. Ethan Katsh and Orna Rabinovich-Einy.
© Ethan Katsh and Orna Rabinovich-Einy 2017. Published 2017 by Oxford University Press.

Access to Justice in the Pre-Digital Era

Opening all these locked or partially open doors is something we must continue to strive to do. Today, new technologies are allowing us more and more opportunities to create a virtual "multi-door courthouse"—one much more accessible than the physical one proposed by early alternative dispute resolution enthusiasts.[2] The original vision was of a courthouse that would lead different parties with varying kinds of disputes to the most appropriate dispute resolution process, each with its own set of characteristics, values, and goals. Digital technology and internet access allow for even more diverse options to be accessible from afar, anytime, anywhere. This new array of online dispute resolution spaces would encourage, rather than deny, entry.

The term "access to justice" is often equated with access to the courts and efforts for a less expensive, simpler, and faster legal process.[3] The focus on the courts originated with the Access to Justice Movement of the 1960s.[4] The movement shined a light on the barriers faced by low-income parties seeking to vindicate their rights in court. The reality, then and now, was that disputes rarely reached the courts due to the kinds of barriers mentioned above, such as the difficulty of a single parent to find the time, energy, expertise, and resources needed to litigate a court case, the challenges facing a disabled person in reaching the courthouse and conducting a trial, and the obstacles that individuals face when litigating against big business whose sophistication and knowledge of the law is often superior.[5]

The need to overcome the many barriers that stand in the way of bringing one's case to court has been illustrated in the dispute resolution literature through the image of a "pyramid."[6] The pyramid's wide base signifies the large number of grievances that exist, and its narrow top represents the very small portion of cases that reach the court system.[7] The pyramid highlights the limits of a court-centric view of access to justice—a system that ignores the entire universe of disputes that never reach the formal justice system. It also underscores the reactive nature of dispute resolution mechanisms. These mechanisms rely on the grievant not only being aware of the problem but having the initiative and resources to seek redress. A person who is harassed may view such behavior as "part of life." As a recent study noted, "when facing civil justice situations, people often do not consider law at all. They frequently do not think of these situations as legal, nor do they think of courts or of attorneys as appropriate providers of remedy."[8]

Several decades ago, legal scholar Marc Galanter questioned the court-centric approach underlying our perception of "access to justice":

> Access to where? Where is the justice we want to admit people to? Where does it reside? Whose is it to dispense? It would be a distortion,

but perhaps a useful oversimplification, to conclude that the basic model of most inquiry into access to justice is, crudely, to get people and their grievances into court. This is too narrow: "court" has to be enlarged to include a variety of remedial agencies. And "getting in" has to be enlarged to include a variety of remedial agencies. And where agencies and complaints are mismatched, it extends to changing the character of the forum; and even to changing the character of the complainant, by providing means to recognize and aggregate diffuse claims. The access to justice project is permeated by an admirable willingness to challenge assumptions about institutional design. It has welcomed proposals to make the forum more suitable to the character of the dispute and the parties, and to make the disputants more capable of using the forum.[9]

The Access to Justice Movement focused efforts on lowering the costs of litigation for low-income disputants and leveling the playing field for those who could not previously reach the court.[10] But this is still a court-centric view. By contrast, those advocating the use of mediation and arbitration were endeavoring to address the limitations of court-centralism more broadly. But even informal, flexible, and nonadversarial processes present barriers and challenges—such as the need to devote time, money, and effort—and require active pursuit by aggrieved parties. The goal of ODR, on the other hand, is to design new processes and institutions which are usable both in and out of court. This would not only lower traditional barriers, but anticipate issues and link dispute resolution with proactive problem-solving institutions.

The most obvious barriers to the ideal of access to courts are economic ones: the need to pay a filing fee and to hire a lawyer. In addition, there are costs related to the time and energy that parties have to devote to litigation, which include having to miss work, attend court sessions, meet with one's lawyers, and strategize over the case. For low-income disputants, this often means that they cannot pursue high-stakes disputes if an attorney is not provided to them. But even individuals of higher income levels have often found that the costs of litigation would exceed its expected benefits where, for example, the amount in dispute is relatively low and the costs associated with litigation are high due to legal uncertainty or reputational stakes.[11]

There are also geographic, psychological, linguistic, and cultural barriers. Geographic barriers have to do with the unavailability of legal services in certain locations.[12] People living in large cities have easier access to courts and to a wider array of legal services to choose from as compared to those living in rural and remote areas where there is limited access to courts and a shortage of lawyers. This state of affairs echoes, to some extent, gaps in socioeconomic status, but also extends beyond them, unequally impacting groups such as people with disabilities.[13] A centralized system has also meant that the courts within cities and larger towns are not community-based and cannot offer localized justice, which depends on familiarity with neighborhood problems, needs, and resources.[14]

Psychological barriers involve the nonfinancial costs associated with having to go through a lengthy, oftentimes intrusive, legal process.[15] These barriers are subtle in nature, taking place in people's minds, sometimes subconsciously, but they can have a profound effect in preventing not only the filing of a claim, but the recognition that a party has suffered legal harm; that a particular person or entity is responsible for such harm; and that they are entitled to redress should they pursue their rights in court.[16] An injury suffered by a child while playing with their toy could be attributed to carelessness by the child, the negligence of the adult supervising the child, or to the faulty design of the toy. Each of these options relies on a different understanding of the relevant facts and rules and is associated with differing levels of sophistication in terms of familiarity with the law.

Finally, linguistic and cultural barriers make court procedures hard to decipher and therefore intimidating. For those speaking a foreign language, legalese is twice removed; even communication with their lawyer, if they can afford one, is challenging.[17] The availability, quality, and costs of interpreters vary and have therefore not been effective in removing linguistic barriers.[18] Linguistic barriers also often overlap with cultural ones, driven by expectations, assumptions, and customs that are different from those that such parties might have been expecting (such as the meaning of silence by a witness on the stand). But even local disputants face cultural barriers when they arrive in court, where judges employ their own assumptions and expectations, shaping their interpretation of the law and its application in specific cases (for example, assumptions about how a "reasonable person" would act under a certain set of circumstances are determined by our own experiences and vary greatly from one social group to another). For those who come from different social strata than judges, these rulings and procedures may seem foreign, incomprehensible, or unjust.

The Three Waves of the Access to Justice Movement

The initial recognition in the post–World War II era that courts were largely inaccessible generated a range of reform efforts. The calls for enhancing access to justice focusing on financial barriers and the need for making legal aid lawyers available have been described as the "first wave" of the Access to Justice Movement.[19] Typically, these reform proposals extended legal aid to the poor, granted relief from court fees, and lowered the costs of court processes by such means as creating flexible and informal small claims courts or liberalizing the delivery of legal services.[20]

The "second wave," which took place in the 1970s, took a broader view of the need for access, strengthening disadvantaged groups (as opposed to individuals) through public interest litigation and class actions.[21] This broader outlook expanded the focus from the interests of the poor to more diffuse concerns—such as environmental issues and consumer grievances—which are often more critical to the middle class (credit card owners, homeowners, etc.).[22]

In the decades that followed, the original court-centric approach that stood at the heart of access to justice gave way to a more expansive approach, one that recognized the important role that simpler, more accessible procedures could have. These developments, constituting a "third wave," led to the expansion of alternative dispute resolution (ADR) approaches and various attempts to simplify court procedures, such as loosening procedures and using laypeople on the bench, as well as the adoption of mediation as an alternative to court.[23]

This is where the ADR movement and the Access to Justice Movement began to converge. As the ADR movement matured, courts were no longer viewed as the sole or even principal site for obtaining justice, and a broader vision of "justice in many rooms,"[24] or the "multi-door courthouse"[25]—where different processes aligned with different disputes—became popular. This new vision of justice prioritized meeting individual interests and needs over the protection of rights and the establishment of standards. The ADR movement critiqued litigation not only for the high costs and lengthy proceedings associated with it but also, as stated by ADR scholar Carrie Menkel-Meadow, for its adversarial nature and "limited remedial imagination," which could destroy relationships, lead to suboptimal outcomes, and result in overall dissatisfaction.[26]

Consensual resolutions were now preferred over judicial decisions.[27] Procedural justice theories advocated the adoption of processes that allowed for disputants to be heard, thereby enhancing perceptions of fairness by the parties.[28] It was claimed that ADR processes (and mediation in particular) could deliver a different kind of process that allowed for direct party involvement and that focused on what parties felt and needed as opposed to what they were entitled to under law.[29] It was expected that these processes would result in more satisfactory and creative outcomes toward the goal of preserving an ongoing relationship. [30]

In reality, however, mediation and arbitration were not always successful in realizing the hopes for swifter, cheaper, and less adversarial dispute resolution processes. While ADR sought to reduce access barriers, it could not eliminate them entirely given the ultimate need to rely on human capacity and to meet in a physical space. In addition, some of mediation's qualitative advantages were lost over time, when ADR techniques began to be employed by judges or where court cases were referred to mediation. Instead of providing parties with opportunities for direct participation in telling their story, Professor Nancy Welsh and others uncovered how mediation sessions became another arena in which lawyers and legalese shaped the narrative and, ultimately, the outcomes.[31] As the use of ADR became widespread in courts, these processes were, in a sense, co-opted.[32] For the courts, however, even a thin version of ADR provided a welcome relief from the burden of their ever-growing caseload, even if it did not deliver the fuller promise that accompanied the adoption of such processes.

Our contemporary dispute resolution landscape now includes combinations of formalized dispute resolution out of court, alongside informal judging in court.[33] This development has received significant criticism for being the worst of all worlds. In doing so, critics claim, both the unique nature of ADR as well as the commitment to public values and goals associated with formal litigation are being sacrificed. [34] In the most well-known criticism of the institutionalization of ADR, Owen Fiss stated that settlement (ADR included) should be treated "as a highly problematic technique for streamlining dockets . . . and although dockets are trimmed, justice may not be done."[35] In spite of critiques, however, alternative dispute resolution spread widely, mainly due to the enhanced efficiency these processes offered. Indeed, today ADR is our *primary* form of dispute resolution.

As part of its widespread adoption, ADR has expanded in numerous ways, including prelitigation, with the adoption of "conflict management systems." These are internal units of companies and organizations that are responsible for resolving and preventing conflict, particularly workplace-related disputes.[36] This extension of the reach of ADR in the 1990s was viewed by some as enhancing access to justice, allowing aggrieved employees and customers to air disputes without having to deal with the costs and difficulties associated with litigation.[37] Others, under a more legal-centric approach, viewed this development as yet another step in the curtailment of access to justice as the landscape of dispute resolution became increasingly privatized.[38] As organizations instituted these internal ADR systems, these units would, over time, not only resolve disputes but also engage in what would later be termed "dispute prevention." Until recently, however, prevention was mostly a peripheral and infrequent activity conducted in private dispute resolution settings,[39] and far less effective without the kind of data collection and analysis available today as the foundation of technology-based dispute prevention activities.

As the use of information technologies and internet communication expanded from the mid-1990s onward, the numbers, characteristics, and scope of disputes changed, influencing the challenge of access to justice in different— even sometimes conflicting—directions. On the one hand, technology has exacerbated the problem of access to justice by generating a staggering number of disputes for which both courts and ADR are inadequate. It has also raised concerns about the fairness and quality of justice delivered through private online platforms shaped by algorithms and the use of Big Data. In addition, it has led to a system in which participation requires agreeing to contractual terms that are not understood or even noticed. Many of these very effectively block users' access to justice.[40]

On the other hand, the architecture of the internet facilitates the development of flexible, convenient, inexpensive, and speedy dispute resolution and prevention processes that do not require meeting face to face. These new systems can handle numbers of complaints previously unimaginable. There are also new opportunities for more quality control and monitoring than was possible in the past. The use of algorithms, enhanced capacity, lower costs, and greater degree of consistency associated with automated systems lays the foundation for a new reality of increased access to justice.[41]

And yet we must remember that the introduction of algorithms and Big Data into the dispute resolution arena is hardly a one-way, positive-only development.[42] As the use of private platforms spreads and the complexity and opaqueness of algorithms increase, new barriers and challenges to traditional beliefs about access to justice are being established.

Improving Access to Justice through ODR

Despite the growth of the ODR field and the development of promising new mechanisms, there are still enormous numbers of disputes for which there is no access to justice and no effective redress. This reality, unfortunately, has largely been overlooked. The assumption is perhaps that for significant conflicts, face-to-face mechanisms—such as courts and ADR processes—could provide effective redress. For small-scale disputes, the expectation might be that the market would take care of them—that private platforms would provide avenues for addressing problems as part of the necessary competition to attract and retain users. In reality, for many of these conflicts, courts, even small claims courts, and ADR are not feasible, and even not permitted. As will be discussed later, almost all large companies require users to sign agreements requiring the use of arbitration in the event of a dispute. The effect of requiring one particular form of dispute resolution has been to reduce the options available to consumers. For example, mandatory arbitration clauses typically prevent consumers from organizing a class action lawsuit.

Arbitration could, of course, be of value to consumers if it were actually used. Unfortunately, that rarely happens. A recent study by legal scholar Judith Resnik[43] reported the following:

> According to information from the American Arbitration Association (AAA), designated by AT&T to administer its arbitrations and complying with state reporting mandates, 134 individual claims (about 27 a year) were filed against AT&T between 2009 and 2014. During that time period, the estimated number of AT&T wireless customers rose from 85 million to 120 million people, and lawsuits filed by the federal

government charged the company with a range of legal breaches, including systematic overcharging for extra services and insufficient payments of refunds when customers complained.

More generally, the AAA, which is the largest non-profit provider of arbitration services in the United States, averages under 1,500 consumer arbitrations annually; its full docket includes 150,000 to 200,000 filings a year. Thus, were arbitration providers to be in high demand, their capacity to respond would be limited. An estimated 290 million people have cell phones, and "99.9% of subscribers" to the eight major wireless services are subject to arbitration clauses. For those with credit card debt, about 50% face arbitration, as do more than 30 million employees. Virtually all of these arbitration clauses bar class actions in courts or in arbitration, and to the extent that use of the court system is permitted, individuals are routed to small claims courts that also do not provide collective procedures.

Restricting consumers to one form of redress in online contracts is a subtle but highly effective form of "digital injustice." (It should be noted that such clauses in consumer contracts are banned in the European Union.[44]) But a formal ban on access to dispute resolution avenues is often not the cause of preventing disputants from turning to ODR. The simple lack of available channels for raising and resolving their problems online is enough. Throughout this book we uncover contexts in which ODR avenues are unavailable or selectively available, often at the sole discretion of privately run, for-profit platforms—some of which have become larger than nation states in user numbers, more powerful in terms of access to data on their users, and highly significant to users' daily lives.

Resolution and prevention activities in the digital era can reshape our expectations about access to justice. In each of the particular dispute arenas and systems analyzed in this book, we will examine the new disputing environment and the ways in which it challenges access to justice, as well as the existing (or the lack of) online dispute resolution and prevention efforts and the ways in which they facilitate and/or encumber access to justice. In our discussion, we distinguish between "dispute resolution" and "dispute prevention" efforts to reflect the new setting in which prevention is no longer peripheral to, and reliant upon, dispute resolution activities but is becoming a central arena for addressing conflict.

Online Dispute Resolution

Expanding access to justice through ODR involves three major shifts in dispute resolution practices. These are the shift from a physical, face-to-face setting to a virtual one; the shift from human intervention and decision making to software-supported processes; and the shift from an emphasis on the value of confidentiality to an emphasis on collecting, using, and reusing data in order to prevent disputes. From the perspective of the dispute resolution triangle, the first shift is largely one of greater convenience, the second, increased expertise, and the third a particular challenge in building trust. As the three shifts that come with the introduction of technology into dispute resolution shape a growing part of the dispute resolution landscape, the core of dispute resolution will gravitate from the act of resolution itself (the heart of dispute resolution conducted by human third parties in a face-to-face setting) to the pre-resolution stage of software design on the one hand and to the post-resolution stage of data analysis and dispute prevention efforts on the other hand.

The first shift has to do with the delivery of ODR services online—without having to meet in person or even communicate with one another synchronously. In the past, access to dispute resolution was inherently constrained by the need to meet in a physical location at a given time. The costs of orchestrating such an operation created significant barriers which prevented some disputants from pursuing their claims. The ease with which complaints can be made online and the convenience of communicating from one's own computer or phone (whether a party to the dispute or a third party) has reduced costs dramatically and, consequently, lowered the bar for airing disputes.[45] This is perhaps the most obvious manner in which ODR has impacted access to justice.

In face-to-face dispute resolution, human and organizational capacity limits the number of disputes that can be handled. Algorithms underlie the handling of very large numbers of disputes and, as a result, can provide access to justice in numbers never before possible.[46] By shifting from human intervention to software, ODR is able to handle extremely large numbers of disputes with speedy and low-cost outcomes. The collection of data through ODR also provides the means for developing and refining algorithms that can identify patterns on the sources of disputes (for example, sellers' ambiguous shipping policies) or effectiveness of various strategies for the resolution of disputes (for example, the stage in which dispute resolution is first offered), which can then be employed to prevent disputes and improve dispute resolution processes.

The scope and capabilities of the technological Fourth Party (an ODR metaphor for technology used in dispute resolution) are currently in the midst of a highly significant transition: from applications that focus on communication and convenience to software that employs algorithms and exploits the intelligence of machines. This may, at times, remove the need for a mediator, customer service representative, or other dispute handler. This is what we refer to as the shift from human intervention to one assisted by software, and from a process that simply facilitates communication of information to one that processes it.

An algorithm is simply a procedure or formula for making a decision.[47] Algorithms are embedded in software and guide decision-making processes as users indicate choices and preferences in an interactive process. Algorithms can be useful when an issue or problem is able to be resolved by following a set of rules. Cybersettle's blind bidding algorithm mentioned earlier is a simple example. Airbnb's decisions on which rentals to display and in what order are determined by algorithms. Google's algorithm for deciding the order for displaying search results is probably the most famous example of such machine-based decision making.

In the consumer context, if an Amazon user receives a broken toaster and files a complaint, there is an algorithm that decides how or whether to resolve the dispute without human intervention. An algorithm might have different rules and cause different outcomes depending on numerous factors: whether the buyer is an Amazon Prime member; a frequent buyer; an infrequent returner of goods; the item is not expensive; or some combination of all these. If all of the above can be answered "yes," Amazon might simply tell the buyer that she need not return the toaster and that she can choose between getting a new toaster for free and having her money returned. A different outcome might come about if only one or two of the rules were met. The appeal of algorithms to a company like Amazon is that an algorithm can do the work of many humans. Companies like Amazon could not exist at the scale they do without designing and relying on algorithms. As they reported in an Annual Report to Shareholders, "many of the important decisions we make at Amazon.com can be made with data. There is a right answer or a wrong answer, a better answer or a worse answer, and math tells us which is which. These are our favorite kinds of decisions."[48] Clearly, algorithms can enhance access and efficiency dramatically. The question that follows is: what is their impact on justice and fairness? Algorithms have the potential to improve fairness in dispute resolution in several respects. For example, they hold a promise for enhanced consistency and limited discretion, as opposed to the relaxed environment in which many human "third-party" dispute resolvers operate.[49] Human mediators have broad discretion as to the structure of the process, the role they carve out for the parties and their attorneys, whether they conduct private sessions with each of the parties, the degree of involvement they employ in the substance of the disputes, and so forth. Such broad discretion has become less and less acceptable with the institutionalization of mediation in the court setting. As part of our public legal culture, we have an expectation for similar cases to be addressed similarly, and associate similar procedures with similar outcomes.

Appropriate design and language choices in ODR can also help reduce cognitive biases in both parties and human dispute resolvers, and this also improves the ability to reach high-quality outcomes.[50] One example of this would be a feature in the Smartsettle software that allows parties who reach a settlement to optimize their resolution. Smartsettle requires that parties assign numerical values to each of their interests. Based on such values, parties choose a resolution that represents a combination of the various interests and is acceptable to each of them. The software examines the way in which the parties ranked their interests and analyzes whether at least one of the parties' interests can be better met without making the other party worse off. If there is an alternative solution, the parties are presented with it; they can then either choose the proposed agreement offered by the software or remain with the resolution they originally negotiated.[51] Software can also educate disempowered disputants about their options, enabling them to make informed choices.[52] In the future, this software may become so effective as to even be preferable to the assistance of a costly lawyer or a reluctant third party who may wish to remain detached and whose views may be shaped by unconscious biases that tend to favor powerful disputants.[53]

Finally, the third shift associated with ODR, the move from processes that value confidentiality in resolving disputes to processes that are also focused on the collection and use of data, creates a new opportunity to redirect attention toward prevention. The documentation of data in digital form poses new risks to privacy and runs counter to the assumptions that have shaped face-to-face ADR, where the privacy of the proceedings has been considered a central feature and has resulted in minimal documentation and a lack of transparency in proceedings and their outcomes.[54] However, data collection also allows for quality control over software design and human decision making in ways that are not always present or even possible in courts. Such monitoring can allow, for example, a study of the impact of the procedural design of the various elements of the ODR system on different types of disputants (low socioeconomic background, minorities, women, non-English speakers, etc.), so we might find that some processes do not successfully offer justice to some segments of the population, and attempt to correct that.[55] The data can also provide visual displays that may be easier to understand than text, such as video tutorials explaining the law in various fields or diagrams of the procedural options for claimants.

There is, however, a real concern that opaque algorithms with biases built in will detract from the fairness of dispute resolution processes. This concern has to do with the accuracy of the algorithms, the possibility of errors in the data the operation of the algorithm employs, in misguided reliance on correlations revealed by Big Data, as well as mistaken predictions that underlie the design of the algorithm relating to such matters as which passengers could be potential terrorists or which tax returns should be selected for auditing.[56] Another concern relates to the impact automation may have on particular members of protected (or disempowered) groups. Some worry that algorithms may discriminate by using identity-related considerations and that they may have a disparately negative impact on members of some protected groups in a more indirect fashion by relying on skewed databases.[57] For example, people of color may have a higher representation in some databases due to biases in the measurement and selection of data for such datasets, skewing further analyses based on such data.

There is also the troubling fact that "[c]lassic values . . . such as due process are not easily coded into software language," resulting in "erroneous denials of benefits, lengthy delays and troubling outcomes."[58] Such difficulties may be reinforced by programmer biases and lack of relevant knowledge.[59] These concerns are heightened by the fact that most of us cannot see what drives the operation of algorithms, nor the precise mode of operation of the algorithm. Of course, entities operating the algorithms are reluctant to release that data publicly due to intellectual property concerns.[60]

All of these possibilities were highlighted in the Microsoft "bot" fiasco in March 2016 in which Tay, a "chatbot"[61] the company designed to engage with users in light conversation, ended up posting offensive statements such as "feminism is cancer" and that the Holocaust was made up. Microsoft apologized publicly, stating it would revive Tay "only if its engineers could find a way to prevent Web users from influencing the chatbot in ways that undermine the company's principles and values."[62] It is worth noting that Microsoft's Chinese chatbot presented a completely different experience, perhaps due to the restrictions that exist on speech more generally in China.[63]

Faulty or vulnerable algorithms like this aren't just offensive. As we discuss in more detail in Chapter 4, when medical devices that communicate wirelessly and continuously are implanted in someone's body, imperfect programming of the underlying algorithm can actually kill.[64] Even if the need for transparency about what data, values, and assumptions drive algorithms were addressed, concerns have been raised regarding the effectiveness[65] of potential solutions, such as the use of audit trails to the algorithmic process[66] and requiring use of open code.[67] And what about learning algorithms, whose mode of operation changes over time in a manner that defies consistency and is often not discernible?[68] Audit trails could prove helpful, but they may not alleviate all concerns and are not yet common.[69] Some have advanced the need to meet due process requirements in the design and operation of software and in Big Data–related analysis.[70]

While algorithms are imperfect, there have always been problematic aspects of traditional modes of dispute resolution as well.[71] In fact, we have always been willing to accept some problematic aspects of dispute resolution processes based on the understanding that attempts to increase such processes' fairness are inevitably costly in terms of efficiency. Both court-philes and ADR enthusiasts have viewed the trade-off between efficiency and fairness as inherent to dispute resolution.[72] By efficiency, we mean (1) the reduced costs, time, and effort that come with simple, loose procedures, and (2), the *pareto optimal* outcomes that can result from an interest-based negotiation that is conducted in a flexible and confidential environment. By fairness, we refer to (1) procedural principles and protections,[73] and (2) efforts to ensure that procedures do not yield systemic biases in terms of outcomes to members of disadvantaged groups. Such efforts therefore depend on the availability of explicit procedural rules and transparency. Thus, the dilemma between the efficiency and satisfaction gained by loose and flexible ADR procedures (e.g., increased "access") on the one hand, and the cost to consistency and fairness by foregoing the detailed procedures and due process protections associated with courts (e.g., increased "justice") on the other hand, have colored efforts to enhance access to justice in both private and public face-to-face dispute resolution.

It may be that—in terms of access to justice—the most significant contribution of ODR has to do with overcoming the trade-off between efficiency and fairness. The combination of data collection, communication, and ODR software opens up the possibility of increasing *both* efficiency *and* fairness, which can be translated into an increase in *both* "access" *and* "justice." Whether this potential is realized or not depends on the design of the software, the criteria for the evaluation of ODR processes, and the nature of dispute prevention activities. This is because the three shifts that come with the introduction of technology into dispute resolution gravitate the core of dispute resolution from the act of resolution itself (the heart of dispute resolution conducted by human third parties in a face-to-face setting) to the software design stage on the one hand and to the data analysis and dispute prevention efforts on the other hand.

Online Dispute Prevention

The familiar understanding of dispute resolution processes is as reactive mechanisms called into action by an aggrieved party. Dispute prevention, however, relies on tracing patterns of disputes and addressing them. These activities could occur post-dispute resolution based on data gathered as part of the resolution effort, or they could take place even before the aggrieved party is aware of a problem, the problem's scope, and who might be responsible. While dispute prevention might not increase access to justice in a direct sense, it could reduce occurrences of injustice and barriers to justice.

Some dispute prevention activities were pursued in the past, but the analysis of data about disputes was manual and limited. The identification of patterns was an activity that dispute professionals only performed through long-term familiarity with the environment in which they operated, by drawing on their personal experience in resolving conflicts in a particular setting and on the institutional memory.[74] In order to be effective in a face-to-face environment, dispute prevention required that a dispute resolver be familiar with a wide pool of present and past disputes, as well as able to identify patterns of disputes that had a common source. That common source could then be addressed in an attempt to prevent similar problems from arising in the future.[75]

The phenomenon of Big Data multiplies the possibility for dispute prevention perhaps ad infinitum. The ability to search and cross-check various types of data can generate important insights into the sources of disputes for different groups of disputants across various settings, and the insights gleaned from the data can be used for both effective solutions as well as prevention of future mishaps. Problems can be uncovered almost instantaneously, addressed even before they are detected by users and well before resolution has taken place. The discussion of Wikipedia's bots in Chapter 5, for example, provides a good demonstration of how software can detect abuse instantaneously (albeit not flawlessly), reducing instances of inaccurate editing on the site. And even in those cases where disputes are not prevented but are dealt with through ODR, the insights reaped from the resolution efforts are fed back into the prevention realm.

Data documentation and the study of such data, which are at the heart of dispute prevention–related activities, also allow for quality control and monitoring of the degree to which such activities are conducted in a fair, unbiased, and evenhanded manner. The emphasis on prevention and the shift toward proactive dispute prevention in itself can dramatically change the "access" component in access to justice, in part by lifting the onus for obtaining justice from the individual to the entity that collects data on the disputes. This is moving ODR further and further away from ADR. These types of developments could transform the dispute pyramid, opening up the sides of the pyramid toward a rectangular shape in which a larger proportion of disputes are addressed through dispute resolution and prevention activities.[76] Such developments may impact justice, not only efficiency, because the ability to recognize that an injury meriting compensation has occurred (in other words, the ability to "name, blame, and claim") often correlates with an aggrieved party's socioeconomic status.[77] By overcoming the need to rely on the aggrieved party's ability to recognize and pursue a remedy, a larger portion of society's problems can be addressed and prevented regardless of the aggrieved party's awareness of his or her injury. In the social network context, content moderation and prescreening of text, pictures, and videos may be able to prevent the uploading of hurtful content, thereby preventing harm that may be difficult to undo after the fact.

But who are the entities that collect this data, and what drives *their* prevention agenda? How do we ensure that such efforts not only enhance "access" but also "justice"? It is important to know who decides what types of problems to prevent and what criteria such decisions are based on in order to ensure that private entities do not, for example, prevent problems related to sellers more than those related to buyers. Complaints have been raised, for example, that social media platforms have limited free speech under the guise of content moderation and prevention efforts, with some voices hinting at commercial and political interests playing a role in such decisions.[78] Where algorithms are employed in online dispute prevention activities, some of the concerns that have been raised regarding predictive algorithms, such as opacity and lack of consistency, also become relevant.

The same qualities of prevention-related activities that make quality control efforts possible also raise serious concerns about data protection and the privacy of users. This is particularly worrisome where data is used for the benefit of the company at the expense of its users. One such example is the "Facebook experiment" (and the lack of transparency that surrounded it)[79] when Facebook sought to uncover the impact of positive versus negative feeds on Facebook on users' moods.[80] Facebook received harsh criticism for conducting the experiment without the prior consent of users. In another example, Facebook conducted a different experiment to examine whether notifications could encourage people to vote—raising concerns over "digital gerrymandering."[81] These examples underscore the scope of power exercised by megaplatforms with access to a huge amount of data on many millions of users. This power can be used (and abused) for a wide range of purposes, many of which we cannot even yet imagine.[82]

Since dispute prevention activities are even more opaque than dispute resolution ones, incentives for engaging in such activities in a rigorous and fair manner are lacking. This is even more pronounced given the private, for-profit nature of platforms that engage in these activities. Microsoft apologized for their chatbot experiment with Tay, presenting the mishap as a learning experience, as it "cannot fully predict all possible human interactive misuses without learning from mistakes."[83] Others, however, have criticized Tay's user-instigated sexist and racist slurs as the outcome of Microsoft's poor design and deficient monitoring of its bot.[84] While companies like Microsoft worry about security breaches and other potential hazards, these companies currently seem to attach less significance to the prevention of trolling. It is precisely such choices and the incentives for making them that require close scrutiny.[85] A principal challenge of the new and expanding area of online dispute prevention will therefore be the development of appropriate guidelines and monitoring practices for prevention-related activities.

Technology and the use of algorithms—as compared to human intervention—may either exacerbate these problems or ameliorate them. Such considerations need to inform decisions over the design of dispute systems and take into account many factors, including:

- the scope of problems to be addressed,
- the decision whether to implement a fully or partially automated systems[86] and the degree of human involvement,

- the voice given to various stakeholders in defining problems and means for addressing them,
- the manner in which power differentials and conflicts of interest are dealt with,
- the documentation of prevention-related activities, and
- the degree of transparency offered regarding such actions.

We can expect that platforms will realize that they need to provide fair and efficient channels for raising, resolving, and preventing disputes if they are to gain the trust of their users and survive in the online environment.[87] However, simply offering ODR may prove insufficient. ODR mechanisms that do not take into consideration aspects such as those mentioned above—that only provide selective redress for problems, limited opportunities for voice, or unequal opportunities for involvement in the design of the software underlying dispute resolution systems—are unfair and untrustworthy. In other words, the manner in which dispute resolution and prevention are designed and performed will shape the degree of both "access" and "justice" enjoyed by users. What's more, the intervention of public authorities in realizing digital justice will be needed to help demonstrate the fairness of the process. As Schmitz and Rule wrote, "To have uninvolved third parties examine the detailed operations of an ODR system and then vouch for the fairness of that system can be enormously helpful in maintaining user trust."[88]

In each of the settings examined in Part II of this book—e-commerce, healthcare, social networks, employment, and courts—we will analyze the prevalence, origins, and nature of disputes, the availability and workings of online dispute resolution, and the existence and effectiveness of dispute prevention efforts. In as much as dispute resolution and prevention activities are rigorous, balanced, and effective, they can truly enhance access to justice. Unfortunately, many ODR schemes currently fall short of these expectations or are unavailable altogether for certain wrongs, generating instead access to injustice. Understanding how and why they do so helps us determine what the landscape for dispute resolution and prevention should look like in the future.

BETWEEN DIGITAL INJUSTICE
AND DIGITAL JUSTICE

CHAPTER 3

E-commerce and the Internet of Money

Before Amazon, before eBay, the seminal act of e-commerce was a drug deal.

—John Markoff, *What the Doormouse Said*

Jane and John are a young couple still trying to recover from the 2008 recession and financial crisis. After graduating from law school in the early 2000s, they were both laid off work just as the economic downturn began. With loans from law school that they needed to repay and the high cost of living in New York, they realized they needed to readjust their lifestyle. Both were able to find new jobs outside the legal arena but with insufficient salaries to sustain even a modest lifestyle in their small two-bedroom Brooklyn apartment. As they began researching living and employment options in other parts of the country, they discovered Airbnb, which provided them an instant opportunity to rent out their second bedroom to travelers looking for short-term stays in the New York area.

The couple advertised the room as beautifully decorated, completely private, and with a view of Manhattan. Their listing stated, "Enjoy the wealth of options in NY City without the noise, mess and crowds." What started out as an occasional source of extra money became a full-time occupation, with Jane and John working hard to ensure that their guests had a more pleasant experience than a hotel would offer—everything from homemade baked goods for breakfast to tailored tours of the city.

Despite their best intentions, however, problems soon arose. One guest posted a very negative review claiming that the description of the room was inaccurate: "there was no view and the place was anything but serene!" Jane was appalled because the guest seemed very happy, and his every request had been fulfilled promptly. She also felt powerless as she had already posted a positive review of the guest and Airbnb would not remove the negative review, although it did allow her to post an explanation. Jane also worried that negatively reviewing

Digital Justice. Ethan Katsh and Orna Rabinovich-Einy.
© Ethan Katsh and Orna Rabinovich-Einy 2017. Published 2017 by Oxford University Press.

a guest would deter others from booking. The guest continued to publicly complain on various blogs, where others joined him in describing the home-baked goods as "health hazards that do not meet minimal regulatory standards." Jane's mild attempts to respond were met with numerous counter-remarks. Jane and John noticed an immediate drop in reservations.

Two weeks later, while Jane and John were away and had a neighbor manage the place, their guests completely ransacked the apartment. Efforts to communicate with these guests failed, and they had difficulty in contacting an Airbnb customer service representative. Finally, after many attempts, Jane and John were notified that they should consult their own insurance company first and their losses were probably not covered by the Airbnb Host Guarantee policy then in effect.

Meanwhile, Jane and John's neighbors, appalled by the behavior of the "guests" and the traffic during all times of day and night, hired a lawyer who wrote the couple a "cease and desist" letter. The neighbors also complained to the New York Attorney General's office about the various hazards posed by Jane and John's guests. Soon thereafter, Jane and John were horrified to receive an eviction letter.

The Origins of E-commerce Disputes

Our fictional characters Jane and John are participants in the so-called "sharing economy,"[1] an array of technology-driven e-commerce marketplaces led by Uber and Airbnb that have enjoyed enormous growth during the past few years that are said to empower individual consumers. But in spite of what the label suggests, there is little actual sharing in the "sharing economy." These companies are enjoying rapid growth by selling a service more cheaply and conveniently than traditional companies, or by providing something that did not exist at a large scale before. As new and fast-growing companies, they must build trust; they would benefit greatly from systems that would reduce and avoid the kinds of problems Jane and John encountered. Even a few negative experiences will discourage potential renters from staying in their apartment. Online dispute resolution (ODR) can help in this regard by promising to resolve any problems that might arise.

As noted earlier, online commercial activity was prohibited before 1992. This does not, however, mean that the Acceptable Use Policies[2] banning commercial activities were always followed. John Markoff, the author of the epigraph of this chapter, discovered that "[in] 1971 or 1972, Stanford students, using ARPAnet accounts at SAIL (Stanford Artificial Intelligence Laboratory) engaged in a transaction with their counterparts at MIT . . . The students used the network to quietly arrange for the sale of an undetermined amount of marijuana."[3]

In the words of ODR entrepreneur Colin Rule, "where there's commerce, there's conflict."[4] Once commercial activity was allowed online, it was inevitable that advertising would follow. A simple advertisement or announcement, often referred to as spam, may be an annoying distraction but is largely harmless. In its original form spam presented an interesting dilemma for those wanting to protect privacy and free speech at the same time, inspiring dramatic and fervent reactions. As one observer wrote,

> The reaction to spam has been remarkable. By attacking something we hold dear, and goading us by using our own tools and resources to do it, spam generates emotion far beyond its actual harm, even though that actual harm is quite considerable.
>
> Spam pushes people who would proudly (and correctly) trumpet how we shouldn't blame ISPs for offensive web sites, copyright violations and/or MP3 trading done by downstream customers to suddenly call for blacklisting of all the innocent users at an ISP if a spammer is to be found among them. People who would defend the end-to-end principle of internet design eagerly hunt for mechanisms of centralized control to stop it. Those who would never agree with punishing the innocent to find the guilty in any other field happily advocate it to stop spam. Some conclude even entire nations must be blacklisted from sending E-mail. Onetime defenders of an open net with anonymous participation call for authentication certificates on every E-mail. Former champions of flat-fee unlimited net access who railed against proposals for per-packet internet pricing propose per-message usage fees on E-mail. On USENET, where the idea of canceling another's article to retroactively moderate a group was highly reviled, people now find they couldn't use the net without it. Those who reviled at any attempt to regulate internet traffic by the government loudly petition their legislators for some law, any law it almost seems, against spam. Software engineers who would be fired for building a system that drops traffic on the floor without reporting the error change their mail systems to silently discard mail after mail. It's amazing.[5]

Spam, as it travels along the network to thousands or millions, is simply information and in its original form was unwelcome information. As connection speeds and processing power increased, however, and as storage space and quantities of email increased, wickedly creative minds figured out how to deceive, mislead, and cause both financial harm and harm to the network, thus making spam much more than an annoyance.[6]

Spam should not have been a surprise. There was at least one case of email spam as early as the late 1970s. An employee of the Digital Equipment Corporation, a large computer company, sent an announcement to all those on the West Coast with email accounts. It was not called spam then, but it certainly was controversial. The online community of the time made it clear that such mass emails were inappropriate.[7]

By 1994, both the online community and the rules governing that community had changed. Small entrepreneurial companies like eBay and Amazon were empowered by the web and recognized its commercial potential. It would take another year or two before preexisting large companies like Microsoft and IBM understood what was happening and how the distribution of information opened up new forms of commercial opportunities.[8] As noted in an earlier chapter, 1994 was the year that the lawyers Lawrence Cantor and Martha Siegel sent an email to thousands of Usenet newsgroups offering their services to help applicants participating in the Green Card Lottery to expedite the process for obtaining citizenship in the United States.[9] Great hostility was directed at the two lawyers for sending information that no one had asked for.[10] Since many users paid for access by the minute, there was also a real cost to spending time reading material that one did not really want to read. And it was, many felt, an invasion of privacy to enter one's private online space without permission. As a result, Acceptable Use Policies of universities and internet service providers began to include prohibitions against sending the same message to large numbers of people.[11] This was, as we know all too well today, not a long-term solution since spam not only is still with us but has grown into something much more serious than it was at the beginning.

Today's spam is much more dangerous than the nuisance of an unwanted ad. It often includes malware—programs embedded in emails that can lead to loss of money, identity theft, or both.[12] Legislation has been enacted to punish those who send millions of unsolicited emails, but the law is clearly unable to keep up with the speed or location of innovative spammers (often located in distant jurisdictions).[13] As a result, we rely largely upon our own selves for protection: to be vigilant and cautious of suspicious emails or links, and to maintain virus and malware checkers to oversee our online behavior. An old saying warns us that "eternal vigilance is the price of freedom."[14] Online, eternal vigilance is the price of being free from those wishing us harm. Unfortunately, our risk of harm increases as spammers become more devious; as the number of sensors and devices we are connected to—and our reliance on the network—grows; and as the formal legal and regulatory system fails to provide us with relief.

The epidemic of spam has continued almost unabated, exposing us to different forms of advertising constantly. The descendants of the original Cantor and Siegel spam advertising model are now a much broader threat, including cyberattacks that can cause huge financial losses and inconvenience to millions. Email spam was, for example, the trigger for one of the largest data breaches of 2014, that involving Target stores: theft of the data began with a phishing email sent to a heating and air conditioning company doing work for Target with a link to their network.[15] The goal was typical of most spam today, namely to spread viruses, malware, and, more recently, ransomware, in order to cause financial and other harm.

One of the best existing safeguards for consumers actually came about almost twenty years before Cantor and Siegel, when the idea of individuals being connected to a network was still fanciful, with the passage of the Electronic Funds Transfer Act of 1978.[16] The act limited the liability of consumers if a credit card was stolen. It also initiated the idea of the chargeback system[17] which enables consumers using credit cards to contest a transaction. In such cases, a dissatisfied consumer notifies the issuer of their credit card and requests a reversal of the transaction. If the charge is removed, the credit card company receives payment from the merchant. Debit cards are not subject to the act but banks have put in place the same protections the law provides.

The chargeback system is the most frequently used dispute resolution process in the United States, but it can be slow and unsatisfactory to consumers protesting a charge.[18] In addition, the chargeback system is not required for many of the new payment systems that are being developed. PayPal, for example, is not technically a credit card and is therefore not subject to the Electronic Funds Transfer Act requirements. It has, however, installed the same requirements in its own regulations[19]—PayPal rightfully realized this would be necessary for consumers to be willing use the PayPal system, although the chargeback system is hardly a solution to the wide range of problems that arise from e-commerce transactions.

Whenever new opportunities for using and communicating information appear, disputes will follow. This is particularly true when, first of all, money is involved; and second, when it is difficult to employ the formal legal system to regulate those who are empowered with new and complex tools or who are difficult to find or located beyond the jurisdiction.[20] Spam is important not only because of what it has developed into but because it is something we need to learn from. It has been more than twenty years since Cantor and Siegel, and the state is still searching for a role that will effectively protect consumers. We have, over time, figured out how to preserve trust in credit cards (on which our economies depend), but it is nonetheless a fragile trust. There is little reason to have faith in government being able to prevent harm caused by sophisticated frauds and large-scale cyberattacks. Spam is a constant reminder that "no matter what you do online, you're trusting someone to tell you the truth—whether it's your bank giving you your statement balance, your email service provider telling you your message was delivered, or your antivirus software assuring you that everything's A-OK."[21] It is also a reminder that all the assistance provided to users through spam filters and other resources are aimed at prevention. They have been developed by private companies who recognized that email would have no value and online commerce would suffer if users were not provided some protection from malicious acts and innocent errors.

RESOLVING DISPUTES

The domain name system—and the process established for resolving disputes over them—also give us clear and important lessons about the relationship between e-commerce and dispute resolution and prevention. Domain names, which are linked to internet protocol (IP) addresses such as 128.20.0.1, are like street addresses and are the only piece of the internet that must be regulated. This is handled by the Internet Corporation for Assigned Names and Numbers (ICANN), which was established in 1998.[22] Domain names provide us with an essential map—perhaps even the street structure itself—in the infinite global city that is the internet. They are a significant piece of the online infrastructure that is needed for e-commerce to function. The system was established before there were easy-to-use search engines. Without domain names, we would have the equivalent of a city without recognizable street names, and it would be difficult to locate anything. Without regulation of domain names, there might be more than one entity with the same domain name. In that case, we would also not know how to locate what we are looking for.

The domain name system was invented in 1984 but only grew rapidly starting in the mid-1990s. As noted earlier, the number of .com domain names increased from 1,151 in October 1990[23] to 1,301,000 in July 1997, to more than twenty million in November 2000.[24] Today, there are over three hundred million top-level (such as .com., .net, and .org) domains.[25] It was during the 1990s that companies began to realize that domain names were valuable and could bring business to the company's online presence. At the same time, businesses were concerned that their trademarks would be damaged if someone registered a domain name that was the same as the trademark.

Disputes over domain names were a consequence of not anticipating the popularity of and demand for the .com domain. In the physical world, trademark law allows different entities to have the same name if consumers would not to be confused. Thus, the Delta Faucet Company, Delta Airlines, and the Delta Technology Company can all use the word Delta in their corporate names because they are in different industries and one will not be confused with the others. Unfortunately, the domain name system allows only one entity to have the .com domain. In the mid-1990s, when Google did not exist and other search engines were in their infancy, a domain name was the primary means to find a website of a particular business. Not only was there competition among trademark owners for the same name but individuals who understood this began registering the names of businesses who did not understand this. Domain names were sold on a first come, first served basis, and purchasers hoped to resell the domain name to the highest bidder. This also opened up the possibility for litigation by trademark owners against those who had registered the domain name and hoped to attract business meant for a competitor.

Domain name disputes, therefore, arose out of several key factors. First was a simple supply-and-demand issue: there was more demand than supply for names in the .com domain. Second, few anticipated how domain names would become a critical advertising, marketing, and search vehicle for companies, therefore valuable in and of themselves. Third, they were not understood to be investments whose value could increase over time. Some who did understand this began to try to manipulate the system. One example of this was "typosquatting":[26] buying a domain name with a common typo—such as MicrosOft with a zero instead of the letter O—and hoping that users might not notice and click on the link, which would lead them to a competitor, a porn site, and so forth, thereby bringing revenue to the domain name owner. Another category of disputes was generated by domain names that were employed to express criticism, like Walmartsucks.com or AOLsucks.com. Should these be considered worthy of free speech protection or were they a violation of trademark law?[27]

What had at first been a very simple system became increasingly complex over time. The idea of considering domain names as a kind of street address and not subject to trademark law at all seems to have never been considered, nor were other creative attempts to avoid domain name disputes. Domain names, for example, could have been shared. All of the companies with the word Delta in their name could have been linked to a single site, which would have then led the user to Delta Airlines, Delta Faucets, or whatever. Scrabble actually did this, and still does. The ownership rights to Scrabble are held in the United States by Hasbro and in the rest of the world by Mattel. Hasbro and Mattel together registered the scrabble.com domain name, and the website scrabble.com links to both companies.[28] They have been living peacefully with this arrangement.

The Internet Corporation for Assigned Names and Numbers (ICANN) recognized when it was founded that a process and a set of rules for resolving domain name disputes was sorely needed. They established a nonbinding arbitration system, meaning that whoever lost could still go to court and assert a trademark claim. In actuality, few losers would.

The arbitration process itself consisted of one arbitrator, paid for by the complaining trademark owner, or three arbitrators, paid for by both parties.[29] The complainant chose the dispute resolution organization that would provide the arbitrator. Why would domain name holders agree to this process, which could potentially result in their loss of the domain name? In short, because there was no choice. Acceptance of the process is required by the agreement everyone signs when registering a domain name.[30] One also agrees that if the arbitrator finds in favor of the trademark owner, the database of domain names is modified, with the old owner being replaced by the trademark owner. This is an instance, in other words, in which enforcement of the arbitrator's ruling is quick and easy.

The rules established by ICANN for the arbitrators were relatively straight forward. The domain name had to be identical or confusingly similar to a trademark held by the complainant and the domain name had to have been registered and used in bad faith.[31] The following excerpt from the policy provides guidance on what is "bad faith."

(i)   circumstances indicating that you have registered or you have acquired the domain name primarily for the purpose of selling, renting, or otherwise transferring the domain name registration to the complainant who is the owner of the trademark or service mark or to a competitor of that complainant, for valuable consideration in excess of your documented out-of-pocket costs directly related to the domain name; or

(ii) you have registered the domain name in order to prevent the owner of the trademark or service mark from reflecting the mark in a corresponding domain name, provided that you have engaged in a pattern of such conduct; or

(iii) you have registered the domain name primarily for the purpose of disrupting the business of a competitor; or

(iv) by using the domain name, you have intentionally attempted to attract, for commercial gain, Internet users to your web site or other online location, by creating a likelihood of confusion with the complainant's mark as to the source, sponsorship, affiliation, or endorsement of your web site or location or of a product or service on your web site or location.[32]

But what should the arbitrator do with the person who registers a domain name like Walmartsucks.com? For the arbitrator to rule in favor of the trademark owner, it must be found that the domain name is being employed for commercial gain and creates "a likelihood of confusion with the complainant's mark."[33] Is Walmartsucks.com likely to confuse a user about who owns the domain name? There have been many of these "sucks.com" cases. Somewhat surprisingly, in 62 percent of these cases the arbitrators have ruled in favor of the trademark owner and have transferred the name.[34]

Although the domain name dispute policy appears fair and reasonable on its surface, in fact it illustrates precisely the kinds of challenges in designing and implementing a dispute resolution process able to satisfy the dispute resolution triangle elements of trust, convenience, and expertise.[35] In this case, the element of convenience has been achieved. The process takes place online, is unquestionably less expensive than going to court, decisions are made relatively quickly, and the ruling is easily enforced. The main element of concern with this process is fairness. One early study, titled "Fair.com,"[36] concluded that the process was anything but. Studies since have shown that the two main providers of arbitrators—the World Intellectual Property Organization (WIPO) and the National Arbitration Forum (NAF)—rule in favor of the trademark owner approximately 85 percent of the time.[37]

Why does this happen? Are the arbitrators biased in favor of the trademark owners? This is not an easy question to answer, but it is hard to trust in the fairness of a system that finds, in most instances, that a "sucks" domain might be confused with the original company name domain. In addition, there is the experience of a third dispute resolution organization, eResolution, that handled domain name disputes from 2000 to 2003; arbitrators for eResolution found in favor of trademark owners only 61 percent of the time.[38] Since all decisions are published, this became common knowledge, and trademark owners stopped choosing eResolution as a provider, selecting instead a provider they were confident would find in their favor. By 2003, eResolution was out of business.[39]

There is an additional complication in that approximately half of all respondents fail to respond to complaints.[40] An arbitrator is still allowed to find in favor of the domain name holder despite a lack of response, but that rarely happens. Defaults may occur because the respondent feels that its case is weak or, alternatively, feels that it is unlikely to receive a fair hearing. ICANN accredits the providers, but imposes almost no standards that would persuade domain name holders that the process is fair. So although it's true that the domain name dispute resolution process has been a success in terms of convenience, questions of fairness as well as trust remain unresolved.[41]

Also, the ICANN system was premised on an understanding of ODR as online ADR—arbitration was imported online without using the "intelligence of the machine," and the process was (and still is) premised on the role of a human arbitrator in deciding the cases. While this approach may be feasible in the domain name context, it cannot satisfactorily address the many millions of disputes that are arising in the e-commerce arena. eBay understood this early on. Alibaba, the Chinese mammoth e-commerce marketplace, also realized that it would have to rely on automated processes, allowing for human assistance only where absolutely necessary.

The Alibaba dispute resolution system is based on automated negotiation in the eBay spirit as a first stage, and, if unsuccessful, disputing parties may turn to either a user-based jury system, or, as a last resort, to a human customer service representative. Strikingly, 99 percent of disputes are resolved through negotiations between buyers and sellers without intervention by Alibaba representatives.[42] This statistic is significantly higher than the eBay one and may be attributed to the strong incentives provided by Alibaba in the form of a reduction in both the buyer's and the seller's reputational rating if their dispute requires the involvement of a customer service representative.[43]

Alibaba has also introduced incentives into its "User Dispute Resolution System."[44] This is a public jury system that is based on volunteer registered users who serve as decision-makers. Jury members cast their vote in favor of one of the disputants, and are rewarded with positive reputation credit based on their participation.[45] Alibaba compiles a credit rating for each user, using various data which includes financial and non-quantitative data, going beyond what the U.S. credit industry would include in such rating,[46] bringing us closer to a "scored society."[47] The credit rating can be translated into donations for a public cause, paid for by Alibaba,[48] something that ultimately benefits the jury member, and may be used to determine eligibility for financial transactions.[49] The jury system allows for quick and effective resolutions.[50] Alibaba also employs various algorithms to ensure jury members' fair decisions. As of March 2016 there were 920,000 active jury members, rendering 150 million votes.[51]

Most important, by adopting a dispute resolution system that goes beyond discrete ODR tools, Alibaba's case data feeds back into their operations. As stated by Ms. Jing Li, a senior legal adviser at Alibaba, "this is valuable input for us. It allows us to better understand customer expectations, the market etc., and improve the design of our operations."[52] In other words, Alibaba's data-centered mode of operation allows for online dispute prevention, an activity which lies at the heart of the new dispute resolution landscape, as further explained below.

PREVENTING DISPUTES

Let us return to the fictional story of Jane and John. Airbnb is part of an e-commerce phenomenon that has a variety of names. Most commonly called the "sharing economy," it is also frequently labeled the "on-demand economy," the "gig economy," and the "1099 economy."[53] Each of these labels captures a quality of e-commerce activity with some novel elements. None of the labels, however, is a perfect fit. For example, it is hard to find instances of sharing in the traditional sense in the "sharing economy." Airbnb refers to customers most often as "guests" rather than renters, but it is a mistake to infer that the relationship is anything but commercial. Airbnb hosts do not offer space in their homes or apartments for free. These are "guests" even less than Facebook "friends" are true friends.

The "sharing economy," at least when the label was originally employed, tended to be described in highly positive terms, referring to such values as sharing, collaboration, responsibility, trust, cooperation, and accountability.[54] In the aftermath of the economic downturn, such values were embraced and celebrated. New technologies, mainly the growth of social media and the increased availability of smartphones, fed into these developments and reinforced them. Law was often viewed as an intruder to this newly emerging paradise of sorts.[55] This is actually ironic, since the larger and richer these enterprises became, the less collaborative they became, and the more they came to rely on traditional contractual relationships.[56]

The terms "gig" and "on-demand" economy generally refer to providing services rather than goods. All of these companies use technology to manage unused space or unused time. When services are sold, the novel employment relationship opens up opportunities for disputes to occur. It has been estimated that disputes occur in 3–5 percent of online transactions, leading to over seven hundred million e-commerce disputes in 2015.[57] If one considers every Airbnb rental or Uber ride an e-commerce transaction, this is not an unreasonable estimate, which leads to the further estimate that the number will rise to a billion disputes in a few years.[58] Unfortunately, as the number of disputes rises, start-ups tend to not take advantage of opportunities to prevent disputes.

What is novel about on-demand enterprises is not the particular goods or services offered. One was always able to rent a room in New York, purchase an old baseball card, or find someone to mow a lawn. What is novel is the level of speed and degree of convenience offered to the consumer, and the use of technology that allows the marketplace to operate at a high scale. As one of Airbnb's founders noted, "You can write one line of code that can solve a problem for one customer, 10,000 or 10 million."[59]

Descriptions of "sharing economy" marketplaces should emphasize the word "economy" more than the word "sharing." Airbnb, for example, enables buyers to pay sellers and renters to pay hosts. No one is giving anything away. The combination of novelty and payments are, in any context, two good ingredients for generating disputes. Initially, though, the sharing economy enterprises have not been as creative in developing measures to prevent disputes as they have been in selling their product. The principal means employed for preventing disputes in the Airbnb context when it first began were contracts involving the host, Airbnb, and the "guest," a reputation system, and a kind of insurance protection for the host. This is a "kind of insurance protection" because even Airbnb reminds users that the Host Guarantee is not insurance, despite being referred to as such in the media.[60]

Whatever kind of services they offer, disputes are a topic that most start-ups would generally prefer to ignore. Any new company's primary goal is to scale revenue; dispute resolution is often viewed as either a distraction or an investment of funds that are needed elsewhere. Advertising the existence of a dispute resolution process also acknowledges that disputes occur—something, we have often been told, entrepreneurs think can be hidden or at least not explicitly referred to.

Lastly, these companies often assume that reputation and feedback systems are sufficient to deter bad actors. However, in the context of providing a service rather than a product, reputation ratings can be more problematic given the physical proximity and interaction between the parties, and the nature of the work performed. Such ratings, of course, are a major dispute generator themselves. As stated in a recent book,

> Sharing Economy reputation systems have become fronts for hierarchical and centralized disciplinary systems, which have nothing to do with notions of 'peer-to-peer' reputation or 'algorithmic regulation' or regulation with a 'lighter touch' through ratings. We trust strangers on the Sharing Economy platforms for the same reason we trust hotel employees and restaurant waiters: because they are in precarious jobs where customer complaints can lead to disciplinary action. The reputation system is a way to enforce 'emotional labor'; service providers are compelled to manage their feelings and present the face that the platform demands, to become that 'friend with a car' or that 'neighbor helping neighbors.' It's the fast food worker's 'Have a nice day' taken to the next step.[61]

Preventing disputes—or stopping a dispute from escalating—is best achieved by establishing an ongoing relationship with users, and understanding how disputes occur and why positions harden, anger increases, and the dispute escalates if it is not anticipated or dealt with early. In other words, it requires ongoing and clear communication by the platform with its users, as well as a rich database on disputes and ongoing analysis of the data. In some instances, preventing one type of dispute can give rise to new types of problems. On the Airbnb website, for example, the attempts to expand the scope of information provided to guests and hosts about one another before they enter a transaction was seen as an effective means for enhancing trust and safety in transactions between strangers. At the same time, increased information about one another has allowed hosts to discriminate against guests on the basis of race, as one study has found.[62] This happens because "[d]ata acquisition shifts the place where racism happens from the street to the database query."[63] The publication of the aforementioned research findings has, in turn, stimulated Airbnb to attempt to prevent instances of discrimination on the website through a variety of measures, including the expansion of instant booking opportunities (without host approval) and enriching information about guests beyond photos.[64] Airbnb's serious effort to combat discrimination on its platform is laudable, but also underscores the importance of studying the operation of large-scale platforms and, in our context, the impact of their design, operation, and the manner in which they address actual and potential disputes.

Jane and John's experience was novel to them, but some of the elements of this dispute have undoubtedly occurred among the millions of rentals Airbnb facilitates every month. The Airbnb site has advice and recommendations for hosts, but these need to first be found by the hosts. None of the data accumulated by Airbnb that might have been helpful to Jane and John was efficiently passed on, nor were processes in place to help respond to the problem quickly and effectively.

To understand Airbnb's level of involvement with its users, or lack thereof, one must start with the agreement that all users of the system must accept. It would not surprise us if the two authors of this book are the only humans (other than Airbnb's lawyers and employees) who have fully read these rules. This user agreement contains over 30,000 words. Much of it is in a very small font, essentially fine print in digital form. (Airbnb is not at alone in having lengthy and difficult-to-decipher agreements. PayPal's agreement is 36,275 words. As a comparison, Hamlet contains 30,066 words.[65]) On the other hand, anyone who has used Airbnb or searched for a listing has agreed to these rules. To quote the terms of service, "If you are using the Site, Application or Services and you reside in the USA, you are contracting with Airbnb, Inc. with respect to use of the Airbnb Site."[66]

If one did thoroughly read this agreement, it might be found disturbing to potential hosts. The main thrust of the user agreement is to limit the potential liability of Airbnb and limit the recourse available to unsatisfied users. Consider the following excerpts:

> If a Guest requests a booking of your Accommodation and stays at your Accommodation, any agreement you enter into with such Guest is between you and the Guest and Airbnb is not a party to it.
> YOU ACKNOWLEDGE AND AGREE THAT, TO THE MAXIMUM EXTENT PERMITTED BY LAW, THE ENTIRE RISK ARISING OUT OF YOUR ACCESS TO AND USE OF THE SITE, APPLICATION, SERVICES AND COLLECTIVE CONTENT, YOUR LISTING OR BOOKING OF ANY ACCOMMODATIONS VIA THE SITE, APPLICATION AND SERVICES, YOUR PARTICIPATION IN THE REFERRAL PROGRAM, AND ANY CONTACT YOU HAVE WITH OTHER USERS OF AIRBNB WHETHER IN PERSON OR ONLINE REMAINS WITH YOU."[67]

What exactly does Airbnb do? According to the user agreement, "Airbnb provides an online platform that connects hosts who have accommodations to rent with guests seeking to rent such accommodations." By declaring that it is only providing a platform, the company is saying that it is not itself selling anything or actually involved with the parties. Without being a party to the host-guest arrangement, it seeks to avoid any liability for any problem that arises.

This is an approach that eBay attempted in early versions of its terms of service. There are two flaws to this approach. One is that Airbnb provides more than a technological means to find or publicize information about a listing. It handles all the money and use of credit cards; it has a Resolution Center and handles complaints; it has a process for compensating hosts in certain circumstances;[68] in some countries, Airbnb even provides liability and property insurance.[69] In addition to already being involved with the guest and host in several different ways, it is likely, as time passes, that the corporation will feel pressure to become even more involved with guests, in all likelihood by instituting systems for avoiding and resolving disputes. This pattern of greater engagement with dispute resolution as the company grows has been seen in eBay and other marketplaces that at one time tried to avoid liability by claiming to be just a "platform."

Having a process for engaging the parties as the dispute is emerging is far superior to telling the parties to work it out themselves or to ignore it. Asking parties to try to negotiate a solution themselves without providing assistance for such interaction, often as not, leads to parties getting even angrier with each other. Email is a poor form of communication for resolving differences between angry parties because the free text form of email and the very rapid exchange of emails are not really conducive to reducing anger and finding common ground.

Another part of the problem has to do with the authority that user reviews and feedback are given on each site. Jane and John's problem stemmed from a guest posting negative feedback. When one of this book's authors conducted a pilot project for eBay in 1999 to see if mediating buyer-seller disputes were possible, he was told that he could not resolve disputes over the feedback system. In other words, eBay's policy at the time was never to remove any feedback. Sometime later, eBay did realize that developing a process to handle reputation disputes over feedback was something it would ultimately benefit from. In fact, the context of feedback disputes was an arena in which eBay experimented with creative process design, producing the "eBay community court" pilot in late 2008. Under the community court scheme, sellers disputing negative buyer feedback could submit their complaint to a randomly selected panel of jurors. This represented one of the first attempts to use crowdsourcing in dispute resolution. It also allowed eBay to address the challenge of handling the relative small percentage but still significant number of disputes that required human determination.[70] For many of the same reasons, this model was also adopted by Alibaba more recently, at a much larger scale, as described above.

Airbnb also has an arbitration process in place to help address disputes over feedback. However, it can only be employed after fourteen days of trying to resolve the dispute. This is not a process that is likely to build trust or prevent parties from getting angrier and angrier with each other. As happened with Jane and John, such anger is not only reflected in the host's reputation on Airbnb but spills over into complaints on social media sites like airbnbhell.com, in which Airbnb becomes the target. If there is no intervention, in other words, the online environment speeds up emergence, escalation, and broadening of the dispute.

This is only one prong of the many types of disputes over Airbnb's interactions. Outside of the reputation feedback system, Airbnb's main attempt to prevent disputes was implementation of a "host guarantee." This is the process that looks like—but is not—insurance. In order for a host to collect on the guarantee, there are many conditions that must be met:

- You must have provided the Responsible Guest with clear written instructions on how the Responsible Guest and any Invitees should conduct themselves while staying in your Covered Accommodation, including informing them that they will be responsible for all Covered Losses.
- You must ensure that any agreement you enter into with the Responsible Guest with respect to the Covered Accommodation includes an express obligation to pay you for damages or losses for any Covered Property caused by such Responsible Guest or Invitee.
- You must provide Airbnb with proof of ownership of, or legal responsibility for, the Covered Property in the form of receipts, photographs, videos, documents or other customary forms of proof (including, but not limited to, appraisal or valuation forms or notices addressed to you) certified by you as true and correct and reasonably acceptable to Airbnb.

The "guarantee" also does not cover jewelry, cash, securities, or pets.

In January 2015, Airbnb began providing actual insurance but only for listings in the United States (it has since added other countries).[71] This is liability insurance for injuries and also property insurance for any damage to the building. A well-known claim[72] in which a guest clogged a toilet that then caused water to overflow and $10,000 worth of damage to someone else's apartment would seem to be covered by the new policy. Unfortunately, that event occurred in October 2014, before the insurance was in place.

In general, on-demand websites selling services have a more complex dispute resolution challenge than those, like eBay, that sell goods. There are usually more things that can go wrong with providing a service than when selling something tangible. It isn't as easy to return a service as it is to return a tangible object; issues of trust and personal safety also become central in the services area. Most disputes in eBay's dispute resolution process involve something not delivered, something not paid for, something broken, and so forth. Nevertheless, Airbnb probably knows the ten kinds of disputes that arise most often in the space-renting context, and in all likelihood could design an appropriate dispute resolution process to resolve and prevent them.

In this context, dispute resolution and dispute prevention are closely linked. An online dispute resolution process sends data to the company and provides a learning experience for users. Airbnb may legally be just a "platform," but to users Airbnb is also a kind of host providing an array of services. If Airbnb helps to solve problems for a user, the user is much more likely to use the system again, as can be seen in eBay's experience described below.[73] But dispute prevention is also occurring at the data (or, Big Data) level, at the predispute resolution stage, and even at predispute phase, where data allows megaplatforms to structure interactions in a way that reduces the likelihood of disputes occurring. Airbnb, for example, may base its decision on which listings to display first, on data analysis that indicates that such transactions are less likely to generate problems.

After an initial reluctance to assume responsibility for user-to-user disputes, Airbnb has realized it must play a role in addressing conflicts between users. A variety of options allow the site to detect bad actors by monitoring activity on the site, authenticating identity, better matching guests with hosts, and mentoring parties on appropriate behavior and on how to deal with problems once they arise—all activities directed at prevention.

Identifying data that can assist in prevention may in fact be the most important lesson the Airbnb experience has to offer. The effortless recording of large amounts of data relating to anyone operating on the site creates a huge database that can be cross-checked with information on problems and resolutions, generating unique insights on how to structure more satisfactory transactions, what problematic patterns need to be dealt with, what rules and practices require clarification or amendment, and which participants require mentoring or instruction. In all of these, the line between prevention and resolution becomes more and more fluid: learning opportunities extend to the dispute resolution avenues themselves, producing insights on such issues as the effectiveness of certain avenues or certain dispute resolvers over others.

In establishing a dispute resolution process, the primary goal for a large e-commerce marketplace is actually not to resolve an exceptionally large number of disputes. The main goal is to maximize the number of *successful transactions*. Resolving disputes is essential to building trust and increasing that volume. By monitoring host and guest behavior and extending the expertise side of the triangle, the company can provide fast and fair resolutions that encourage users to engage in more transactions. This collection and analysis of the data generated by very large numbers of disputes can enable techniques and approaches that are not possible in traditional offline dispute prevention efforts. In the tragic instances of Uber drivers who commit crimes, for example, the first question usually asked is about background checks. This is certainly appropriate. However for drivers who have been driving for some time, Uber may have other data about driving habits that, in some cases, would have even more predictive value. One carmaker, for example, has stated that "we know more about how and when a driver brakes than the driver does."[74] Uber, if not now, then in the very near future, will have a great deal of data about driver behaviors that was never before available.

What is the scope of dispute prevention activities? At what frequency and scale do they occur? Which principles guide the company in designing and conducting them? Much remains unknown about e-commerce entities' dispute prevention policies. They are typically conducted internally, discretely, are not part of a "process" (which is subject to due process or other, similar expectations) and do not necessarily reflect the input of relevant stakeholders.

Over time, eBay and others learned something that the new generation of sharing economy companies will also need to understand: disputes can actually be a good thing and benefit a company. The most obvious reason for this is that dispute resolution represents a promise to users (and potential users) that if something goes wrong, it will be fixed. It helps build trust and reduce risk, thus influencing a user's willingness to try the system. In addition—and perhaps more important, from the company's point of view—dispute resolution is important in identifying bad experiences. eBay's former director of online dispute resolution has explained the value of responding to bad experiences:

> [I]magine you were buying gifts for your family and friends over several weeks leading up to the holiday season . . . imagine that one of the items arrives and there is a problem. Maybe it was damaged in shipping, or maybe the wrong item was delivered. When that happens, you as the purchaser must pay individual attention to that particular transaction. You go back to your e-mail, search for the item receipt, and determine which marketplace the item was purchased from. Then you go to the website of the marketplace and try to determine what you need to do to get the problem resolved. That is the moment at which the buyer experiences an in-depth and unexpected interaction with an e-commerce marketplace. That is the moment where loyalty is imprinted. If the marketplace provides an easy to find process for resolving the problem, a strong impression is made in the mind of the buyer. If the marketplace does not provide any easy to discover process for resolving the problem, the buyer's experience instead is one of frustration, which creates a strong impression in the other direction.[75]

eBay has learned what should be a fairly obvious lesson: that disputes occur in any large-scale enterprise and can provide opportunities to generate loyal customers. This should be even more obvious when those transactions and relationships occur at a distance.

Customer satisfaction is desired in any context. In the alternative dispute resolution (ADR) world, various studies have measured the satisfaction rates of users of different ADR systems.[76] In actuality, these are measurements that derive from what the parties say about how they feel after participating in a mediation or arbitration. Companies that have access to every click made by a user can examine satisfaction in a much more granular manner. In 2010 eBay and PayPal conducted a study that was not intended to measure satisfaction in the traditional manner, for example, by surveying disputants before and after participating in a dispute resolution process.[77] Instead, it would measure customer loyalty by comparing the *behavior* of participants before and after the dispute resolution process—something it could easily measure with data they routinely collected. In other words, eBay would not look at what users said but at their actions as buyers or sellers after participating in an online dispute resolution process.[78]

eBay randomly assigned several hundred thousand users to two groups and compared their buying and seller behavior for three months before and three months after the ODR experience. This activity ratio indicated not only how much more or less active the party became on the site after winning or losing a dispute, but could also calculate how much the company gained or lost financially as a result of someone participating in the ODR experience. It did this by knowing the exact value of each transaction the person engaged in before and after the dispute resolution process.

The study's designers had hypothesized that parties who "won" their dispute (e.g., received a reimbursement) would have increased activity and that parties who "lost" their dispute would have decreased activity. It assumed, in other words, that parties who won would be more satisfied than parties who lost and would adjust their transaction volume accordingly. This did indeed occur. But the most meaningful lesson of the study, and the most counterintuitive, was that participation in the ODR process led to increased activity even from the losers. What it found was that

> [t]he only buyers who decreased their activity after filing their first dispute were buyers for whom the process took a long time, more than six weeks. This lesson affirmed feedback we had heard previously indicating that buyers preferred to lose their case quickly rather than have the resolution process go on for an extended period of time.[79]

Airbnb's Resolution Center requires users to wait fourteen days before filing a complaint. Granted, this is a lot less than six weeks, but the time is unlikely to build trust or positive opinions, particularly if the decision is negative. Over the years, eBay's ODR system has received its share of complaints, but it is nonetheless one that attends to all three sides of the triangle. The few clicks necessary to file a complaint enhances convenience. The automated negotiation process developed by eBay, as well as the capability to analyze data, extract information, and use that data to improve the user experience, provides a kind of expertise not possible with systems that rely solely on human labor. Trust is the overarching and primary goal. The data on usage patterns can bring to light new information as to what is needed to build that trust, and to attract and maintain users. It is yet another way in which the maxim "justice delayed is justice denied" holds true.

ANOTHER STORY AND LESSON

Professor Katsh once asked a class to read a short story called "Assembly Line," by B. Traven,[80] an author known primarily for the book (and later movie), *Treasure of Sierra Madre*. "Assembly Line" tells the story of a tourist named Winthrop who was vacationing in Oaxaca, Mexico. While walking around town, he discovered what he thought might be a successful commercial opportunity: a craftsman making and selling baskets. Finding the baskets both incredibly beautiful and inexpensive, Winthrop thought that he could import them, mark them up, and sell them in New York at a nice profit.

Winthrop returned to New York, found a buyer willing to purchase ten thousand baskets at a good price, and traveled back to Oaxaca to give the craftsman the good news. Closing the deal, however, turned out to be difficult. Winthrop's profit calculations assumed that the price per basket would decline as more baskets were produced. The craftsman, however, wanted to preserve the distinctiveness of each basket and was not eager to mass produce them. He told Winthrop, therefore, that the price per basket would have to increase as the number of baskets ordered increased. In other words, if Winthrop wanted ten thousand baskets, each basket would cost more than if one hundred were ordered. Winthrop had assumed that there would be economies of scale, but the opposite was occurring.

In discussing this story with students, it was suggested that if something like this were to occur today, the mix of variables in the storyline would be completely changed by technology. In Traven's version, the tourist Winthrop travels back and forth to Mexico to negotiate the details. It is Winthrop who finds the craftsman and his baskets, it is Winthrop who finds a buyer for the baskets in New York, and it is Winthrop who is positioned to make the largest profit. One student's reaction to this was, "Who needs Winthrop?"

What this student meant by "who needs Winthrop?" was that the craftsman today could simply sell his own baskets via eBay or some other online site; it is now quite possible for someone located anywhere to sell a product to someone else who is also anywhere. The reason for this, she told Ethan, was that "everything is simpler than it used to be."

Most of the students agreed with her. Replacing commerce with e-commerce, they claimed, was indeed simple; some of the students even had their own small businesses online. The entity providing software might charge a small fee and the payment system might take a small percentage, but conducting business online was so simple that it could even be managed with a smartphone.

The truth is, however, that replacing Winthrop with eBay, Amazon, Etsy, or any number of popular sites for selling online is not really simple. Using a smartphone to buy something online initiates a highly complex process, mostly technical, but also legal. Whenever something online appears to be simple, indeed whenever anything at all is done online, there is a great deal of complexity hiding somewhere in the background.

It has taken us half a century to turn the original internet into a network for exchanging information and money in a manner that is easy for consumers at a degree of risk they are willing to accept. The network makes possible a kind of supply chain where information can be communicated, items can be selected, contractual terms agreed to, and money exchanged. Admittedly, in most instances, at least in the developed world, this is a fairly seamless process. The more we use it, rely on it, and build upon it, however, the more complex that process becomes, and the more likely it is that we will encounter a problem. Publicized data breaches are only one element starting to shake up our confidence a bit. Since most services we use require us to agree to a long contract that absolves the provider of liability (and which almost no one reads), legal recourse is not an option. We are left, in most instances, with those online entities that see value in providing easy-to-use dispute resolution options to customers.

Bill Gates once remarked that "[the] magic of software can eliminate . . . complexity."[81] What Gates probably meant was that the magic of software *hides* complexity, thus providing the users of well-designed software with the illusion of simplicity. The interface may be simple to use but the infrastructure is anything but.

It used to be possible to distinguish complex transactions from simple transactions. Today, there are only highly complex transactions and less complex ones. Consider, for example, the element at the heart of any e-commerce transaction: the exchange of money for goods or services. In the Traven story, paying the basketmaker in person is simple. But the basketmaker is in a foreign country and perhaps does not have a credit card or the ability to process credit card transactions. What about using something like PayPal? PayPal does claim that it does business in 203 countries.[82] Complete functionality, however—where there are many options for sending, receiving, and withdrawing money—exists in only about thirty countries. What is easy for us in the developed world may be possible in the undeveloped world but not nearly as easy. We do not yet live in a borderless world where the playing field is even. Items that eBay bans in one country, for example, may be put up for auction in another.[83]

We live in a rapidly changing world in which Bitcoin and other payment systems are appearing alongside PayPal. In addition, we are buying, or attempting to buy, more and more virtual goods. In some contexts, paying for such goods is not as easy as it should be. Time is needed to build sufficient trust before these systems are widely accepted. Consider the following telephone exchange between the journalist Julian Dibbell and a PayPal customer service representative:[84]

"Hi, thank you for calling PayPal. How can I help you?"

"Yes, hi. I just had payment reversed on a sale that I made, and I understand that because the item I sold was a virtual item from an online game, that payment is not covered by your Seller Protection Policy, and I therefore won't be getting my money back."

"That's correct."

"So, yeah, so I just wanted to check in about that and for future reference make sure that I understand just what is and isn't covered under clause 5 of the policy, which requires that 'The seller ships tangible goods.'"

"That means anything that isn't tangible isn't covered.

. . .

"OK, I just want to be absolutely clear about this now. So say I ship somebody tickets to a football game—is that covered?"

"Yes, because you've shipped them tickets. That's a tangible good."

"OK, then what if I ship them tickets to a virtual item?"

"What?"

"Say I write down a password that gives the buyer access to a virtual item—say I write that on a piece of paper or put it on a computer disk and ship that to the buyer and then give you guys the tracking number for that shipment. Would that be covered?"

"I don't think so."

These kinds of conversations—testing definitions, boundaries, mechanisms, concepts, legal jurisdictions, and means of exchange—will happen a hundredfold over as we try to adapt to new and complex transactions and relationships in which the online environment confronts the physical world. In just the same way as users will struggle to understand these nuances, institutions with legal authority will also. The need to provide online avenues for addressing cross-border consumer disputes continues to be a real concern on a national and international level.

Both the European Union[85] and the United Nations Commission on International Trade Law (UNCITRAL)[86] have been engaged in trying to facilitate the adoption of cross-border ODR systems. In Europe, the ADR Directive and the ODR Regulation—which seek to encourage use of ADR and an ODR platform for addressing cross-border disputes between EU consumers and EU traders—have been adopted.[87] While the directive is aimed at encouraging the use of ADR by ensuring minimal quality standards in the delivery of such services, the regulation required that by January 2016 the EU Commission establish a free interactive website, providing information on ADR, and through which consumers can initiate ODR or ADR processes related to cross-border European online purchases. This actually went into effect in February 2016.

In 2010, UNCITRAL established a working group devoted to the promulgation of an ODR procedural framework for addressing low-value cross-border B2B and B2C disputes arising from e-commerce.[88] Since then and until mid-2016, the working group met twice a year, but the pace of advancement has been slow, largely due to an effort to adopt a two-tiered scheme involving mediation and arbitration. This choice was driven by the desire to take advantage of the existing framework for the enforcement of arbitration awards across jurisdictions (the New York Convention). Due to an impasse in developing the two-tiered approach, the working group shifted its focus to create a set of Technical Notes on ODR, which were approved by the Commission in July 2016.

The rift between the United States and Europe has to do with the enforceability of predispute arbitration clauses in consumer contracts. Despite vocal critiques, the inclusion of predispute arbitration clauses in commercial agreements has become a widespread practice in the United States, with the support of the U.S. Supreme Court.[89] EU countries have shunned such practices; for the most part their courts will not enforce predispute arbitration clauses on consumers.[90] It may be that the very design that emerged through UNCITRAL was reflective of old-world paradigms and power relations, failing to address new phenomena associated with e-commerce—such as the blurring of the consumer-business distinction, wherein individuals are increasingly both buyers and sellers. Consumer organizations object to such clauses because they make it impossible to pursue claims as a class action, but mandatory arbitration clauses are present in almost every U.S. e-commerce site. Airbnb, in its 30,000 words terms of service, is just one example:

> You and Airbnb agree that any dispute, claim or controversy arising out of or relating to these Terms or the breach, termination, enforcement, interpretation or validity thereof, or to the use of the Services or use of the Site or Application (collectively, "Disputes") will be settled by binding arbitration.[91]

While the EU and UNCITRAL frameworks have yet to be fully developed, they are indicative of the growing awareness of ODR and the recognition of its centrality for addressing disputes that arise online—themselves on the rise and bound to grow further as more and more of our daily lives take place online.[92] As consumers rate retailers they encounter in the face-to-face setting, exchange experiences regarding brick-and-mortar businesses on online forums, and order food online from their neighborhood restaurant or market, the distinction between an online consumer dispute and an offline one becomes less and less clear and the appeal of resolving such disputes through online means becomes more appealing. Indeed, use of ODR for traditional consumer disputes, alongside commercial e-commerce ones, is growing. Various bodies are now offering such services, allowing consumers to pursue low-value complaints that were previously in the "lump it or leave it" category, and by doing so enhancing access to justice for offline disputes.

Conclusion

As commercial relations in the last several decades have evolved, so have the types of disputes and conflicts and the development of new tools and systems for addressing such conflicts. The novel dispute resolution and prevention landscape in ODR manifests the shift from a physical to a virtual setting, the shift from human-based to automated processes, and the shift from processes that value confidentiality in resolving disputes to processes focused on collecting, using, and reusing data in order to prevent disputes.

The first shift, from a face-to-face to an online environment, made ODR a necessary avenue for addressing what are often mass-scale, low-dollar-value disputes whose resolution has been essential for sustaining commercial activity online. The efficiencies associated with ODR and the scale at which automated processes could operate, have allowed large entities like eBay, Airbnb, and Alibaba to handle many millions of disputes a year.

Both the potential and limitations of the second shift—the substitution of human intervention with algorithms—can be learned from the shortcomings of those ODR ventures that did not employ them and relied instead on human decision makers, such as the ICANN domain name dispute resolution system. Algorithms may be able to overcome precisely the types of human discretion–based biases that have cast a shadow over the ICANN process. The opacity that surrounds the design and operation of algorithms, as most evident in the so called "sharing economy," also raises its own set of concerns.

Finally, the third shift—from processes that value confidentiality in resolving disputes to processes focused on collecting, using and reusing data in order to prevent disputes—is enabling e-commerce companies to learn from such data about sources of disputes. Such learning, never before possible at such enormous scale and low costs, is helping companies like eBay and Airbnb assess what makes transactions successful and what gives rise to failure; how to better structure transactions and disclose information to users; what training and mentoring needs to take place; how to better incentivize users to collaborate and abide by their agreements; and how to identify and weed out "bad seeds." All of this suggests a better, more trustworthy, less risky experience for the user. At the same time, however, data is being used (and abused) by big companies to assign consumers evaluative scores, which can be discriminatory and inaccurate, but are rarely made known to consumers and cannot be challenged and corrected by them.[93] In addition, dispute prevention-related activities are conducted discretely and are not subject to any kind of principles or guidelines that would ensure their fairness and accountability.

These three critical shifts embedded in ODR are inevitable and are a central component of what defines the new dispute resolution landscape. Each of these represents opportunities and risks, benefits and disadvantages. The e-commerce environment has been an innovator in ODR; despite some misgivings, it provides positive examples of ODR. This is, in part, due to innovations from eBay and other nontraditional e-commerce companies. It is also due to the presence of some new tools that empower consumers to find low prices more easily, spur competition, and encourage the building of e-commerce platforms with novel means of building trust. These are far from perfect systems but are still more advanced than the ODR efforts that are described in the chapters that follow.

CHAPTER 4

The Internet of On-Demand Healthcare

Medical errors kill more people each year than plane crashes, terrorist
attacks, and drug overdoses combined.
—Sarah Kliff, "Fatal Mistakes" (*Vox*, March 15, 2016)

Jamal and Mira are a couple who moved to Hartford, Connecticut in 2015.
In her first visit to her primary care doctor, Mira was given information about
ElectronicPatient.net, the website the physician used that allows patients to see
their electronic health records (EHRs) and the doctor's notes about the visit.[1]
After her old records were transferred to the Electronic Patient system, she
noticed that a former doctor had written "SOB" in describing her. She had gone
to the doctor for treatment of a chest cold and could not fathom why the doctor
had written something so insulting in his notes. Mira called her new doctor's
office to ask about the notes. SOB, it turns out, is a common shorthand for "short
of breath."

Jamal, meanwhile, also visited a new doctor and also encountered a problem.
When he accessed the "patient portal" of his EHR and read through the previous
notes, he found the word "prostitute." This was strange and troubling, so he, too,
called his new doctor's office. They explained that sometimes the program used
by the former doctor automatically finished words to make typing easier and
faster. In this case, the intended word was likely "prostate," not prostitute.

Shortly thereafter, Jamal experienced chest pains and called 911, and an
ambulance took him to Rockville, the local hospital. Jamal told the emergency
room doctor that his records could all be found online. It turned out, however,
that the primary care doctor used different EHR software than the hospital and
records from his primary doctor's EHR system could not be transferred electronically to Rockville. Hoping to solve the problem, Jamal offered to register for an
account on Rockville Hospital's system and copy his records into this account
himself. The doctor told him that this could not be done since they did not allow
patients to enter information directly into the EHR. In the end he was treated and

Digital Justice. Ethan Katsh and Orna Rabinovich-Einy.
© Ethan Katsh and Orna Rabinovich-Einy 2017. Published 2017 by Oxford University Press.

released, but all that medical information was stored in a new record, in a new system, at Rockville Hospital. A paper report was sent to his primary care doctor.

Later, in 2015, Jamal was notified that a data breach had occurred at the Anthem insurance company.[2] Jamal had never heard of Anthem but soon learned that it managed his health insurance. Given his experience with the "prostate/prostitute" mistake, he was concerned not only that his private data was in someone else's hands, but that some entity also had false information about him. Jamal was surprised that Anthem had not encrypted the eighty million records stolen, something that might have made it harder for the thieves to access the data. Nor were they required to do so under the Health Insurance Portability and Accountability Act of 1996 (HIPAA)—the main federal effort to protect medical privacy.[3] The only thing Jamal felt relieved about was that he had not been a Rockville patient in 2012 when a physician's unattended laptop was stolen from his desk at the hospital. The laptop contained health information about 3,800 patients and employees, as well as the personal information—including addresses and Social Security numbers—of a few hundred more Connecticut residents. None of these files had been encrypted either, thus facilitating use by the thieves.[4]

Generating Disputes

Medical errors are the third-leading cause of death in America, after heart disease and cancer.[5] Over a decade ago, the Institute of Medicine published "To Err Is Human," a report that attributed 98,000 deaths each year to hospital mistakes. A few years later, in 2010, the Office of Inspector General for Health and Human Services reported that 180,000 hospital patients in Medicare die each year due to poor hospital care. The number continues to grow. A 2013 study in the *Journal of Patient Safety* estimated that in the next year 210,000 to 440,000 patients who are hospitalized would suffer some sort of preventable harm that would contribute to their death.[6] Many of these would be caused by bad information.

The ever-increasing level of complexity in healthcare means that there are many more opportunities for mistakes to occur and problems to arise. Misinformation that was buried in manila folders is being revealed to patients as they gain access to their electronic files for the first time. Technology is supporting not only the use of new tools but creating a new environment with new participants, new interactions and new relationships. Continuous streams of data are being produced and communicated by apps outside our bodies and by sensors inside. The validity of some of this data, however, is open to question. Modern healthcare is data intensive; we need processes for assuring that data about us is of high quality. Abigail Zuger, a physician and writer, wrote in the

New York Times about the increasing complexity of healthcare and the challenge of achieving accuracy and security in online data:

> It is increasingly critical for patients to be sick in the right place, and increasingly difficult for them to do so. As the great plates of medical care heave and split in cash-based tectonics, the options are multiplying in confusing plenty. There used to be the doctor's office and the hospital. Now we have street corner wellness centers and urgent care centers, free-standing emergency rooms with no hospital attached, chain pharmacies with occasional doctors attached, and nursing practices with no doctors attached. We have hospitals that have merged and split and merged again into configurations that put all the cardiologists uptown, all the neurosurgeons downtown, and all the pediatricians somewhere that keeps changing. Accordingly, we spend a lot of time and energy getting people to where they need to be, launching them according to condition, severity and, always, insurance. Predictable mix-ups occur. Doctors leave insurance plans, patients forget appointments. Or they see the kidney guy, who sends them to a vascular guy, but they already have a vascular guy, and then the cardiologist recommends yet another vascular guy, and now what?[7]

This observation is, in effect, a recipe for generating problems and disputes. In the environment described, there is complexity, novelty, economic value, social impact, professional status, and—underlying everything—rapid change. Physicians have often been described as persons who "deliver" care. The logistics and quality of such delivery may or may not have been better in the past, but they were certainly simpler. In our new environment, the goals for both individual and public health are ambitious, and the reliance on technology to achieve these goals is extensive. but, as noted above, "[p]redictable mix-ups occur." And, of course, so do the unpredictable ones.

In the past, the landscape of healthcare "mix-ups" and disputes was dominated by the issue of malpractice, of large monetary awards for horrendous injuries. The position of malpractice on the map of health-related conflicts, however, is different today. This is not because negligent treatment has been eliminated but because numerous problems that were generally ignored in the past or that had never before occurred are being noticed and acted upon. The landscape previously monopolized by malpractice and high-value disputes is now increasingly being populated with a variety of other problems and issues, often technology-related, that were previously either too small or too few to merit taking action, or that simply did not exist.[8] But in a time of rapid communications, ignoring small disputes can quickly lead to big ones.

Identifying and addressing small (but potentially serious) medical problems is also part of the growing "patient engagement"[9] movement. With novel tools and online access to their medical records, it is hoped that patients may discover problems at an early stage when the medical issues can be responded to more easily, or prevented. An essential element of these tools is online communication with physicians and access to the patient's own medical record, as well as to data collected by tracking devices and apps. Even more novel is the goal of "personalized medicine," a growing field that prescribes different treatments to persons with the same symptoms, often on the basis of genetic differences. As this field grows and opportunities to learn from the experience of other patients multiply, a change in the doctor-patient relationship is also occurring.[10] All of this, in order to improve care and treatment, requires technology that works well and provides information of high quality. In short, it requires an EHR that manages access to data, monitors information quality, communicates across traditional boundaries, and involves patients in novel ways.

Two decades ago, in his 1997 State of the Union address, President Bill Clinton stated that "we should connect every hospital to the Internet, so that doctors can instantly share data about their patients with the best specialists in the field."[11] This theme was resurrected by President George W. Bush almost a decade later in his 2005 State of the Union address, when he asked Congress "to move forward on a comprehensive health-care agenda with . . . improved information technology to prevent medical errors and needless costs."[12] Unsuccessful in moving forward on this in 2005, President Bush urged again, in his 2006 State of the Union address, to "make wider use of electronic records and other health information technology, to help control costs and reduce dangerous medical errors."[13] But still no major progress was made. In February 2009, President Barack Obama stated in an Address to a Joint Session of Congress about the financial crisis, "Our recovery plan will invest in electronic health records and new technology that will reduce errors, bring down costs, ensure privacy and save lives."[14] President Obama was speaking about the American Recovery and Reinvestment Act (ARRA), frequently called the "stimulus bill."[15] One section of that legislation was given a subtitle: Health Information Technology for Economic and Clinical Health Act (HITECH). HITECH authorized $19.2 billion to be used as incentives for physicians and hospitals to adopt and use electronic health records.

EHRs are in much wider use today than ten years ago. They are, however, still not something a president of the United States might brag about in a speech to Congress. It is still not possible, for example, for doctors to "instantly share data about their patients with the best specialists in the field." Linking systems so that data can be transmitted accurately and securely among physicians, patients, and machines remains an ongoing challenge. Patient access to parts of their own EHR is limited, and many physicians remain uncomfortable with much EHR software. The potential for EHRs remains great, but the level of frustration among hospitals, physicians, and patients is also great.[16] As John Palfrey and Urs Gasser note in their book *Interop*,[17] "it is hard to fathom why we have not yet solved this problem."

Any president talking about EHRs today would be speaking about something vastly different from the EHRs of 1997 or even 2006. The practice of medicine and the organization of healthcare are far more complex than they were a decade ago. The hope is that EHRs would assist physicians, hospitals, patients, and others to manage this complexity by collecting, processing, and communicating the information needed for efficient and accurate diagnosis and treatment. To effectively do so, the EHR needs to be something altogether different from the old manila folder and not only store information but also monitor and improve the quality of communication and the processing of information. If this were to actually occur, the EHR would be a primary cornerstone of quality improvement in healthcare.

Dr. David Blumenthal, one of the architects of recent government policies on EHRs, has stated that "[i]nformation is the lifeblood of modern medicine. Health information technology (HIT) is destined to be its circulatory system."[18] With some exceptions, physicians in the past only saw sick patients, and patients only saw doctors when they were ill. That was a poorly operating "circulatory system" since information did not flow continuously or often. The medical technologies that most patients see and experience today, such as machines that provide internal imaging, deliver medications through the skin, enable complex surgeries, or function in a variety of ways to assist or carry out directives from doctors, can be expected to improve, grow in use, and be of greater and greater importance. Improved healthcare, however, relies not only upon these technological breakthroughs but on something less visible: HIT.

HIT, according to the Department of Health and Human Services, "involves the comprehensive management of medical information and its secure exchange between health care consumers and providers. Broad use of HIT has the potential to improve health care quality, prevent medical errors, increase the efficiency of providing care, reduce unnecessary health care costs, increase administrative efficiencies, decrease paperwork, expand access to affordable care, and improve population health."[19] Interoperable HIT, in which information flows seamlessly among patients and providers, can improve individual patient care in numerous ways, including:

- Complete, accurate, and searchable health information, available at the point of diagnosis and care, allowing for more informed decision making for the patient, and enhancing the quality and reliability of healthcare delivery.
- More efficient and convenient care, eliminating the wait for the exchange of records or paperwork and unnecessary or repetitive tests or procedures.

- Earlier diagnosis and characterization of disease, with the potential to thereby improve outcomes and reduce costs.
- Reductions in adverse events through an improved understanding of each patient's particular medical history, potential for drug–drug interactions, or (eventually) enhanced understanding of a patient's metabolism and genetic profile, and therefore the likelihood of a positive or potentially harmful response to a course of treatment.
- Increased efficiencies in administrative tasks, making room for more interaction with and transfer of information to patients, caregivers, and clinical care coordinators, and monitoring of patient care.[20]

This list reveals how extensively the goal of quality healthcare is dependent upon high-quality data, something that requires high-quality communication and information processing.[21]

Improvements in healthcare depend on a large and highly complex transition from a medical-record environment that used paper records—and was deeply shaped by norms and expectations about information presented in physical form. If it is true that the broad use of HIT has the potential to improve healthcare in the ways stated, this potential can only be reached with precise and careful attention paid to the new processes that will be employed to collect, utilize, and distribute that information. Data quality, in other words, needs to be a much higher priority than it is today. Otherwise, as Dr. Doug Fridsma, president of the American Medical Informatics Association has stated, "If you've got unreliable data, you're going to make unreliable decisions."[22]

For the kind of technology-supported "circulatory system" envisioned by Blumenthal, data must flow smoothly and accurately through patients, physicians, other healthcare providers, and institutions, as well as the apps and medical devices whose goal it is to increase the use and quality of information. It requires the patient to attend to her health as conscientiously and as often as she attends to her financial affairs or to keeping her electronic devices updated and bug-free. Technology and the work of professionals are a critical component in generating data for patients, the ultimate goal being a new model of patients who are also conscientiously monitoring their own health. This is all part of the larger shift in the medical field away from reactively treating disease to actively preventing it.

For more than fifteen years, patients have had online access to information about illnesses. Indeed, the main value of technology for patients during this period has been that it provided convenient access to previously inaccessible information. Google, WebMD, and the like have provided information about ailments that patients will often read and bring with them to doctor visits. Patients could also visit websites such as patientslikeme.com or e-patients.net to consult with other patients with similar symptoms.

There is no question that use of the web in the health arena will grow, and greater involvement of patients in their own treatment is the core of "patient engagement." However, as Jonathan Darer, chief innovation officer at Geisinger Health Systems, has stated, "if we don't have accurate data we can't take care of patients appropriately."[23] Accurate data has an enormous impact on the transition from treatment to prevention as well—in fact, this shift is driven by the need for a communications network that provides information conveniently and continuously, interacts with the patient, relies on the patient for input, and provides guidance and advice.

Unfortunately, the transition to and adoption of powerful information technologies and EHRs has not been smooth. Indeed, errors in healthcare records are a "growth industry" themselves, and healthcare cannot continue to improve if the accuracy of the information needed to support quality healthcare does not improve. Malpractice will still be part of the picture in the future—indeed, malpractice may even grow as a problem, since there are so many more opportunities to be negligent in the use or transmission of information, or the use of a new technology or technique. Malpractice may no longer, however, be in the center of the canvas. That canvas is becoming both larger and more crowded with a greater number disputes and new kinds of disputes.

In the same way that technology brings us numerous new opportunities for health benefits, it also presents us with an array of new opportunities to resolve the problems it introduces. Identifying, understanding, and responding to these challenges requires less the assistance of lawyers and courts than the use of informal technology-based dispute resolution and prevention processes.

What we call "on-demand healthcare" closely parallels some of the ideas discussed in Chapter 3 about technology used to assist consumers in efficiently resolving and preventing disputes in a commercial setting. Patients, after all, are consumers of healthcare—a costly and complicated service, but a service with commercial aspects nonetheless. In both healthcare and e-commerce, the on-demand world contains expectations that goods and services will be delivered faster and more efficiently than before, in a higher quality manner that allows assistance to be provided at a distance. The goal is "anywhere, anytime"[24] monitoring, diagnosis, and treatment and "healthcare in the palm of your hand,"[25] just the same as the goal is "anywhere, anytime" ordering of goods and services. Such a mindset is not likely to be tolerant of long waits for appointments to see physicians, laboratory results, or feedback on concerns that arise. This on-demand culture is also reflected in pressure for government agencies to approve new treatments more quickly than before.[26] Pressure from consumers and the world of online commerce may be a factor in the Food and Drug Administration's determination that tracking devices such as Fitbit and other mobile apps that receive, transmit, store, or display data are generally not considered "medical devices" and can therefore be marketed without prior FDA approval.[27] When patients experience problems in this new and broad technological context, speed of response and technology-based dispute resolution will be expected. In the words of one health attorney, "[c]onsumers want on-demand, easy access and low-cost care."[28]

On-demand healthcare and the technology that enables it challenges established business models and regulatory systems, transforming long-established patterns, relationships, and rules with a new influx of information and data, and ways to use that information and data. We are seeing these new capabilities transform healthcare and the authority of the medical profession in many fascinating ways that can make some forms of care an immediate, real-time feedback loop of analysis, diagnosis, and treatment. Medical devices that create streams of data from sensors inside and outside of our bodies are a critical part of this, as are devices that employ algorithms to guide and monitor treatments, as well as support Big Data approaches to improving public health. For example, researchers are now building a platform to enable smartphones and smartwatches to collect data from sensors worn by children and placed in various locations at their homes and schools. The sensors will transmit data to a cloud-based system where it will be integrated with patients' electronic health records and real-time reports on weather conditions, air quality, pollen count, and other factors that can trigger asthma attacks. Apps will analyze patients' behavior and incidences of asthma over time, so that it can predict and alert users when conditions might be ripe to trigger an attack, allowing them to take steps to prevent attacks.[29]

We are also witnessing the very rapid expansion of "telemedicine," interactions with physicians and others at a distance, and new forms of providing care.[30] A growing number of companies now provide remote interaction with a physician, instead of or in addition to a face-to-face visit. Many health insurers have agreed to pay for such "visits,"[31] validating their use. The University of Mississippi Hospital, for example—Mississippi's only academic hospital—has remote connections with 165 sites, providing specialized services to some of the state's most medically deprived areas.[32] The University of Pittsburgh Medical Center had almost 16,000 telemedicine visits in 2014.[33] Start-ups such as Heal[34] and Pager[35] have "home visit" apps that will bring a doctor to your home in less than an hour. One of the founders of Pager, not surprisingly, was involved with designing Uber.

We also now have robots in homes and operating rooms. In the future, these robots will take on more tasks and increasingly difficult tasks.[36] Predictions for robotic and artificial intelligence–derived technologies that will be commercially available in the next decade include intelligent walkers, smart pendants that track falls and "wandering" for seniors, room and home sensors that monitor health status, balancing aids, virtual and robotic electronic companions, even drones that can transport supplies or assist the infirm. One current experiment focuses on small drones that would perform simple household chores for the elderly such as retrieving a bottle of medicine from another room. The roboticist carrying out the research has stated that "within 20 years drones will be today's cellphones."[37]

The in-depth awareness of our individual genetic makeups will have an enormous impact on the health field in a myriad of ways. This includes being helpful in diagnoses and predicting health issues and management, as well as the possibility for genetic treatments, a fast-growing and promising field. However, knowledge of our genetic makeup also leads to discovering new risks to our well-being, and presenting society at large and individuals with difficult choices.[38] Use of Big Data to find patients whose genome puts them at risk for various diseases or bad drug interactions is ongoing but this kind of analysis, as Professor Tal Zarsky has pointed out, yields correlations between two factors rather than a causative relationship between them.[39] Also, the "personalized medicine" movement—which aims to increase the use of genetic information to find the best treatment for a particular patient—is predicated on the idea that the data can be anonymized and studied en masse. Unfortunately, anonymity is something that cannot be expected in all cases, nor can it currently be perfectly guaranteed of protection from data breaches. In various contexts, including health, Latanya Sweeney and others have demonstrated that one cannot guarantee that re-identification of "anonymized" data is impossible.[40] A 2015 survey of 271 professionals who handle protected health information found that

> while 62 percent of respondents indicated that their organizations currently release data for secondary purposes, more than two out of three of these organizations lack confidence in their ability to share data safely in order to protect individual privacy. Nonetheless, more than half (56 percent) are planning on increasing the volume of data they share in the next 12 months.[41]

Linking all these examples together—figuratively and literally—is the EHR. The EHR may be the most important, and perhaps most challenging, of technological developments since it is (or will be) what links and adds value to all the scientific and entrepreneurial efforts listed above. As Professor Glenn Cohen has pointed out,

> the health care system stands on the edge of a breakthrough: New technologies will soon be available that can harness the power of large data sets to help identify which medical interventions will benefit which patients. . . Predictive analytics could be that technology. . .[and] with the advent of the EHR, it has become possible to apply predictive analytics to health care.[42]

Accuracy of the data in the EHR, therefore, is a key element in the new landscape of patient-related conflicts. While each of the above developments may generate its own set of problems, processes for coordinating data generated by telemedicine, robots, and other applications and discoveries will, if not addressed, generate even more. If efficiently and securely designed, the EHR will be the resource that will make all the data that is being generated both useful and valuable to the health of individuals and to public health as well. In its current state, however, it is as much a cause of problems as a resolver of them.

On-demand healthcare, like other parts of the on-demand economy, is data-driven. Data which we did not have before is the resource around which software-based decisions affecting our well-being will be made. To function effectively, therefore, the EHR needs not only to store and communicate information but to reliably process information. We need to be able to trust that data received from many sources is accurate and that errors, inconsistencies, and data of poor quality can be quickly fixed. This, as we shall see, is not yet the system we employ.

The EHR, like many records now in electronic form, was originally intended to be an efficient replacement for the once ubiquitous manila folder (still, in many offices, the place where a patient's medical history is stored). Like electronic replacements for paper records in other fields, however, the EHR has taken on a life of its own. It is, in its functions, something altogether different from the manila folder. Calling what appears on the screen to be an "electronic health record" suggests that a piece of information about some event is now being placed into an electronic container in lieu of a physical one, thus bringing benefits in how much information can be stored and how easily it can be accessed.

This is, however, a bit of a mischaracterization. The rapid means for storing or retrieving information is not in fact the *most* important quality of the EHR. To understand the reach and novelty of the EHR, one should focus less on new efficiencies of storage capacity and speed of access and more on new capabilities. The EHR is much more than simply a new kind of container or an extension of a physical object. It is, in many respects, closer to the operating system of a computer or smartphone: something that manages inputs and outputs of data and provides a framework for other applications. As one physician has noted,

> Communication lies at the root of medicine and can take many forms. EHR's have not only replaced their paper predecessor for narrative documentation, but they are becoming the central hub for all clinical, administrative and quality aspects of healthcare. Although EHR's were not designed as a communication tool, the EHR is encroaching on this role as well. When looked at from this perspective, we must be careful of the unintended consequences this may lead to.[43]

When an operating system works well, it supports a lot of programs working together. When it works even better, it coordinates a continuous stream of data, facilitates the processing of that data, and then advises, guides, or alerts the user. It is intelligent in that it makes sense of interactions among patients, physicians, and others involved in the patient's care. The system's boundaries grow not only in quantity but in functionality, as data enters from various medical devices of diverse, new types. Like an operating system, the EHR is an enabler that allows and facilitates new opportunities for building onto it. It is, therefore, not a single or simple tool but a highly complex system with many capabilities and functions. Like a supply chain, it requires all the links to function properly and be upgraded regularly in order to avoid problems.[44] When it works as planned, we can trust in the treatments prescribed or monitored, but when it is not working as planned, problems spread quickly and widely.

Because of its increasingly wide reach and complexity, today's EHR is generating problems that did not exist in the manila folder era, and it needs to be able to provide solutions that were not needed in the paper environment. The EHR is changing both the environment in which it is being used and those who are using it. It is creating new roles and responsibilities and must accommodate the needs and responsibilities of those working in a new and evolving environment. As one author has written about EHRs, they contrast with traditional practice by relying on "personnel trained in different disciplines, working in different settings, on different sites and in different languages."[45] These include:

- patients themselves and their appointed caregivers,
- clinicians, in therapeutic or anticipatory care roles,
- groups of clinicians working in primary or secondary care,
- paramedical colleagues working with the patient,
- clinicians and clerical or research staff undertaking clinical audit or quality assurance,
- hospital and general practice managers and healthcare purchasers (health authorities or insurers) undertaking quality assurance,
- healthcare planners at hospital, practice, district region, or national level,
- legal advisers for the patient or the clinician,
- clinical researchers,
- medical students and medical teachers,
- commercial product developers for market research (e.g., the pharmaceutical industry),
- insurance companies for determining payment, or assessing risk,
- politicians, health economists, and journalists.[46]

While EHRs are still largely employed as convenient and powerful artifacts for storing and retrieving information, it has been understood for some time that putting information into electronic form opens up opportunities for providing care in new ways. In 2003, for example, the Institute of Medicine identified eight core functions of EHRs, only a few of which involve the kind of clerical tasks typical of health records in the manila folders of the past:

- health information and data
- result management
- order management
- decision support
- electronic communication and connectivity
- patient support
- administrative processes and reporting
- reporting and population health

Almost all of these go beyond what paper files are capable of by serving as a kind of "Fourth Party" or electronic assistant, which, ideally, will help build trust, provide convenience, and deliver expertise. In other words, technology will satisfy the goals of the dispute resolution triangle. Because of its increasingly wide reach and complexity, however, today's EHR is generating problems that did not exist in the manila folder era. It needs to be able to provide solutions that were not needed in the paper environment as well. With an ever-growing number of parties needing to interact with each other but having different levels of access, experience, and training, problems are inevitable, and attention to providing systems to respond to them should be a high priority. EHRs need to provide access to justice by incorporating processes that resolve and prevent problems in a fair and efficient manner.

Unfortunately, this has not been happening. The increase in lawsuits due to EHR errors has highlighted various problems stemming from many different areas of interaction with EHRs. One such area is the manner in which data is entered. Prepopulated checkboxes and default choices in drop-down menus

> can be a physician's nemesis. It's easy to click on checkboxes, and often they are pre-checked in templates. EMRs have been presented in court that show, through checkboxes, daily breast exams on comatose patients in the ICU, detailed daily neurological exams done by cardiologists, and a complete review of systems done by multiple treating physicians on comatose patients.[47]

Lawsuits have alleged "a broad range of mistakes and information gaps—typos that lead to medication errors; voice-recognition software that drops key words;

doctors' reliance on old or incorrect records; and nurses' misinterpretation of drop-down menus, with errors inserted as a result in reports on patient status."[48] Other examples of mistaken EHR entries, reported by health law attorney Kim Stanger, include, among many others[49]

- Skin: somewhat pale, but present
- Discharge status: Alive but without permission
- Rectal exam revealed a normal size thyroid
- Patient was alert and unresponsive
- The patient had no history of suicides

And yet the contracts most purchasers sign with EHR developers exempt the software vendor behind the EHR from liability and impose responsibility on the doctor and hospital.[50] As a result, EHR companies aren't being sued because of these errors—doctors and hospitals are.

It was only in 2016 that the Office of National Coordinator for Health Information Technology issued a guide with the following warning:

> Consider, for example, the situation where your EHR software has been programmed to translate narrative diagnoses for outpatient physician visits into ICD-10 codes. You notice and alert your EHR vendor to errors in the crosswalk, including the incorrect mapping of a narrative diagnosis of diabetes to a code representing a diagnosis of diabetes associated with ESRD. Your EHR vendor responds to the error by implementing software corrections as part of non-urgent periodic updates and does not correct any previously misreported diagnoses. The effect of such a software error on your business could be significant, especially if your EHR contract does not provide protections against your exposure to such risks and associated liability. If your medical record entries are populated with incorrect patient diagnoses, your patients are at risk of associated treatment errors, and you are at risk of incorrect patient diagnoses, your patients are at risk of associated treatment errors, and you are at risk of potential medical malpractice liability as well as exposure for false claims liability if governmental insurers were billed using incorrect diagnoses codes. If your EHR vendor's liability under your EHR contract is limited by the exclusion of certain types of damages and by a low liability cap (as is the case in many standard form EHR contracts), you may be able to recover only a fraction of the amount of financial damage suffered by you, despite the cause of the damage being the EHR vendor's defective software and inadequate support.[51]

Unfortunately, "EHR systems may generate errors rather than prevent them, especially early in the adoption process."[52] In one study, 176 physicians from various U.S. hospitals with implemented computerized physician order entry (CPOE) systems reported "new kinds of errors" associated with using CPOEs, including "entering orders for the wrong patient, errors of omission, nurses not knowing an order had been generated, desensitization to alerts, loss of information during care transitions, wrong medication dosing, and overlapping medication orders."[53] Medication lists, in particular, have been identified as a source of low-quality data that can lead to errors.[54] One review reported medication list omission rates of between 27 percent for ambulatory oncology patients[55] and 53 percent for primary care patients.[56] In another study, the authors reported that some piece of inaccurate information was present in 81 percent to 95 percent of patient records.[57]

In a sense, all software is an experiment in that data learned in using it leads to new versions and improvements. According to one software company,

> It's easy to think that with enough testing a program won't fail (but who ever thinks their software has been tested enough?). But "normal accident" theory holds that, as a system gets more complex, its chances of failure increase, no matter how careful you are with all the requisite components, because of unexpected interactions between them. Even putting in checks and balances looking for failure adds complexity and makes the system more prone to failure . . . "Programmers are making mistakes all the time and constantly," John Carmack, the primary programmer behind games such as Doom, said in a speech, while pointing out that today's games are more complex than the software that sent us to the moon, "the problem is that the best of intentions really don't matter. If something can syntactically be entered incorrectly, it eventually will be."[58]

Like all other software, EHRs are evolving as we experiment with them. We are, in effect, in the middle of a large-scale societal experiment in which we are learning where improvements are needed not only in the features provided but in the manner in which use occurs. What is concerning is that we are currently relying heavily on EHRs without understanding the full scope of this experiment— an experiment in which the risk of harm is quite a bit more serious than a lost package or an overpriced room rental. On-demand healthcare that links patients with physicians and data-processing machines is much more complex than the exchange of goods, services, and money in the e-commerce world. There are, as will be explained below, governmentally authorized quality control efforts in healthcare, but these do not cover all problems. Unfortunately, EHRs do not yet facilitate the reporting or repair of errors. This places an undue burden on patients to focus on quality control because "[i]n the not-too-distant future, our lives will depend upon how our health information is accessed and used."[59]

The case of Thomas Duncan, the first patient in the United States to die from Ebola, presented the public with a dramatic example of the nuanced challenges of the introduction of the EHR. Mr. Duncan had gone to the emergency room of Texas Health Presbyterian Hospital on September 25, 2014, with a temperature of 100.1F, dizziness, nausea, abdominal pain, and several other symptoms. Three and a half hours into his visit his temperature rose to 103F, but later dropped to 101.2 degrees. The patient rated his "severe pain" at eight on a scale of one to ten. His travel history from Liberia, a country highlighted in recent news, was recorded in the nurse's notes.

Mr. Duncan was sent home and told to take antibiotics and Tylenol. Two days later he was admitted to the hospital again; he passed away a week and a half later. Mr. Duncan was clearly misdiagnosed, something that occurs with 10 percent to 15 percent of outpatients.[60] His EHR came into play when the hospital blamed the EHR for the fact that the physician did not know that the patient had recently traveled to the United States from Liberia. This turned out to be false, but it is true that several features or lack of features in his EHR may have impacted the mistakes that were made. The EHR, for example, could have highlighted the fact that Mr. Duncan had very recently come to the United States from Liberia. We would not expect a manila folder to provide such information, but technology changes our expectations and the EHR is much more than a replacement for the traditional manila folder.

The issue of data quality was present but at a far smaller scale in the manila folder era. The manila folder had managed patient logistics by storing paper records and reports from laboratories and other doctors and hospitals. It was efficient in an era of limited data because it was cheap, simple, and unquestioned. Using it required no training, and the folder itself, unlike some electronic medical device or smart software, could not itself do any harm. It also had a side effect that was desirable, at least to the physician, in that it created a kind of distance between patient and doctor that emphasized their knowledge and status difference, and deterred patients from looking in the file. Other than in malpractice cases, there was little opportunity to find errors in the paper record. Ironically, there have been regulations in place for over twenty years for finding and handling errors in medical records. As already noted, in 1996 Congress passed the Health Insurance Portability and Accountability Act (HIPAA). It gave patients the right to see their medical record and to request an "amendment" if they discovered an error. This was an instance, however, in which the law had little effect since few patients looked in their manila folder or encountered any physician's office that encouraged them to do so. If there were errors in the record or mistakes in the doctor's notes, they were likely to be revealed only in the course of a malpractice case involving a serious injury. Technology, however, in the guise of online "patient portals" and easy online access to one's EHR, is accomplishing what HIPAA had never been able to do. Making records available online has lowered the psychological barriers that discouraged anyone from asking to look at their manila folder. Our experience today is that almost everyone who looks at their EHR finds some kind of error. People we know who have looked at their EHRs have seen such examples of incorrect information as their having diabetes, breast cancer, anxiety disorders, and being listed as a smoker. Medication lists, as noted above, are notorious for being out of date. One acquaintance of ours describes what it's like to find and then try to correct these errors as follows:

> After returning home, I accessed my electronic health record to obtain a visit summary from my primary care doctor. As I read it, I found 3 significant errors: A problem I didn't have, a procedure I hadn't had, and a medication I wasn't taking. I called to report the problem, and no one even knew how to route my call. On day 2, call #3, I got hold of the office manager. She understood the issues, but her hands were tied. There was no policy about how to handle my request to address these needed changes. She said she would take care of them, but we agreed that was not a scalable solution.

The manila folder never really evolved—it remained what it was when it was first introduced and used. The EHR, however, is always evolving. What it is today is not what it will be tomorrow. As an operating system, it needs to be constantly updated to provide new capabilities to address new practices, new tools, new sources and kinds of information, as well as new relationships and roles. In April 2015, eClinicalWorks, a large vendor of EHRs, announced capabilities for Fitbit data to find its way into an EHR. This is potentially very valuable information, but how to deal with this extra layer of complexity and risk—complex new information, and new risk for errors that cause unknown possible damage? Wearable devices such as the Fitbit haven't been clinically validated to perform at the same standards for reliability that the U.S. Food and Drug Administration uses for medical devices, such as a traditional blood-pressure cuff in a doctor's office. Marketed under the FDA's less rigorous "wellness-focused" rubric," consumer wearables have not been proven to be consistently reliable in the quality of data they capture. One skeptic noted that "what makes most fitness trackers extremely suspect is their complete lack of technical specifications. Take Fitbit, for example: I have not seen any specifications on their heart rate or even distance trackers, internal or otherwise.

Without even trying to explain the accuracy of the product in a concrete way (e.g. error bars and sampling rates), I can only imagine most of these companies are capturing data of poor quality."[61] In a study performed for NBC News, "half of the fitness trackers underestimated energy expenditure and the rest overestimated it."[62]

It is also necessary not only to collect and validate the data generated by tracking devices but to make it meaningful to physicians. Visual representations that help make sense of numerical data—that communicate an analysis of the data and suggest treatment—are important. But these analyses increasingly involve decisions that are driven by algorithms, and those algorithms are not transparent. In fact, they can be as harmful to some as they are helpful to others. Lastly, the EHR must be configured to make sure that the data is appropriately managed: that it does not go to persons or others who have no need or right to it. Genetic data, for example, is beginning to become part of the EHR. Genetic data from a company like 23andMe can find its way to an insurance company. In 2010, human error at 23andMe led to a mix-up in their lab, leading almost one hundred customers to get incorrect DNA information. In several cases, even the gender was wrong.[63]

In all these changes in the collection, use, interpretation, and display of patient data, disputes are an inevitable side effect. While bad data in electronic form may be more likely to be discovered than when it was in the manila folder, it is also more likely to be passed on and affect not only the individual but public health data and decisions.

Resolving Disputes

The need to correct errors and improve data quality was recognized by the Office of the National Coordinator for Health Information Technology (ONC) almost ten years ago. It wrote:

> Individuals should be provided with a timely means to dispute the accuracy or integrity of their individually identifiable health information, and to have erroneous information corrected or to have a dispute documented if their requests are denied. Individuals have an important stake in the accuracy and integrity of their individually identifiable health information and an important role to play in ensuring its accuracy and integrity. Electronic exchange of individually identifiable health information may improve care and reduce adverse events. However, any errors or conclusions drawn from erroneous data may be easily communicated or replicated (e.g., as a result of an administrative

error as simple as a transposed digit or more complex error arising from medical identity theft). For this reason it is essential for individuals to have practical, efficient, and timely means for disputing the accuracy or integrity of their individually identifiable health information, to have this information corrected, or a dispute documented when their requests are denied, and to have the correction or dispute communicated to others with whom the underlying information has been shared. Persons and entities that participate in a network for the purpose of electronic exchange of individually identifiable health information, should make processes available to empower individuals to exercise a role in managing their individually identifiable health information and should correct information or document disputes in a timely fashion.[64]

In 2010, when the healthcare reform legislation commonly referred to as Obamacare was enacted, the White House expressed its hope that the legislation would "make health care more affordable, make health insurers more accountable, expand health coverage to all Americans, and make the health system sustainable, stabilizing family budgets, the Federal budget, and the economy."[65] It also made clear that these ambitious and challenging goals would require not only changes in regulatory policies and financing, but equally ambitious and challenging uses of technology. For healthcare reform to be successful, in other words, the current system would not only need to be more efficient and work better, it would also need to be innovative and work differently. New uses of technology, particularly EHRs, would be at the center of this transformation.

We have already made significant progress in improving on the capabilities of the manila folder by employing software that easily stores and provides access to medical data. By providing patients with online access to their records, we are providing a means to identify and expose errors. However, most EHR software is lacking in efficient means to document and report mistakes (beyond just suggesting that a patient contact the doctor). "Patient engagement" has led to greater capability to find errors but not to being able, in an easy way, to report and fix errors. "Patient empowerment" is needed to move forward. "Patient empowerment" would provide patients with access to software that would allow them to enter and correct data easily themselves (with the final attention and approval of the doctor or other professional in charge). "patient empowerment" might also help to move beyond gaining access to one's record to being able to download one's whole record.[66]

Studies continue to reveal large numbers of errors and very few attempts to correct them. Patients can and should play a central role in identifying errors, but this requires both higher levels of EHR usage by patients and a friction-free means to communicate the error to the physician's office. It should be as easy to correct an error in a medical record as it is to correct a mistake in a checking account deposit. Yet a study of Medicare data found:

> 2.7 percent of the nearly 11.9 million records in the database, approximately 321,300 records, contained coding errors. Such errors can impact the clinician's and/or the patient's insurance reimbursement and/or cause additional time to be spent correcting the errors. The study also identified the immediate benefits of addressing the errors. According to the Medicare study, the top 10 coding errors accounted for 70 percent of the total errors. By focusing on those 10 coding errors a high percentage of the problem can be addressed instantly, saving time and money.[67]

In spite of such studies, the de facto assumption still is that data quality in EHRs is high and generates few errors. In fact, as the quotes from Presidents Clinton, Bush, and Obama earlier in this chapter indicate, this has been a key selling point for EHRs.

In order to overcome physician resistance to EHRs and accelerate adoption, the HITECH Act[68] authorized payments of $44,000 (for Medicare Eligible Professionals)[69] and $63,750 (for Medicaid Eligible Professionals) to help purchase EHR software.[70] Congress did not simply hand over $44,000 to every doctor to purchase an EHR system. It wanted assurances from the recipients of the grants that the systems would be employed and that patients would benefit from them. To do this, it required that doctors and hospitals requesting the funds meet a set of regulations known as "meaningful use."[71] The Office of the National Coordinator for Health Information Technology has, for the last eight years, been overseeing the process of drafting and implementing the meaningful use regulations and determining standards for certifying EHR software. It was envisioned that there would be three stages of meaningful use and that adopters would proceed from stage one with fairly basic requirements to stage three with more complex requirements. Although the intent of these regulations is sound—to ensure "meaningful use" and protect patients—the process has proved to be very difficult and lengthy. One of the requirements included in a draft of the stage three recommendations was the following:

> Provide patients with an easy way to request an amendment to their record online (e.g., offer corrections, additions, or updates to the record).

Unfortunately, providing some online capability for patients to correct errors did not remain a priority and was removed from the final version of stage three.[72] This is difficult to understand since HIPAA already requires that patients have the ability to see their records and request an amendment to it in order to correct an error. That was appropriate to records in a paper environment. One should reasonably expect that requests for amendments would now be in a manner appropriate to records in electronic form: online and with a quick response time.

How could this be accomplished? An example of how patient-generated data might be handled is present in a website run by the company Acxiom. Acxiom, a data collection and marketing business, also runs a site called AboutTheData. com in which they provide forms to check the accuracy of various pieces of information. Users can fill in boxes when incorrect information is noted. There is very good reason to be skeptical about the privacy and other data use policies of a very large data collection company like Acxiom, but its process in this one instance does illustrate a possible approach to error correction in factual records. Ironically, hospitals have used Acxiom to obtain data about patient lifestyles in order to make predictions about future use of health services.[73]

As this book was nearing completion, the EHR called Patient Gateway, which is employed by the Partners HealthCare and Massachusetts General Hospital and is developed by Epic Systems, began allowing patients to indicate on a form which medications they were taking and which they were no longer taking. Physicians could easily see two groups of medication, one with the medications currently being taken and one with medications that the patient indicates should be removed from the list. At the same time, the Patient Gateway Terms of Service absolves itself of any liability for inaccurate information in the EHR. In bold uppercase letters, the Terms of Service states:

IN THE EVENT OF ANY PROBLEM WITH PATIENT GATEWAY OR ANY OF ITS CONTENT, YOU AGREE THAT YOUR SOLE REMEDY IS TO CEASE USING PATIENT GATEWAY. UNDER NO CIRCUMSTANCES SHALL PARTNERS OR ANY PARTNERS AFFILIATE BE LIABLE IN ANY WAY FOR YOUR USE OF PATIENT GATEWAY OR ANY OF ITS CONTENT, INCLUDING, BUT NOT LIMITED TO, ANY ERRORS OR OMISSIONS IN ANY CONTENT . . .

It is hard to imagine a physician's office with manila folders requiring patients to agree to something like this.

You may recall from the introduction to this book that when "e-patient Dave" discovered that he was listed as a female, the hospital would not change his gender.[74] Instead, it added the fact that he was male to the end of the record. To find out that he was a male required one to scroll down several screens. Beth Israel's behavior was a result of a long-standing legal prohibition against deleting any information from a medical record. In the event of a lawsuit, preservation of an accurate record that can be relied on to document treatment history is necessary. A physician at Beth Israel would have been able to correct an error on paper by making a note in the margin; a mistake in the manila folder record was hard to find but easy to fix. With EHRs, errors are easy to find but hard to fix. It is ironic that, at present at least, it is often easier to make a correction to a paper record than to an electronic one: to this day, patients at Beth Israel are told to call the doctor's office or send an email through the patient portal to the doctor.

Factual errors in an EHR should be the easiest errors to correct. Some, like a mistake in gender or in a Social Security number (which inevitably occur in a small percentage of cases), are the medical equivalent of an eBay dispute over a purchase: they are commonplace and easy to correct and verify, and resolution should require little human oversight. The magic of software is that it can display a new and accurate Social Security number while preserving, out of sight but still accessible if needed, the mistaken number, managing the legal need to document all changes to a medical record. In fact, in some ways, correcting factual errors in EHRs should be even easier to resolve than eBay or e-commerce disputes: there are far fewer disputes, the parties are generally not very angry with each other, and the solution concerns an empirical fact. Most notable is that there are growing numbers of patients who are concerned with the accuracy of their record and can easily report errors—engaged patients have been called "an army of free fact checkers."[75] The more efficiently this is handled, the better for everyone. It is, therefore, hard to understand why the developers of EHR software have been uninterested in including easy-to-use correction capabilities.

As with many e-commerce sites, there seems to be a reluctance to acknowledge that errors occur. This may change as malpractice cases caused by poor software design begin to focus on the companies building the software rather than on the physician using it. As noted earlier, many contracts between hospitals and EHR software development companies "limit the vendor's liability, require that the EHR software be taken 'as-is,' prohibit class-action lawsuits or require arbitration."[76] This parallels the clauses imposed on consumers that we described earlier and that restrict class actions and require arbitration.

In November 2011, the Geisinger Hospital System initiated a project designed to use technology to reduce errors in medication lists. The goals of the pilot project were threefold: (1) to assess the impact of online patient contributions to the accuracy of the medical record; (2) to assess if patients can be effectively engaged using a networked health record; and (3) to assess the efficiency and reliability of an online system for receiving and processing patient feedback data. Patients included in the study had specific chronic conditions (i.e., chronic obstructive pulmonary disease, asthma, hypertension, diabetes, or heart failure) that the Agency for Healthcare Research and Quality (AHRQ) listed as being among the top ten most costly illnesses in the U.S. healthcare system.[77]

To obtain and process online feedback, the patients were sent a link to a medication feedback form prepopulated with the currently active medications listed in their EHRs. Patients had the opportunity to indicate which medications they were no longer taking and which they were taking differently from the way the instructions were presented, and to add medications that were not listed at all. Their responses were routed to a Geisinger pharmacist who reviewed the patient's input and followed up with the patient. After the pharmacist review and patient contact, the pharmacist updated the medication record, then notified the patient's physician and case manager about any changes by completing a note in the EHR.

Between November 2011 and June 2012, Geisinger sent out a sample of 1,500 feedback forms and received 457 completed forms. In category 1 of patient feedback forms (feedback on medications from the prepopulated medication list), patients identified discontinuations or changes in frequency or dosage on 281 submitted forms (67.9%). The 281 forms included a total of 661 requests for changes to medication entries, for an average of 2.4 requested changes per patient form requesting any changes. In category 2 (feedback received on prescription medications missing from the prepopulated medication list), patients listed additional prescription medications on 82 submitted forms (20%). The 82 forms included a total of 141 requested additions to the Geisinger medication list, for an average of 1.7 requested additions per patient form.

In addition to errors in patient records, persons who survive hospital stays are generally faced with large medical bills that are both hard to decipher and far from error-free. One recent study found that up to 80 percent of hospital bills contain errors.[78] Everyone who has had a hospital stay recognizes that understanding a medical bill is beyond the capability of most. The *Cleveland Plain Dealer* found that "[t]here are lots of places where something can go wrong with your hospital bill. By our count, 289 of them . . . The opportunities for mistakes are astronomical, and a mistake early on can compound exponentially. Mistakes can be as simple as human error or as complex as interpretation; some seem inexplicable."[79] Errors cannot be fixed if they cannot be found, and these errors are costly in more ways than one.

The rate of errors in billing—and the large amounts of money involved— have led to a number of entrepreneurial efforts to address the issue. The start-up Copatient analyzes medical bills for free and, if an error is found, represents the patient in appealing the bill. They also claim that over 80 percent of the medical bills they review contain a billing or coding error.[80] When a bill is contested, the company receives 35 percent of any reduction in the bill. A similar company called ELAP analyzes a hospital's own financial filings, then uses software to determine what is a reasonable charge for a procedure done. ELAP pays that amount plus what they consider a reasonable profit to the hospital in lieu of the actual amounts on the hospital bill. Hospitals have generally accepted what was offered to them.[81]

The first prerequisite to correcting EHR errors is acknowledgment by medical providers both that this is a serious problem and that EHR software vendors should make fixing errors a highlighted feature in the EHR. This pressure needs to come from both patients and physicians. Physician complaints about EHRs have largely focused on usability and design; poor usability and bad design often lead to errors. It is remarkable that it has not been widely recognized that errors and problems are inevitable in an electronic system which does not sit self-contained on a shelf like a manila folder but is a shared system with many different levels of access. We have also not properly recognized how much disputes can harm the level of trust that physicians and institutions continuously strive for. Institutions that do not provide quick remedies are interfering with the fragile trust-building efforts of doctors and hospitals.

Prevention of Medical Errors and Prevention of Conflict

The need for accurate information has not escaped government regulators. At a hearing before the House Energy and Commerce Committee, Dr. Jeffrey Shuren, director of the Food and Drug Administration's Center for Devices and Radiological Health, stated:

> The "linchpin" for effectively using big data to customize individual care and to personalize medicine—while finding cures faster and at lower costs—is accurate information . . . The stakes are even higher as we move into the world of big data as we're able to pool large amounts of information and sift through it, not just with the eyes of a human, but with the smarts of analytical software and other technologies . . . If the information is wrong about the individuals when we put it together, we're now wrong about the population and we go after the wrong cures or we don't develop cures and miss the opportunities . . . We want to make sure the information is accurate, reliable and meaningful because—if not—doctors and patients make the wrong decisions.[82]

Preventing harm caused by incorrect information is a responsibility of the Food and Drug Administration (FDA). Yet, there are gaps in the regulatory structure that raise doubts about the quality of data in many medical devices. As already noted, most wearable tracking devices and phone apps related to healthcare are not regulated at all. The move from physical to virtual involves not only increased human access to records created by the healthcare system but to the software-generated patient data that is communicated, collected, and processed wirelessly and automatically from implanted devices, like that from pacemakers, cardioverter defibrillators, insulin pumps, and continuous glucose monitors. Unfortunately,

> hundreds of deaths have been attributed to software failure in medical devices, resulting from errors including software lockups, premature shutdown, failure to restart, unexpected depletion in battery life, faulty detection of patient events, and miscalculated safety alarms. As the software on devices becomes more complicated, the odds increase that errors will be present. An internal report from the Food and Drug Administration ("FDA") concluded that between 2005 and 2009, 18% of recalls on all medical devices were related to a software problem. The economic costs of such errors are enormous as well; a 2002 study by the National Institute of Standards & Technology estimated that inadequate software testing and resultant bugs cost the economy $59.5 billion per year. This figure has no doubt increased since then.[83]

In many cases, the data from implanted devices flow to private companies and not to a hospital or a patient's EHR. Nor is the data in any form that could be monitored by patients. The impact of this is that while patient access to EHRs has improved, other patient-related health data is now distributed by a variety of companies in ways that the patient may be unaware of or have no access to.

If patients owned and controlled their own medical data, this would not be such a significant problem. At present, however, those who produce the data own it. HIPAA, which requires patient access to one's own health record, does not require access to data held by anything not considered a "covered entity." Further, if the data is encrypted, research may be prohibited by copyright's anticircumvention laws. These laws state that, with few exceptions, no person may circumvent technological protection on a copyrighted work (e.g., by decrypting an encrypted work) without permission from the copyright owner. This leads not only to an inability to discover what the device is reporting about a user but an inability to study the software generating the data and monitoring treatment.

Consider the case of Hugo Campos, a computer scientist researching the security and safety of medical devices. He has an implantable cardioverter-defibrillator, but he and others like him have not been able to study data from devices implanted in their own bodies. The data, after all, does not belong to them. In a recent request for an exemption to the copyright anticircumvention prohibition, it was argued by lawyers at the Harvard Law School Cyberlaw Clinic that Campos and others researchers

> each study the safety, security, and effectiveness of medical devices. Some look at the devices from a system design perspective, analyzing the hardware and software of the devices for misconfigurations or vulnerabilities. Others look at the devices as they are applied to a particular patient's care, and help patients retrieve important information off the devices that the device otherwise would not share, or would only make available through periodic checkups with doctors once every several months. Their research has helped patients and doctors better tailor care, the public understand the nature of medical device risks, and regulatory agencies like FDA improve government oversight of devices.[84]

This request for an exemption was granted in October 2015[85] and is a significant step forward in furthering patient safety.

The most anticipated efforts to treat individual health problems involve genomic data and "personalized medicine." As described by the Food and Drug Administration,

> [most] medical treatments are designed for the "average patient" as a "one-size-fits-all-approach," that is successful for some patients but not for others. Precision medicine, sometimes known as "personalized medicine" is an innovative approach to disease prevention and treatment that takes into account differences in people's genes, environments and lifestyles.[86]

Advances in precision medicine have already led to powerful new discoveries and several FDA-approved treatments that are tailored to specific characteristics of individuals and "use genomic information from cancer cells to provide individuals with targeted treatments."[87]

President Obama's Precision Medicine Initiative seeks to advance these developments by identifying genetically based drivers of disease in order to develop new, more-effective treatments. Regulation of laboratory-developed tests, however, is discretionary for the FDA and

> [g]etting to the next stage of precision medicine requires comprehensive, reliable genetic tests . . . But due in part to the lack of regulation by the FDA, the commercialization of diagnostic tests based on advanced sequencing has outpaced the underlying science of collecting

and analyzing the data. Though high-quality tests are indeed available, many of the products on the market are questionable. Different tests can produce different results from the same DNA sample, says Elizabeth Mansfield, the deputy director of personalized medicine and molecular genetics for the FDA.[88]

The FDA needs to play a more significant role in ensuring the accuracy of genetic tests, many of which are derived from new, rapid, and increasingly inexpensive technologies that may collect data on a person's entire genome. The goals of the president's initiative also evoke concern over the security, accuracy, and use of genetic data that will become linked to an EHR for the purpose of providing medicine appropriate to a particular patient's needs. We have not yet had any large-scale breaches of genetic information of this type, but we can expect to see it: as the cost goes down and the amount of genetic data collected and held by different entities increases, the more likely problems are to arise. The more sources that contribute data to an EHR and the more data available in or through the EHR, the more complex will be the process of managing the data and the more likely it is that problems will surface.

The Precision Medicine Initiative involves collecting genetic data from one million volunteers in the United States. Ownership of results is a critical issue because it affects not only who benefits financially but whether the individual has any control over the use of the data.[89] President Obama has indicated his personal belief that "if somebody does a test on me or my genes, that [information is] mine, but that's not always how we define these issues." Indeed, the president added, "[r]ight now, what happens is the best researchers and the best universities, oftentimes they're kind of hoarding their samples." If ownership is decided by an agreement between the institution collecting the data and the individual whose data it is, the contract, unlike almost all the consumer-oriented contracts described in this book, should ensure that the person involved understand the consequences of what is being agreed to and how the data will be used. At a minimum, it should provide options for opting out at a later date if the data is not being used for the benefit of the patient.

Genetic data employed for treatment is a young field, and disputes in the area are just beginning to surface. One notable dispute that suggests how difficult it is to predict the variety of disputes that will surface involved a sixth grader in Palo Alto, California. The student, Colman Chadam, was removed from his sixth grade class without any warning because of an issue with his DNA. Colman has genetic markers for cystic fibrosis, an inherited lung disease. Multiple children with this disease should not be near each other, because they can give each other contagious infections. Two other children with cystic fibrosis were attending Chadam's middle school, so, in 2012, he was removed from the school.

While Chadam had a genetic marker for cystic fibrosis, he did not actually have the disease and was no more contagious or vulnerable than anyone else. Chadam eventually was returned to school. His was a case of genetic discrimination, something that was in fact anticipated in the federal Genetic Information Nondiscrimination Act (GINA) of 2008, which bars genetic discrimination in employment and health insurance. GINA, however, does not cover public education. As disputes are a consequence of complexity, disputes involving the use of DNA are likely to be varied and many.

Conclusion

Healthcare in the digital era is centered on data, and much of this data will be documented in EHRs. While medical records used to be seen as an internal document prepared by and for the medical team—a team whose members applied their expertise to address an acute medical condition—this view is slowly changing. Gradually, the EHR is viewed as a platform for patient participation in the diagnosis and treatment of medical problems and, hopefully, for the prevention of future medical problems. This becomes all the more important as healthcare services grow more and more entwined with the digital environment, whether that takes the form of online information, telemedicine and apps for the management and monitoring of medical conditions and medications, or the experimental use of sensors and even robots in the medical context.

Each of these processes requires reliance on data that may not be accurate. Unfortunately, data quality has not been a priority of EHR software developers and vendors. This has not led to more serious problems largely because communication between systems is still limited. While the use of EHRs has increased greatly in the last decade and the generation of data is also a growth area, developing systems to manage the resulting complexity and growing numbers of disputes remains a serious and significant challenge.

CHAPTER 5

The Challenge of Social and Anti-Social Media

Please refrain from being a nuisance.
—Reddit

Dixi was a woman in her late thirties. She had been born to a religious family and given the name Deborah. Until the age of 18 she lived at home and remained devout. While in college she discovered her sexual identity. However, she was respectful of the values and feelings of her loved ones, and therefore never admitted to her family and childhood friends that she was gay. While they realized she was no longer religious, they were completely in the dark in terms of her sexual orientation, social milieu, and even the nature of her work as an independent publisher of gay literature. Dixi was living a double life. Her sexual preference was a central component of her identity in her social and work circles. Indeed, her friends, partner, and colleagues did not know that her birth name was Deborah. She was known to all of her current social circle as Dixi, and had been Dixi during all of her adult years.

It was therefore only natural for Dixi to open her Facebook account under the name "Dixi." She became an avid user for several years, with several hundreds of friends on Facebook, posting numerous entries a day. In fact, Facebook was not only a way for Dixi to connect with her friends but was also an important work tool for soliciting manuscripts and marketing published works. Over time, Dixi was able to drop other marketing channels and focus exclusively on Facebook as a means for promoting works published by her.

One day, without prior warning, Dixi received a notification from Facebook that her account was frozen due to a violation of Facebook's "Authentic Name Policy." Her account was anonymously flagged as "fake," and she could not activate it again until she provided some form of ID proving that "Dixi" was her "real name." Dixi was devastated. She no longer was able to connect with many of the people she was friends with online. For most of them she had no other

Digital Justice. Ethan Katsh and Orna Rabinovich-Einy.
© Ethan Katsh and Orna Rabinovich-Einy 2017. Published 2017 by Oxford University Press.

contact details. Facebook had become her principal lifeline to friends and colleagues. It was also where she stored a significant portion of her personal photos and work-related materials, all of which she needed for future use. She could not even begin to imagine how she would cope with the loss of these materials and contacts.

Her attempts to restore her account were met with automated notifications that she must provide a valid ID, as it is Facebook policy to "ask everyone on Facebook to use the name they go by in everyday life so friends know who they're connecting with." This is because "[h]aving people use their authentic names helps protect our community from dangerous interactions."[1] Her attempts to appeal the decision were rebuffed, and she was nearing the deadline at which, Facebook told her, her information would be lost forever. Even her requests for an extension of the deadline were met with a response that failed to convey any degree of concern and sensitivity to her situation. She could not believe that this catastrophe was initiated by an anonymous complaint, the credibility of which was in essence given more weight than that of her own attestation that Dixi was the name by which she was known "in real life."

The irony was that Dixi was indeed the name by which she was known in everyday life, as her Facebook friends could easily confirm. She was constantly reminded of how much she was missing out on, as Facebook reminders of whose birthday it was and who posted new pictures and information online continued to flow into her inbox. But even more worrisome to her than the loss of all her information was how she would be able to maintain her social and work ties without revealing her sexual orientation and lifestyle to her family, a prospect she could not even begin to digest. As complaints similar to Dixi's began to surface, the people at Facebook began looking at the issue more carefully and realized that their policy needed to be revisited. An apology issued a while later by Facebook's chief product officer was appreciated but did not compensate for what she had lost nor did it provide her with confidence about using social media in the future.[2]

Introduction

Another story, this time not fictional. Clay Shirky begins his important book on the power of organizing, *Here Comes Everybody*,[3] with the case of Ivanna, who left her cell phone on the seat of a New York City taxi.[4] At first, technology seemed to provide a solution. The person who took the phone began taking pictures with it and these pictures popped up in the new phone that Ivanna had bought to replace the lost one. Some of the pictures contained enough information to enable Ivanna to obtain the person's email address. Unfortunately, the exchange of emails did not help. The person who now had the phone refused to return it. Ivanna considered the other person a thief. The other person thought she had simply found a lost object, and was following the old adage, "finders keepers."

This was in 2006, a year before the iPhone was introduced, before it became possible to track a phone via the iPhone's "find your phone" feature or some other app.[5] Ivanna, however, was fortunate enough to have an extraordinarily dedicated and technically adept friend. This friend, Evan, understood how to use the web to create a virtual community for Ivanna, and then to employ that community on her behalf. It was a temporary community but one that became dedicated to correcting what it perceived to be an injustice. The group that formed became a phenomenon, one that was able to bring pressure on the police and the *New York Times*[6] to help bring about the return of the phone. To paraphrase the title of Shirky's book, "everybody"—or at least a huge number of people—did "come" and provide pressure on the person to give back the phone. The *New York Times* "came" by writing a story about the theft and the effort to get the phone back; the police, after initially refusing to get involved, "came" and began to pursue the case; hordes of individuals from all over "came" to the website Evan had built, with the intent of using the online world to bring pressure and secure the return of the phone. Eventually, by employing the force of something novel, a large online collective, as well as the New York City police department, that is what happened.

Just as large-scale interactions can help resolve a dispute, however, large-scale interactions can be the cause of them—as we know from the trolls active in public comments or the collaborative editing process on Wikipedia. We are still not well prepared to handle disputes involving large-scale online social interactions. Clearly, networks can be employed to build relationships, foster positive interactions, and be pro-social. The same networks, however, at other times can be employed to erode relationships, generate conflict, and become anti-social. When people who are strangers to each other find ways to connect and communicate, both helpful and harmful relationships can result.

The early internet was largely populated by research scientists who had a very limited set of tools for interacting. The network did accelerate some collaboration over distances and, in that sense, could be considered a pro-social network. But it was a network linked to a well-defined professional community where participants were not only connected but shared many values and goals—often, they already knew each other. While the network may not have originated the relationships, it did help strengthen them in that it fostered opportunities for exchanging information. It was largely a closed environment with boundaries that were hard to cross, and this helped to limit disputes and deter anti-social behavior. At the same time, without any way to connect to users it did not already know, it did not support growing numbers and different types of relationships. It was a safe place, but a relatively uninviting place.

This all changed as use of the web expanded and as the population of the internet began to not only grow but became increasingly diverse. Later, with the emergence of Facebook and other popular applications, connections among individuals and the formation of groups became easy, thus increasing the range of and opportunities for both pro-social and anti-social behaviors. The two parties in Shirky's lost phone story belonged to the same large wireless communications network, which is why pictures taken on one phone appeared on the other, but they did not belong to the same communities. At that point, the only link was through their internet service providers (ISPs) and wireless carriers—entities that facilitate social and anti-social behavior, but assume no responsibility other than providing an entrée to the Net.

The process of securing the return of the phone to its rightful owner raises some challenging questions. It illustrates, for example, how difficult it is to resolve problems in a setting that has no structured supportive formal institutions. In this regard, today we are only slightly better prepared to handle problems involving online social interactions in very large virtual environments. Ivanna's friend Evan was extraordinarily dedicated and able, in a relatively short time, to create a group or crowd that was eager to apply pressure on Ivanna's behalf. This was, however, more self-help than institutional help—and a show of force rather than a demonstration of process. Outside of asking the police for help, there was, in fact, no process that could be standardized and employed in the next case of someone who refused to return a phone found in a taxi. The line between the crowd and a mob—between pro-social and anti-social behavior—was somewhat ambiguous.

Social media support relationships but, as we shall see, also generate problems and disputes involving relationships. Part of the reason for this is that the relationships enabled by social media are often quite weak. In many instances the relationships formed are not much stronger than the relationship we have with a fellow subscriber to a magazine. Even on Facebook, where most relationships involve some level of interaction prior to declaring someone a friend, the category of Facebook "friend" is really the lowest common denominator of a positive relationship. All of this affects the range and number of conflicts that arise on social media and the challenge of responding to and anticipating them. The numerous applications that constitute social media also make it much easier to generate a conflict than to resolve one (at least thus far). Evan's approach is one of many possibilities for resolving problems. We are only just beginning to see the need to develop multiple institutions and processes that allow us to revive or restore a friendship as easily as we can acquire a "friend."

Conflict as a Growth Industry

Today, no special skills are needed to create a group to support a cause or to find members interested in a cause. The means we have for communicating and organizing online allow us to easily and quickly form communities, crowds, mobs, and a great many other kinds of groups. Some of these labels imply pro-social activity and some anti-social. All, however, when compared to their offline equivalents, can emerge very rapidly and at a very large scale. All of these different kinds of groups support incredible numbers of varied relationships, and all create the possibility of problems occurring between members and groups. It can't be expected that every online platform or application will establish an online court or dispute resolution process. There is, however, a need for those who manage the platform to take on some responsibility for problems that arise. eBay, Amazon, Alibaba and others have learned that facilitating the resolution of disputes is actually profitable—that building trust and reducing risk can translate into increased participation and revenue. As discussed later in this chapter, Wikipedia, a joint venture by many thousands of contributors, devotes considerable resources to reducing conflicts; by doing so, the site is reinforcing our trust in the quality of its entries. As tools and systems for resolving and preventing disputes become more and more available, their value will inevitably become clearer and improve over time.

Some large social networks, while often challenged by users, are at least making some movement in the right direction. Facebook touches relationships in so many ways that this will be a long term effort. Facebook has a "Compassion Team" that, as we shall describe below, is developing applications that help those who are being targeted by a current or former "friend"—either bullying or harassment, or helping to air misunderstandings. These are attempts to help resolve the range of interpersonal disputes we know will continue anywhere there is interaction. The online gaming world, as another example, is starting to get serious about dealing with conflict among players—inspired to do so by an industry-wide, particularly nasty conflict called "Gamergate," which we shall discuss later.

Those tasked with dealing with the conflict generated by social media have a much more difficult challenge than those working in any of the environments we have discussed in previous chapters, such as health and e-commerce. As noted in Chapter 3, there are elements that are inherent to the exchange of goods that make the task of resolving a transaction dispute simpler than resolving an online relationship dispute. For one, the feedback systems involved are a risk-reduction tool that increases the willingness to interact with someone whom the buyer or seller does not know. That, in turn, reduces the likelihood of a dispute occurring (although of course there are disputes over feedback ratings and there are commercial contexts in which feedback ratings are less effective). Second, the kinds of disputes that need to be resolved are limited. Most involve something broken, not paid for, not delivered, and so forth. Third, the disputes are two-party disputes rather than involving many different parties. It's also difficult for parties to hide who they are, since identities are linked to some payment process; similarly, discovering who is at fault is easier with mechanisms such as shipment insurance and tracking. And last but far from least, monetary exchanges can occur immediately once an agreement is reached.

In both transaction and relationship disputes, parties may be extremely angry. In the transaction situation, however—and particularly when the value of the item is not great—anger tends to stem from a belief that one has been defrauded. The level of anger can be high, but it can also be reduced relatively quickly by facilitating communication between the parties in a way that avoids a great deal of venting and accusations. (That is why, as we noted earlier, email is a poor vehicle for such a process—its format is far too conducive to such venting and accusations). In most cases, reduction in anger comes as the parties recognize that what has occurred is not fraud but an accident or a misunderstanding, which also contributes to making resolution easier. In a relationship dispute, on the other hand, anger may have been brewing for a longer period of time and be of a more emotional nature, thus making it harder to address.

In addition to these elements, there is an existing infrastructure that can help in some kinds of transactions. For example, credit card charge disputes can be handled by the credit card chargeback system. There are also limits on liability in place for stolen credit cards. Participants in e-commerce disputes are consumers and sellers, categories for which there may be offline consumer assistance.

Social media disputes have almost none of the qualities or systems mentioned above that assist the e-commerce companies. The array of problematic behaviors is far larger, often deriving from an intentional act such as harassment, invasion of privacy, communicating false information, accusations, criticisms, bad reviews, or threats. The context in which the dispute may arise can also have a huge range, from a small group of known acquaintances or associates to large numbers of unknown participants in games and public environments. Those problems are also more likely to be serious and impactful, sometimes involving monetary loss but more commonly involving disagreements over the use of information—something that may have an immediate impact on someone's personal life or work environment. The speed of communication is also more likely to contribute to an escalation of the problem in the social media context. Intervention needs to occur at a very early stage. Time often does not heal all wounds. The problems themselves are also more complex, and complexity leads to a higher likelihood of unintended consequences. While e-commerce involves monetary loss, and restitution is often sufficient to achieve a resolution, relationship disputes often require attention to emotions. In the physical world, mediation has become a preferred process for managing family disputes because relationship disputes that go to court often result in more anger between the parties. Anger, in other words, poses more challenges in relationship disputes than in monetary disputes. Even the basic step of identifying parties involved may be more difficult in social media disputes. Disputes may involve groups or many parties. While Facebook requires users to provide their name in the hope of preventing disputes or making them easier to resolve, sometimes mistakes occur in names (or, disputes arise out of the complex nature of identity online).

There is one very important aspect in which relationship disputes may be easier to resolve than monetary or transaction disputes. The parties in a transaction of goods need a process that will work when there is no opportunity to settle the problem face to face. Parties are almost always located at a distance. Relationship disputes are more likely to involve people who know each other. They may have once been actual friends and may still be "Facebook Friends." The problem may be that the relationship has deteriorated and one party has done something online to anger or embarrass the other party. In such cases, a social group might be able to apply pressure to overcome differences, or there may be opportunities to resolve the problem face to face. Many cases of cyberbullying involving students and schools, for example, are as much physical-world bullying as online bullying and would be best resolved through a serious face-to-face intervention. More effective offline processes in schools and other contexts in which there is some spillover from disputes that originated online is sorely needed.

In the case of the missing phone, the dispute could be seen as ending positively. The phone was, indeed, returned. Violence, which had been threatened at one point, was averted. Although the police missed an earlier opportunity to contribute in a positive way, they did finally have a hand in bringing a degree of order. On the other hand, no process emerged that might be used over and over again for other online disputes. It is unlikely that another phone left in a taxi and taken home by the next passenger could be retrieved in the same way, with the anger of millions directed at a teenager whose moral compass was not functioning well. There are only so many times the crowd can be galvanized to find one person's device, and we don't even understand all the factors that caused it to happen. Which is, in fact, fitting: informal justice has always valued flexibility more than consistency, and confidentiality more than almost anything. It is almost in the nature of informal justice that the creativity employed in the resolution of the case needs to be kept secret if it is to be duplicated. At the same time, as we show below, new online forms of dispute resolution are emerging which do not always conform to the well-established principles, assumptions, and values associated with face-to-face alternative dispute resolution (ADR).

Dispute Resolution as a Growth Industry

One thriving arena for social disputes, but also a setting in which online dispute resolution (ODR) is slowly being introduced, is Facebook. Facebook was first established in 2004 as an internal social platform for Harvard students.[7] It expanded shortly afterward to additional campuses, then to high schools, then to everyone. In 2004, it had one million users and by 2016 had expanded to a staggering 1.23 billion monthly active users.[8] Over the years, all of this traffic has generated quite a few disputes. Some of these disputes are among users, while others are between users and the platform.

Facebook now is so ubiquitous that, as the story about Dixi at the beginning of this chapter illustrates, disputes connected to it can involve almost any part of one's life. It can even generate disputes after a user has passed away. Families, for example, today face the issue of who owns or can access a user's Facebook account after they die. They can request access, for example, in order to shed light on the circumstances that may have led to a family member's decision to commit suicide. Attempting to meet the requirements of federal privacy laws, Facebook has a policy of deactivating an account after family members provide proof of death; the page then becomes an online memorial for friends and family to post messages (but unwelcome messages cannot be deleted or edited).[9] In some cases, digital assets left on such accounts, such as client lists and music downloads, can also have substantial economic value, again opening the question of who should or can have access to these accounts posthumously.[10]

In other instances, families are driven by the desire to have ongoing access to a loved one's digital legacy in order to access and save pictures, messages, and other memories. Jaclyn Atkins' access of her deceased sister's Facebook account (as well as Tumblr, Twitter, and Yahoo accounts) to which she was still logged on for some time on her personal computer after her death, was a violation of the sites' terms of service, and she was eventually locked out from all and prevented from accessing the pictures and writings of her beloved sister.[11] As a result of a series of failed passwords to her sister's accounts, the Facebook account was removed. Later, after a plea to Facebook, the account was reactivated and memorialized, but this was not quite what the family wanted. "If she herself were to die . . . [Ms. Atkins] would want her boyfriend or parents to have access to her accounts,"[12] not, in other words, a "right to be forgotten" that is discussed below but a "right to be remembered." "But there is no system to make that happen.

The Internet seems like a scrapbook and memory book that is going to be there forever—but it isn't . . . it could all be gone in a second."[13] There have been some beginning legislative efforts in a few states toward granting executors power over digital estates, but national action has yet to take place.[14]

It is very apparent how difficult it is to establish procedures for these types of cases. Some, for example, may want a site preserved, while others want to secure the right to remove something from the online world. In Europe, Google was forced to institute a process for removing information from its search results in the aftermath of the "Right to be Forgotten" case, decided by the European Court of Justice in May 2014.[15] The decision mandated that Google (and other search engines operating in Europe) allow users to have information about themselves removed from lists of search results under certain conditions. The right is not absolute, and the information remains on the website pointed to by the search engine. It also must be balanced against competing rights of other parties and interests on a case-by-case basis. Google developed a form for its European users to request the removal of links that revealed personal information about them and met the conditions specified in the Court's decision relating to the adequacy, accuracy, and relevance of the information contained in such links.[16] Among other things, the person requesting removal needs to demonstrate why the information is irrelevant, inaccurate, or otherwise objectionable.[17] In the year following the European ruling, some internal Google information on certain patterns and trends relating to the 280,000 requests for removal of search results was unintentionally included in source code on Google's Transparency Report. Analysis of those patterns and trends revealed that unlike the selective requests disclosed by Google relating to criminals and public figures, the vast majority of requests came from the general public relating to more mundane privacy-related concerns.[18]

Twitter, established in 2006, boasts more than three hundred million active monthly users with roughly five hundred million tweets a day as of 2015.[19] With its 140-character messages, Twitter has been an active site for voicing complaints, generating conflict, and even harassment. It has also been employed to deliver apologies and implement conflict resolution and prevention efforts, as further described below. Twitter's mix of traits makes it a thriving site for disputes and misunderstandings, particularly due to the combination of frequent and thin communication, delivered instantaneously to numerous recipients, often anonymously or pseudonymously. These phenomena have been referred to as "trolling"—the online posting of offensive or abusive content, purposefully, and often repetitively and anonymously.[20] These features also make escalation in disputes more likely, allowing for other individuals to pile on and aggravate the situation. Indeed, statistics show that more than any other media platform, Twitter has become closely identified with online bullying and harassment, with 88 percent of abusive social media mentions taking place there.[21]

However, Twitter isn't alone in engendering harmful social behavior. According to a PEW Research Center 2014 Report, 40 percent of Americans have experienced some form of online harassment.[22] Text messages have also been used for bullying, whether it be with exclusion and hateful language, doxxing (the unwanted sharing of private personal information), the unwanted distribution of "sexts," or "revenge porn." Sexting refers to the sending of sexually explicit graphic messages, while revenge porn involves the nonconsensual distribution and disclosure (not necessarily via text messages) of sexually explicit materials with information on the identity of the person depicted in such materials, all with the intention of humiliating the person.

In one well-known case, teenager Jessica Logan committed suicide after a former boyfriend and other classmates distributed nude photos she had texted her boyfriend, leading to ongoing harassment at school. Following her suicide, Jessica's parents sued some of the youngsters involved, as well as the school and the police.[23] The lawsuit was settled after legislation meant to prevent such cases in the future was passed in Ohio, and the school's responsibility for preventing such harassment was established.[24]

Some social network sites have intentionally cultivated a culture that solicits sensitive information about others. Secret, Yik Yak, and Whisper were purposefully created as anonymous sites so as to engender a culture of gossip and sensationalism. As the dangers associated with such platforms became more obvious, Yik Yak was banned from various schools, and for a certain period of time was blocked in the entire city of Chicago.[25] Several students threatening to commit a school shooting on Yik Yak were arrested and charged, demonstrating the limits of anonymity for those operating on the site.[26] The founder of Secret decided to close it down after sixteen months of activity, due to concern over the impact of the site.[27]

Various forms of harassment like this have proliferated among all age groups, but the rates for young adults (18–29) have been the highest.[28] The *Guardian* analyzed seventy million comments left on its site (including those blocked by it) and found that women, ethnic and religious minorities, and the lesbian, gay, bisexual, and transgender (LGBT) communities experienced a disproportionate share of online abuse and harassment.[29] In these types of disputes, bystanders/ crowds play a key role. It is their presence that increases the pain of disclosure, and they can play an important part in either aggravating or lessening the impact of the harassment.[30] Responses to online harassment and bullying have included education efforts,[31] ODR, formal legislation, and legal action (as occurred in the case of Jessica Logan).[32] Another strategy has been to "out" and "shame" trolls, in some cases turning the harassers into a subject of online scorn themselves.[33]

Over time, platforms and search engines have become more sophisticated in sorting out the type of complaints and problems that tend to arise, and have indeed adopted some procedures for handling them. While the early driver for addressing conflicts was fear of legal liability, thanks to pressure from affected parties, later policies expanded to include other types of problems that did not constitute a legal cause of action but were prevalent and damaging, and could be dealt with more effectively through a systemized approach. Twitter, for example, has an online form for reporting instances of abusive or harassing behavior on the platform.[34] The reporting form is one part of a shift in Twitter's approach to harassment that was implemented as of 2014. It increased the ability of bystanders to report such incidents and recognized doxxing as harassment.[35] Despite these positive developments, the blogosphere indicates that Twitter's handling of such reports has been imperfect. Twitter's policy states that "[u]sers may not make direct, specific threats of violence against others, including threats against a person or group on the basis of race, ethnicity, national origin, religion, sexual orientation, gender, gender identity, age, or disability. Targeted abuse or harassment is also a violation of the Twitter Rules and Terms of Service."[36] Nevertheless, reports on death and rape threats have frequently been dismissed as "not violating Twitter rules."[37] Lindy West reported the following language directed at her: "choo choo motherfucker the rape train's on its way. Next stop you," only to be dismissed by Twitter despite its policy. West pointed out the following threats directed at Twitter users, all of which were also overlooked: "Dude says he wants my colleagues and I to get raped and die in a mass shooting, @twitter says it's not harassment," or "I would love to knock you the fuck out. Not because you're a female or a feminist, but because you're an enormous bitch." Interestingly, West sees the problem as stemming from the acontextual nature of Twitter's reporting (or dispute resolution) mechanism, for example, the fact that Twitter does not recognize the power relations and other relevant attributes within which these statements take place, thereby magnifying their harassing and debilitating impact.[38] Twitter's only option for the harassed is to block their harasser, but the company does not allow the removal of the abusive text altogether.[39]

Twitter's CEO has admitted that they have failed to deal with online harassment effectively, although he also claimed to have significantly increased the resources devoted to combating such phenomena.[40] As part of Twitter's efforts to better address harassment, it granted "trusted flaggers" status to various entities, which can report inappropriate content in the name of others. A report published by Women, Action and the Media following the organization's "trusted flagger status" helped lead to the change in Twitter's policy which now allows bystanders to report online abuse on Twitter.[41] Still, users complain that Twitter fails to effectively deal with trolling, and according to one recent survey "about 90 percent of those [Twitter users surveyed] who said they had reported abuse said their complaints went unheeded."[42]

Facebook employs four teams to handle different types of complaints: Safety, Hate and Harassment, Access, and Abusive content.[43] These complaints are responded to after users report a problem; Facebook uses a support dashboard to allow users to follow their handling of the complaint, as well as receive an explanation of which action was or was not taken by Facebook.[44] There is some indication that Facebook is less tolerant of abusive and harassing language than Twitter is, reportedly having seriously worked with users to understand the impact such content has on them.[45]

In recent years Facebook added another tool for flagging a problem. Unlike its other processes, this mechanism connects users directly. Like other online behemoths, Facebook—which initially shied away from user-to-user disputes— has found that it must step in and assume some responsibility for addressing problems that arise within the Facebook community if it is to sustain user satisfaction and loyalty. By engaging in "compassion research," Facebook discovered that much of the content reported as abusive by users was often not patently offensive. They discovered that often the content that offended users was not blatantly hurtful instances of pornography or hate, but rather photos taken by others and posted without a user's consent.[46]

The research uncovered the significant role language choice plays in determining whether a complaint by a user to their Facebook friend will be positively addressed. This project is connected to the controversial *Facebook Experiment*, which sought to uncover the impact of positive versus negative feeds on Facebook on users' moods.[47] While the Facebook experiment received harsh criticism in light of lack of informed consent to the experiment, the compassion research project resulted in the launching of a dispute resolution system through which users can alert their friends to content that is offensive to them, explaining how it makes them feel and what actions they would like to be taken by their counterpart.

The research resulted in message templates that provide the parties with language that allows for compassionate communication to take place between them. The process also allows young users to send a message to a trusted older friend with whom they can consult on the matter.[48] Some viewed the development of this discussion tool as an effort by Facebook to take responsibility over user-to-user disputes that arise on its platform. Others have critiqued it as a form of unpaid outsourcing, rendering users themselves responsible for "cleaning up" the internet from disturbing, harassing, or offensive content.[49] In fact, user involvement has been seen as a necessary means for addressing complex social problems where platforms either adopt a "hands-off" approach or fail to deal with the problem effectively. In what has been termed "mutual aid accountability," coordinated peer-support is used to hold others accountable by creating systems for coordinating collective judgments about alleged harassers and setting up support networks for the harassed and facilitating the reporting of instances of harassment.[50]

The process developed by Facebook to address user discomfort over content uploaded by other users seems to represent a more advanced understanding of the role of dispute systems design. Crucially, the process instituted by Facebook is a result of an analysis of the types of problems raised by its users and a recognition that no process existed to address the types of disputes users were facing. There was now an important understanding that Facebook had to provide avenues for users to resolve problems that arose between them, not only problems that involved Facebook directly or could render it legally liable.

The new process reflects a recognition of the significance of dispute resolution processes that create a space for users to discuss problems, feelings, and desired outcomes. This moves beyond rights-based processes in which Facebook renders a decision, and allows instead for direct user-to-user negotiation and an option to consult with another user. It is also a process that is tailored to the characteristics of the parties and the dispute, in that it places an emphasis on the feelings of the injured party and takes into account that many of these users are young and could benefit from external advice. In terms of accessibility and use of technology, the ability to initiate the process by clicking on the offensive picture and the prefixed menu of problematic aspects of the image also presents a more advanced approach to the role of the Fourth Party in dispute resolution.

As we have seen again and again, with all new technology systems come new opportunities for disputes. This same new ODR system can also be its own source of disputes, when the reporting system is abused by revenge-driven users reporting on other users. One scandal, reflected in the story that opened this chapter, involved the possibility for anonymous flagging of a Facebook account name as "fake," thereby triggering an identification verification process, which many users find intrusive and offensive.[51] The option to report such instances became available under Facebook's "Authentic Name Policy," as part of an attempt to shut down celebrity imposter accounts, among other problematic phenomena.[52]

The policy has been critiqued for its "haphazard" enforcement and its frustrating attempt to determine whether a name is "authentic," which, under Facebook's definition, means the name used "in real life."[53] This definition has proven elusive and, more troubling, has raised serious critiques claiming that it is harmful to users who belong to marginalized groups and prefer to use pseudonyms (such as the transgender community, or those suffering from abuse) or those whose name is unusual (such as the Native American community). In freezing these accounts, some argue, Facebook is curtailing free speech by removing marginalized groups' speech from the site and by restricting the manner in which such users can present themselves once they are allowed to access Facebook again.[54]

The scandal received significant attention and led, among other things, to a public e-apology by the Facebook chief product officer, vowing to improve the flagging processes and the customer service to those users whose accounts were flagged.[55]

Regardless, it is significant that large social network sites such as Facebook and Twitter are doing some self-analysis. And they enable it in others, too: in fact, the networks have become important arenas for various companies to uncover and address individual complaints against them.[56] For some companies this has been extremely effective, and they have designated employees to handle such complaints. Some customers even find that online complaints are dealt with more effectively than those voiced offline.[57] But not all companies are able to deal with the culture of social media of 24/7 availability; others, such as Charter Communication Inc. (the fourth largest cable provider in the United States), have chosen to cut back on or even retreat completely from addressing complaints raised on social media.[58]

The various types of processes described above are currently the only discrete tools for addressing specific types of problems or disputes that arise on social media sites, search engines, and sharing (or renting) economy platforms. They are not part of a broad *system* offering a wide range of dispute resolution avenues for various types of problems and disputes that arise on a particular site.

One elaborate ODR system (as opposed to discrete tools) that has emerged is the one on Wikipedia.[59] Wikipedia may not be a social media application whose goal is to extend individual relationships. It is, however, a collaborative enterprise with large numbers of interactions among individuals and with many lessons on how to reach consensus through communication among individuals separated by distance. Disputes on well-known social media platforms also seep into Wikipedia as these disputes are described by editors, a process that sometimes leads to more disputes.

The largest free online encyclopedia, Wikipedia, was established in 2001 and has grown impressively since then to just under five million entries in the English version and nearly thirty-five million articles in 288 languages.[60] Wikipedia is edited by volunteers, with most editors operating anonymously. The entire enterprise depends on the positive engagement of a wide base of participants who are able to cooperate and reach agreement on the content of the articles on the site. Abuse of editing authority, low-quality editing, or constant changes in the content of articles would undermine the value and quality of Wikipedia. However, the lack of engagement and discussion of article content would also decrease the site's scope and accuracy.[61] While conflict and argument are an inherent part of any human activity, in Wikipedia's case this is not only true but also necessary. Over a decade ago, the site adopted various measures that would allow for constructive discussion and consensus-building, while ensuring that quality is maintained and abuse is addressed or prevented. These measures have included clear and predetermined rules governing the editing process; a multi-layered ODR system; and a hierarchy of editors with varying levels of authority in determining editing disputes and regulating editor misconduct.

The site prescribes several principles for editing rules. The articles must be written in the style of an encyclopedia, and their content must be verifiable ("V"); their content must express a neutral point of view ("NPOV"); and no original research ("NOR") by the author is permitted so as to enhance neutrality and authenticity. Given the complexity of these principles, Wikipedia operates a large number of talk pages on Wikipedia norms and practices,[62] but these remain both complicated, and at times frustratingly rigid.

The following events reflect the complex and sometimes unexpected ways in which Wikipedia's rules may operate. In a recent twist on the Gamergate scandal discussed below, Wikipedia's ground rules led to the inclusion of an article that was clearly untrue, but correct under the site's own rules. Based on an inaccurate report in the *Guardian*, according to which "Wikipedia Bans Five Editors from Gender-Related Articles Amid Gamergate Controversy," an article to that effect was added on Wikipedia. In reality, no such decision had been reached by the Wikipedia Arbitration Committee, as was well known to the Wikipedia community, but at the same time, the *Guardian* article provided the Wikipedia entry with the verifiability required for publication on the site. A contrasting incident had happened to Philip Roth, who attempted to correct an error about his own book—and was rejected under the "no original research" criterion.[63] As was explained to Roth, the site was after "verifiability, not truth." In most cases, however these guidelines have worked well in ensuring reasonably accurate and well-grounded articles, particularly when operating in conjunction with editor conduct–related rules, the ODR system, and the prevention mechanisms described further below.

Wikipedia has adopted a set of principles and rules relating to editor conduct as well. Wikipedia requires that discussions remain civilized[64] and that editors assume that others are acting in good faith.[65] Editors are therefore not allowed to engage in editing wars (reverting to the same or similar edits more than three times in twenty-four hours), sock-puppetry (editing through several user names), and other attempts to abuse the editing process.[66]

To ensure this goal is met, Wikipedia has instituted an elaborate dispute resolution system which allows disputing parties to employ a variety of processes and tools to settle a disagreement over an article's content as well as police editor conduct (or misconduct).[67] The basic process employed is negotiation over article content. This process takes place on the article's talk page, where editors disagree on whether the article meets the basic principles of Wikipedia.[68] Unlike face-to-face negotiation, which typically takes place privately in a closed space, here the discussion is public (although discrete negotiations can take place on personal user talk pages). If the parties are unable to resolve the dispute on the talk page, they can ask for external assistance. One option is to ask for such assistance informally by submitting a "Request for Comment" (request for a community-wide input),[69] "Editor Assistance" (one-on-one assistance by an experienced editor), "Third Opinion" (requesting another editor's informal opinion in case of a simple dispute between two editors),[70] or informal mediation (by any Wikipedian).[71] In some cases, a vote of all interested Wikipedians is sought.[72] Other formal dispute resolution mechanisms on the site include mediation for content-related disputes (conducted by a member of the Mediation Committee),[73] and arbitration for editor conduct–related conflicts (conducted by elected members).[74] While formal mediation is a private process, arbitration processes are conducted publicly by default. Arbitration is also described as "a last resort."[75] An arbitration decision can even be appealed to Jimmy Wales, Wikipedia's founder, usually by email. In most cases such appeals have been unsuccessful.[76]

A dispute cannot be escalated to external resolution unless the parties demonstrate that they first attempted to resolve the conflict through direct negotiation.[77] Numerous noticeboards exist for assistance on various topics, such as the "Neutrality Noticeboard" or the "No Original Research Noticeboard."[78] When conflicts escalate and external assistance is needed, the history of talk pages and the article page can provide evidence on the conduct of the editors and the changes in the content of the article in question over time.[79]

Wikipedia's dispute resolution system offers its users a variety of online parallels to traditional ADR processes (e.g., negotiation, mediation, and arbitration), as well as some new variants (such as the ability to draw broad input from the Wikipedia community of editors). Interestingly, some of the elements of the Wikipedia system are "bottom up," generated by users with no expertise in dispute resolution. It is the combination of the diversity in dispute system designer identities as well as the unique features of digital technology that have rendered Wikipedia's dispute resolution processes different from the traditional offline dispute resolution landscape. This is evidenced in the relaxed attitude toward confidentiality (e.g., the open negotiation and arbitration processes), as well as in the ease with which input can be drawn from a wide range of editors.

All Wikipedia editors are potential or actual dispute resolvers. These editors are not necessarily individuals with a background in law or dispute resolution, and for the most part contribute to Wikipedia on a volunteer basis. The Wikipedia system provides a good demonstration of the need for online mechanisms to address online disputes, as well as of the ways in which these mechanisms differ from face-to-face dispute resolution. Offline processes are not only impractical in terms of costs and inconvenience (the Wikipedia process takes place entirely online, asynchronously, and at no cost) but also because the disputes rarely constitute a legal cause of action.

Conflict Prevention

Alongside its dispute resolution efforts, Wikipedia has been very focused on dispute prevention. It employs technological tools not only for studying patterns of disputes and effective resolution strategies but also for automatically detecting problems, for example, the illegitimate editing of content on its site and deleting such content immediately, even before abuse has been reported by users.

"Bots" (commonly known as software programs) have played an increasingly significant role in preventing vandalism and spamming to the site's articles. While some editors sign up for vandalism control, following articles on how to detect and address suspicious editing practices,[80] bots have a significant influence on the quality and process of editing.[81] Bots not only detect spam and vandalism on the site but also assist the editing process by automating certain elements in the process, making it more efficient and improving coordination among the large base of editors.[82] Bots comprise seventeen out of the twenty most prolific editors on the site, and are collectively responsible for 16 percent of all edits on Wikipedia.[83] Many of the bots employed on the site have been developed by Wikipedians and are put into use after being approved by Wikipedia's "Bot Approval Group," a committee that reviews bot proposals and ensures that they comport with Wikipedia rules and policies.[84]

One such bot, Huggle, is the most widely used assisted-editing tool against editing vandalism. It also transforms the editing in subtle but significant ways.[85] The program presents suspicious edits to human editors while arranging them in queues according to the degree of suspected abuse. The program removes certain edits from the suspected queue entirely (edits made by bots), and advances the edits that are the most likely vandalism candidates to the top of the queue.[86] So, for example, the more content that is removed, the higher the article is placed on the list (with completely blank text pages being marked with a red X). Anonymous users are treated with more suspicion than registered users, and users whose edits have been previously reverted or received a warning, are considered more suspicious.[87]

Aided by the software program, human editors revert the edit swiftly and easily upon detecting abuse. When an edit is reverted, the software can automatically leave a warning on the user talk page. There are four increasingly severe levels of warnings, which impact the manner in which Huggle and other such software programs will determine the user's edits in future instances of suspected vandalism.[88] After four warnings, users are typically banned temporarily by administrators. Bots also facilitate the process of quickly recognizing the number and severity of warnings the user had received, asking the editor whether he or she would like to report the user as a vandal.[89] While certain obscenities are easy to detect, the adding or deleting of regular but inaccurate text is more difficult. The programs, by linking these edits to user history and characteristics, can uncover vandalism even where a human editor reading the article might not have been able to detect such changes.[90] In this respect, the workings of Huggle and similar programs have been described as "a form of delegated cognition."[91]

These programs allow Wikipedians to—in a matter of minutes—uncover large-scale vandalism attempts and address them effectively in what would otherwise be an arduous, and perhaps impossible, task for humans. Bots may also make mundane interventions and allow average and widely dispersed editors who may lack special technical, literary, or academic skills to detect whether changes to the text were motivated by vandalism.

While bots have been effective in preventing disputes, they have also given rise to new disputes. Reputation based on editing history plays an important part on Wikipedia, and it is highly challenging for newcomers to master the rules and build such a reputation.[92] Concerns over bot operation have impacted newcomers whose edits were mistakenly flagged as spam. In response, one user created Snuggle, a mutual aid mentorship technology that uncovers users who were mistakenly flagged as spammers and coordinates Wikipedians to assist those newcomers who have had editing privileges revoked.[93]

Other conflicts on Wikipedia have also revealed suspicion toward the reach of bots on the site. One such example is an argument over the operation of HagermanBot, a software program that appended signatures to all unsigned comments left in discussion spaces (which is against Wikipedia policy). This seemingly uncontroversial action became "a full-blown controversy about the morality of delegating social tasks to technologies."[94] The argument over the impact of bots and the scope of their operation is not unique to the Wikipedia context. These issues arise in other cases as well, where the introduction of a prevention mechanism's algorithm gives rise to new types of problems that need to be addressed. Whether and how such problems are being addressed is often what distinguishes those engaged in rigorous dispute prevention activities from those driven by other agendas and self interest.

Similar to Wikipedia's attempts to fight vandalism, other social media sites such as Facebook, Twitter, and Whisper have also attempted to prevent the publication of harmful materials—sometimes postpublication but before being flagged by the victim; other times even prior to its widespread publication online.[95] This has been accomplished under what has been termed "moderation" activities,[96] which can be reactive (when content is flagged) or active (real-time screening).[97] These companies now employ many outsourced laborers who review various types of content and have to make difficult determinations in a matter of minutes about which content is offensive to users of U.S. social networking sites and should be removed.[98]

Determining whether the content is permissible or problematic can be tricky, requiring contextual information that is not always available in the tight time frame available for rendering such decisions. These activities require not only language skills but also cultural sensitivity.[99] Sometimes decisions are clear cut, but even then they are by no means an effortless task. There are horrifying reports of content moderators who have been scarred deeply by watching hours of abhorrent material like beheadings and child pornography while cleaning up the internet for us all.[100]

Other moderation activities are software-based, such as the recently added Twitter functions that allow users to share "block" lists. The goal is to block known trolls before they strike, or identify "future banned users" by studying troll-produced posts. Researchers claim to be able to predict with an 80 percent accuracy rate which user will be banned in the future by analyzing just 5–10 posts.[101] Indeed, the future seems to lie in a growing base of automated dispute prevention activities that are driven by internal data analysis, rather than external complaints and disputes.

Another prominent automated prescreening of content is conducted by YouTube. YouTube developed "Content ID"—an algorithm designed to block the uploading to YouTube of content identified as copyright infringing. Content ID is designed to detect a match between materials submitted by a user and copyrighted files. The copyright owner can choose whether to "block, track or monetize the allegedly infringing content."[102] Most copyright holders prefer to monetize the infringing materials rather than remove them, rendering YouTube's Content ID into a facilitating tool for copyright licensing agreements on behalf of copyright holders. Similar systems can be found on additional sites with user-generated content as well as search engines.[103]

Concerns about the Content ID approach have been voiced that such agreements may be entered into even where users have fair use rights to the material.[104] These concerns are magnified in light of the lack of transparency surrounding the underlying algorithm of Content ID; the fact that YouTube has actively created incentives that discourage users from disputing Content ID determinations; and the fact that important accountability mechanisms seem to be lacking in the design and implementation of Content ID.[105]

Recently, Nextdoor, a social networking site for neighborhoods, publicized that it has reduced racial posts by 75% through changes to its interface, by posing additional questions to users who post messages to the site's Crime and Safety forum.[106] Most social media sites have been reluctant to disclose their content moderation activities. Whisper, however, made the decision to allow journalistic reporting on these activities;[107] a leaked manual of content moderation on Facebook given to an oDesk employee also shed some light on the types of dilemmas and controversies that can accompany such activities. For example, moderation activities may raise concerns over the limits of public speech, cultural sensitivities, individual rights, and the virtues and dangers associated with private decision making in this context.[108] As online interactions increase and vast amounts of data accumulate, the scope of automated online dispute prevention activities will grow, becoming, in all likelihood, a primary source of addressing problems and potential disputes, with an increasingly smaller portion of grievances maturing into disputes and being handled on- and offline.

Sources of disputes arising from social interactions extend beyond real-life relations to games and virtual personas. Social games have been an environment of conflict since they first appeared on the internet. In the early 1990s, Julian Dibbell published a story titled "A Rape in Cyberspace"[109] that described a particular incident in LambdaMOO, a text-based virtual world. Unlike the elaborate colorful avatars used in contemporary virtual worlds, identities and actions in text-based environments were described in writing. Even so, users described their engagement as deep, time consuming, and meaningful.[110] Some individuals spent a major portion of their day in those settings, communicating with others, usually amicably. This all changed when the "rape" occurred. A player named "Mr. Bungle" caused two other characters to commit sexual acts against their will.[111] Needless to say, this was all happening virtually, in text format—no one was actually committing physical acts; the offensive acts were executed through textual commands. But the gap between acts in the physical world and words appearing in the virtual setting did not lessen the trauma for the members of the LambdaMOO community. They claimed to experience the event as a rape, and considered seriously what its consequences and implications should be.

Over twenty years later, online games generated another controversy in which threats of violence did spill over into the physical world in what has become known as Gamergate. The story emerged from a blog post of the ex-boyfriend of a female gamer claiming that a game she developed had received positive reviews from a journalist in exchange for sexual favors.[112] Despite its weak (most would say nonexistent) factual basis, the story caught on, infuriating an extreme, misogynist faction within the gaming community.[113] These individuals expressed their anger and aggression toward other women in the gaming industry, inflating the original controversy into a more general attack on female gamers as part of what has become a culture war over the nature and diversity of the gamer community. Reddit groups, Twitter, and other sites became popular venues for expressing harsh statements by the extreme minority within the gaming community against their female targets, with some of these proclamations amounting to threats of bodily harm causing these women to flee their home and involve the authorities. Several female game developers had to cancel public appearances after being threatened and "doxxed" (their home address had been published online) on Twitter.[114] The other side of the argument claimed that this was not a conflict over harassment and the treatment of women in the industry, but over journalism ethics and biased criticisms of the industry by female journalists.[115] The story gained a lot of attention in the media, underscoring the need to address more rigorously the problem of online harassment on social media sites.

It is in this context that Riot Games sought to change the game culture of League of Legends in what has been one of the most ambitious attempts at online dispute resolution and prevention. League of Legends is the most popular video game in the world, with sixty-seven million active players a month[116]—a success attributable not only to qualities of the game itself but also to the active involvement of its publisher, Riot Games, in ensuring a safe and civil environment for the game's users. Online games and virtual worlds have always constituted an intense environment,[117] but at some point Riot noticed that players were dropping out of their game. Consequently, Riot studied the reasons for players' decision to quit and implemented significant changes to the rules of the game and its disciplinary approach.[118] This new approach was developed by a "player behavior team" composed of neuroscientists, psychologists, and cognitive scientists. The team generated insights on what was driving harassment by players and how to best address such conduct.

The single most important discovery was that "persistently negative players were only responsible for roughly thirteen percent of the game's bad behavior. The other 87% was coming from players whose presence, most of the time, seemed to be generally inoffensive or even positive."[119] This meant that the changes would have to impact the entire community; singling out the bad apples would not bring about sufficient change. Two main avenues were pursued: introducing some structural changes to the game that would limit opportunities for negative interaction, and improving the ways in which disciplinary measures were imposed.[120] The first avenue included such changes as automatically turning off the chat option during play. Players were still allowed to turn it on if they wished to, but this simple measure reduced negative chat by 30 percent. For the discipline of players, clear statements describing what offense had been committed were written.

But perhaps more important, the community became involved in disciplining bad players. This took the form of juries composed of voluntary fellow players on a "Tribunal." These juries were empowered to vote on the punishment for abuse, which included anything from warnings to bans. These measures have not only made instances of abuse drop sharply but have brought about a change in the culture of the community, with former "bad actors" demonstrating real understanding of the impact and consequences of their abusive behavior toward others. As Jason Kotkke wrote, "Punishing the offenders and erasing the graffiti is the easy part . . . [F]ostering 'a culture that encourages both personal expression and constructive conversation' is much more difficult. . . It requires near constant vigilance."[121]

Conclusion

Social disputes, online and offline, can be more difficult to address effectively than commercial ones, but early detection and the active structuring of the online social environment in a way that prevents disputes can go a long way in containing the harmful impact negative social interaction can have on users. The quick pace at which such disputes escalate online and the large number of individuals who are involved in these disputes passively and actively make them much more difficult to address, and render their consequences much harsher than offline social conflict. Efficient online avenues of redress are essential, as is an emphasis on preventative mechanisms such as structuring the conversation, prompt removal of inappropriate content, and improving incentives for appropriate conduct online. A concern for invasions of privacy is also critical, but learning from such data about sources of various problems and conflicts that arise on social networks can drive online entities to develop new tools and processes for better online communication between circles of friends and acquaintances.

Each of these developing areas represents a crucial part of future online interactions with friends, family, and colleagues. They offer us many new opportunities for dispute resolution and prevention—as well as new sources of abuse and bias. Some social media sites have recognized that they can no longer ignore conflict and simply enjoy the awareness and engagement that come with sensationalism without devoting significant efforts for addressing and containing conflict; others are still lagging behind.

CHAPTER 6

Labor and the Network of Work

"[T]here's no social contract—only vague terms of service."
—Sam Biddle

Consider the following scenario. Melinda is a single mother, struggling to care for her three young children. She lives with her mother in a crowded two-bedroom apartment in California. After being let go from her job as a part-time secretary several years ago, she has not been able to secure a steady job. Melinda has always been a quick learner but has had limited resources and inadequate opportunities to pursue formal education. After her department was closed down, Melinda searched for a job relentlessly, but was unsuccessful. She realized that the lack of formal education and accreditation posed a real barrier to getting a job and she therefore signed up for a course on ALISON (Advanced Learning Interactive Systems Online), a free online vocational training and accreditation site. Her former manager, who was impressed with her talents, encouraged her to develop her abilities, often lending her books and sending her to get training for computer and internet skills.

With her new credentials, Melinda was able to secure a significant amount of online work as a freelancer. She worked on Amazon Mechanical Turk (AMT), a site in which "micro tasks," such as proofreading and validating automated translations, were posted online. She also worked on TaskRabbit, a site matching clients looking for freelancers to perform various tasks and those looking for short-term work. Here, unlike AMT, the work was performed in the physical environment, typically in the client's home or office. Melinda accepted a wide variety of assignments ranging from cleaning jobs and car washing to secretarial tasks. She enjoyed the flexibility that the work on both sites afforded her, allowing her to spend more time with her children and assist her mother. Being a diligent worker, Melinda received very positive feedback, quickly building up a reputation. But the task-related sites were no panacea for her financial woes. Each assignment provided her with very small sums of money, making it necessary for

Digital Justice. Ethan Katsh and Orna Rabinovich-Einy.
© Ethan Katsh and Orna Rabinovich-Einy 2017. Published 2017 by Oxford University Press.

her to look for additional work. She then registered as a driver for Uber, borrowing a friend's car in return for a share of her earnings.

On her way to return the car to her friend after dropping off her last customer—with her Uber app still on—Melinda had an accident. Thankfully, she was not hurt, but the car was a total loss, as was a parked car into which she had crashed. Her friend's insurance claim was rejected, on the basis that Uber-related activities were not covered under the standard personal insurance policy he was issued (at the time, car owners had a choice between personal and commercial insurance; now, insurance companies have started offering commercial ride-hail policies). In fact, the insurance company filed a complaint against Melinda and her friend on the grounds of insurance fraud. It turned out that Melinda's friend, who recently renewed his policy, was explicitly asked whether he worked for Uber and had replied negatively. Uber, on their end, claimed that the policy in between rides covers a certain amount of the damage, but the driver must first report the claim to his or her insurance company. Melinda's friend also faced trouble with the Department of Motor Vehicles, as his car was registered for private use and not commercial use as required under California law.

What impact has the internet had on Melinda's employment opportunities? Melinda's story illustrates a variety of new kinds of employment relationships. The traditional employer-employee relationship is replaced by "taskers" (or freelancers) and clients, and the distinction between online activities and offline ones is blurred. With the spread of new technologies, global work has expanded from physical work conducted in distant countries, to services and tasks performed online from anywhere in the world for various types of employers, ranging from large companies to individuals. What types of problems can arise in this new work relationship? What is the role of the various platforms such as AMT, Uber, and TaskRabbit in addressing Melinda's conflicts with a "client"? How are Melinda's problems with the platform itself being addressed, if at all?

The internet has opened up many new opportunities for people like Melinda in terms of vocational training and work possibilities. These new work arenas, however, also give rise to problems, some familiar and others less so. For some of these problems, traditional dispute resolution avenues may provide redress. For other issues, however, courts and alternative dispute resolution (ADR) can provide no answer, since these avenues require physical presence, are costly, and operate in the shadow of the law. The global workplace environment involves distant, cross-border and flexible work arrangements, some of which entail very low pay. Such problems therefore require fast, simple, and often automated responses. What types of avenues for addressing disputes have emerged in the new workplace setting in the course of the last two decades? How have dispute resolution avenues adapted to the changing reality of work from home, distant work, and online engagement? And what further changes can we expect to occur in the future?

Technology and the New Workplace

It is hard to imagine a contemporary workplace, or even an individual worker, who does not make use of computers and the internet.[1] Not long ago, however, that wasn't so. It was only in the 1980s that personal computers entered the general workforce. In the 1990s computer use at work expanded, buoyed by the spread of the web and other applications. The proliferation of new communication options in the last ten years strengthened this trend, with smaller, connected, powerful, and mobile devices transforming how we buy and sell, as well as how, when, where, and under what conditions we work.

The growth of an information-based economy has eroded physical boundaries and made it possible for many to work from anywhere. Flexible work arrangements enable employees to perform their work from home, sometimes at a significant distance from the workplace, showing up at the office occasionally or even working exclusively from afar.[2] These flexible schemes were enabled by the availability of technology, particularly mobile devices. These developments have been significant in diversifying the workforce, improving opportunities, for example, for single parents, people with disabilities, and elders.[3]

Typically, flexible work schemes are portrayed as enhancing worker efficiency by reducing travel time and other diversions, but such claims have been questioned by those worried about the ability to monitor employees when working from afar.[4] Another drawback is the lack of interaction with co-workers, which can erode the sense of belonging to the workplace, as well as reduce interaction between diverse groups of employees.[5] Such interaction has proven to be a key element in reducing negative stereotypes toward minorities, people with disabilities, and members of other disempowered groups.

Even for those employees who go to their workplace every day, work has changed dramatically. Much of their work is now conducted online, whether through computers, tablets, or phones. These changes extend all the way to manual laborers and physical work—work that nevertheless requires some digital processing and storage of information such as customer data, stock information, payment systems, and the like. This has meant that various aspects of *all* jobs, not only those that are structured flexibly or rely directly on technology, are being performed from afar.

In another aspect of work conducted online, reviews of that work are also now widely available. Many contractors, plumbers, mechanics, appliance repairmen, and the like are now ranked online, on Angie's List and its competitors, and are connected in some way to the network, if not by a direct web presence, then by use of it. As noted earlier, the Target breach of November and December 2013 involved a heating and air-conditioning company doing work for Target and being connected to its network.[6]

The ability to perform work from any location (including home) has in fact made people work longer hours, blurring traditional boundaries between "work" and "home."[7] Many employees and managers are now constantly online, available for work-related queries and assignments, opening up their time at home on evenings, weekends, and holidays to work-related calls and emails.[8] That's a two-way street, too: technology has not only brought work home, it has brought employees' and managers' personal lives to the workplace exposing co-workers, managers, and clients to workers' ideology, hobbies, and circle of friends.

New models for delivering and performing work have also been generated by the internet. Global freelance sites such as Upwork (formerly Elance-oDesk) have emerged,[9] creating new employment opportunities for some workers but with strong incentives for workers to accept low pay as part of the fierce competition in a global marketplace for work. In some cases, the work is divided into small, menial tasks that can be performed online, often within minutes, on a freelance basis in return for very small sums of money.

This phenomenon has been termed "microtasking" and is the "new assembly line."[10] Software makes it possible to manage a supply chain of work just as it manages a supply chain of goods. Everything can be divided in smaller and smaller pieces, and arranged and ordered in novel ways. Examples include individuals who are willing to perform tasks ranging from verifying information stored on a database to testing a new product received in return for menial compensation. Some Chinese laborers, for example, are online day and night as "gold farmers," receiving meager pay to accumulate value for Western players on virtual game sites such as World of Warcraft.[11] While such activities are banned under the terms of service of the game sites, transactions surrounding them have cultivated a grey industry of trade in virtual goods estimated to be worth approximately $1.8 billion annually.[12] Despite highlighting the flexibility and large number of work opportunities associated with microtasking, the exploitative aspects of such tasks has received growing attention in recent years.

As Melinda's story shows, the internet has also created a market for offline tasks through the "sharing" or "gig" economy. Platforms have emerged that connect individuals in need of certain services with those willing to perform them, typically nonprofessionals who will undertake these tasks for a particular client on a one-time basis. Sites like TaskRabbit and Uber allow individuals to engage in tasks from apartment cleaning and assembling Ikea furniture, to driving people to the destination of their choice. Unlike Amazon Mechanical

Turk or Upwork, this work is performed in the physical world and typically involves an encounter between the "tasker" (the person performing the work) and the "client." But as with work delivered through global sites, reactions have been mixed, underscoring the empowering potential for workers in need of additional income and flexible work structures but also the lack of stability, the power asymmetries between those ordering the work and those delivering it, and the danger of bypassing legal requirements that govern working conditions and delivery processes. The "not really sharing" economy has made more visible a challenge that has accompanied professions like home workers for decades, the need to achieve "full work" and the independence that comes with it.[13]

Another significant development has been the "gamification" of the work-place: the use of video game design and mechanics to recruit and train employees, test products, solve problems, and perform their work.[14] An estimated 70 percent of employers are already using game techniques for these purposes—surgeons, for example, are already performing much of their work in this fashion, away from patients, staring at a screen as surgery now "involves minimally invasive, video-assisted techniques and a robot."[15] Tools like these have the obvious positive impact of allowing for broad-based cooperation and alleviating the burden of certain tedious tasks such as performing repetitive actions, reviewing a large number of documents, or classifying vast numbers of images.[16]

The gamification of the workplace, however, also has troubling implications. By its very nature, gamification exploits the various kinds of pleasure we derive from games.[17] Companies can effectively disguise work as pleasure in "games" that offer participants rewards ranging from reputation and recognition to points and benefits. This may allow these companies to leverage the pleasure we reap from games in return for free labor.[18] As mentioned above, in "gold farms," games have become a site in which Third World cheap labor is used to enhance results scored by privileged developed-country players, thereby gamifying the business of games. Time differences and cheap labor make such transactions particularly appealing, translating into points and rewards, but in some cases also monetary compensation (where affluent Western players wish to earn high scores without devoting the time and effort required).[19] The impact of gamification can be seen as many of these "farmers" spend their scarce free time at internet cafes playing the same virtual games they work on during their long tedious shifts while striving to meet stringent quotas.[20] Other examples have included using games to detect software bugs, induce the performance of household chores,[21] construct websites,[22] and provide effective customer support services.[23] Some of these examples connect gamification with crowdsourcing.

Alongside some of the troubling implications of technology for work laid out above, we've seen a growing array of online courses and training programs that offer employee training and certification, at times free of charge. These developments offer individuals whose job opportunities may be constrained by their low skill level an affordable avenue for enhancing their education and skills. ALISON, for example, offers a range of vocational courses at varying levels, free of charge, seeking to fulfill a vision of freely accessible online worldwide basic education and training. Other advantages of online learning and training include tailored courses, the ability to cater to an individual pace of learning, and the ability to avoid types of discrimination that might accompany traditional vocational training, such as women being directed toward what are considered "feminine" career paths.[24]

No discussion of technology and work would be complete without addressing the displacement of human labor by robots. Robots, drones (flying robots), and other automated processes now perform tasks and occupy positions that in the past belonged to human workers. In hospitals, robots assist in surgery;[25] deliver drugs, linens, and meals; and remove medical waste, dirty linens, and trash.[26] Robotic bellhops are already employed by some hotels.[27] Avatars are even being used to interview and screen candidates for government jobs. Research has found that use of robots in this context not only increases efficiency and encourages interviewee candor but also can overcome the impact of gender and cultural biases in the interviewing process.[28]

Deep concern has been expressed over the "social upheaval" that might erupt as robots displace human labor in a growing number of areas, eliminating a livelihood for some and further deepening the divide between the rich and the poor.[29] Some researchers predict a "jobless future" and offer solutions along the lines of a guaranteed basic income.[30] Others offer a more tempered picture in which areas of employment are shifting, but not disappearing.[31] In any case, the future development of robots will be heavily determined by the design choices made by "governments, consumers, and businesses as they decide which technologies get researched and commercialized and how they are used."[32] Such choices inevitably impact human work opportunities, albeit by increasing or decreasing them.[33]

In the following section, we explore the types of disputes that have emerged in the new workplace. As traditional dispute resolution mechanisms are rendered obsolete by these new technologies, novel avenues of redress and technological options for prevention of these conflicts are emerging. Unfortunately, they usually don't happen at the same time, or in the same measure, and rarely cover the wide range of new problems workers are now facing in the digital environment.

Generation of Digital Disputes in the New Workplace

The new structure of the workplace and the changes in the nature of work have given rise to novel types of disputes as well as variations on familiar conflicts. One of the first sources of conflict between employees and employers in this new environment was over the privacy of personal email communications made during working hours on work computers, or from home on work equipment. In the digital era, this type of information is recorded automatically, making it both tempting and easy for employers to follow their employees' correspondence. This has naturally raised serious concerns over employee privacy; it has also been justified by employers as a way to monitor for various forms of employee misconduct, from slacking off to sexual harassment.[34]

These issues have reached the courts, where the general approach has been that there can be little expectation of privacy where employee communication is done on company equipment and during work hours. The situation has been complicated as distinctions between company and personal email, and between work and home spaces, have become blurred.[35] Questions become even thornier when applied to freelancers, as some freelance sites use tracking software to follow whether freelancers are working the hours they claim to. Freelancers often have to agree to such scrutiny over their performance if they wish to secure work in a competitive market, resulting in a skewed bargain in which clients pay taskers the low pay and lack of constancy associated with freelance work but are entitled to the supervision typically present in employer-employee relations.[36]

Scott Sidell's story is one example of the difficulties in adapting existing conventions, policies, and laws to the digital work environment. Mr. Sidell claimed that his former employer accessed personal emails in his web-based email account after he was fired. This was possible, he claimed, because he inadvertently left his computer logged on at work, allowing his employer to access email for a period of about two weeks. Complicating things even further was the fact that some of these emails contained communications with Sidell's attorney about his claim against his former employer. Sidell's former employer's version of events differed considerably, raising allegations of breaches of trade secrets and confidential company information.[37] Unfortunately, there is no court ruling on these issues as the case was referred to arbitration in accordance with the mandatory arbitration clause in Sidell's employment contract.[38]

Email isn't the only online medium which causes workplace conflict. Social media are also a ripe area for disputes, in particular employee Facebook posts. In one case, the National Labor Relations Board intervened after an ambulance service fired one of its employees for criticizing her boss on Facebook despite a company policy barring employees from discussing their workplace on social media. The labor board viewed the policy as "overly broad" and as interfering with workers' right to organize. The importance of this ruling inspired one law firm specializing in labor and employment to advise its clients, whether unionized or not, to take note of these developments.[39] Similar concerns have been raised regarding employee infringement of copyright law while using company equipment, internet service provider, or email system. Employees can violate software licenses, illegally download music or movies, and upload or distribute copyright-infringing materials.[40]

There have been many other accounts of employees sanctioned or even fired because of personal posts. Thus far, public (or private) Facebook posts and YouTube uploads have not been deemed as protected by a reasonable expectation of privacy. For example, a flight attendant was fired for posting suggestive pictures of herself in her company's uniform. The flight attendant filed a lawsuit in federal court alleging discrimination based on sex. The lawsuit was dismissed without prejudice due to Delta's bankruptcy filing.[41] Another example relates to two pizza chain employees who posted a "prank" video on YouTube that showed them rubbing mucus on the food they were preparing for customers.[42] After the employees were identified, the police and the Food and Drug Administration pursued charges relating to food tampering. In yet another case, two restaurant-chain employees formed a closed Myspace group where they, and other workers, discussed illegal activities and made sexual remarks about other employees and management. Both employees were fired, and though the termination was deemed wrongful (since the manager who found out about the private group did so while coercing another employee to disclose the password), the court found that the employees had no reasonable expectation of privacy in the closed group.[43]

Computer use and internet access at work, whether at a distance or in the office, have given a new twist to all types of disputes involving employee misconduct. For example, as harassment shifts from verbal communication and physical acts to digital communication or display of offensive materials on a computer screen, employers are concerned with how to protect themselves from legal liability. U.S. courts have reached divergent results regarding employer liability for nonsupervisor harassment that occurs outside the physical workplace, though some courts' expansive view of the boundaries of the workplace suggest that employers will be found liable for harassment via social media.[44] One of the first cases where a court recognized an employer as liable for harassment in a digital forum was *Blakey v. Continental Airlines, Inc.*[45] While the court stated that the company did not have a duty to monitor digital media, it nevertheless ruled that a company can be liable if that company had "actual or constructive knowledge" of the content posted in the online forum. It seems, therefore, that a prudent employer might not only prohibit the use of social media and other digital forums at the workplace but also monitor digital forums that could potentially make it liable for harassment.

Some employers have responded to these legal risks by creating policies regarding online use and requiring reading on the subject, as well as the development of employee training in these areas, tailored to the online context.[46] Many employers have also chosen to adopt a wide range of monitoring devices over their employees, such as documenting key strokes and screenshots, thereby raising fierce debates over the legality of such measures and what the reasonable scope of employee expectations of privacy should be in this day and age.[47] While many private employers have taken to limiting and restricting the online social activity and speech of their employees during their off-duty lives by way of contractual clauses or off-duty conduct codes,[48] others are beginning to encourage social networking by employees as a potential asset to firms. This can increase company credibility and positively impact employee engagement and morale.[49] In an era of ever-growing use of social media and other digital tools, and as employer liability grows for acts committed by employees, it is inevitable that new and more intrusive systems and policies of workplace surveillance will emerge.[50]

How are these different disputes—particularly those that do not end up in court—being addressed? What is the role of technology in this new environment? For those employees who deliver their work face-to-face in a physical environment, much has not changed. Legal and face-to-face dispute resolution are still very much present in these settings. As described above, employer policies on appropriate use of employer computers and internet access during work hours create a framework for handling disputes that arise with respect to such issues. In extreme cases, courts and lawyers are involved, while minor problems are, in all likelihood, dealt with through workplace complaint-handling channels.[51]

While the relative dearth of online dispute resolution (ODR) in the more traditional workplace environment may seem plausible,[52] the slow growth of the use of ODR in the context of online labor seems surprising. One would think that sites offering a variety of services online would also provide dispute resolution services online to handle any conflicts that might arise. Thus far, however, relatively few such sites have chosen to assume responsibility for problems that arise between workers and clients interacting through their sites and to address disputes. This picture reflects the greater decline in the broad political and economic context in which worker rights have been eroding the last several decades. There appears to be a growing divide in the digital age between the empowerment of consumers in many contexts and the neglect of the rights of workers on the other.[53]

Dispute Resolution in the Digital Workplace

The National Mediation Board (NMB) is the U.S. government agency charged with helping to resolve labor-management disputes in the airline and railroad industries.[54] The organization employs mediators and arbitrators for disputes over the negotiation of new or revised collective bargaining agreements, as well as for disputes involving the interpretation or application of existing agreements. The NMB also intervenes where an employee's right of self-organization is in dispute. The NMB may be involved through an application for mediation (which may then escalate into interest arbitration), or through voluntary use of its ADR services.

The NMB was one of the first entities to grasp the significance of online tools for addressing employment-related disputes. Their work requires NMB personnel to travel significant distances and to meet with stakeholders and disputants several times a year throughout the United States. Such meetings are naturally costly, making it necessary for people to be away from their main office and for the NMB to cover travel and accommodation costs. This is the context that drove Daniel Rainey, NMB's chief of staff, to initiate a collaboration in 2004 with the National Center for Technology and Dispute Resolution to experiment with incorporating technology into its dispute resolution services.

The NMB began by focusing on cost savings and the convenience side of the dispute resolution triangle of ODR. It was also interested in the expertise side, and a substantial National Science Foundation grant to the University of Massachusetts allowed for the development of "STORM"—a novel ODR tool for online brainstorming.[55] STORM was designed by a multidisciplinary group of computer scientists, ADR practitioners, and legal academics. The group began by conducting in-depth research on the processes and tools employed by NMB mediators as encapsulated by Figure 6.1.

Such research underscored the key role that the brainstorming phase occupied in the mediation process. While brainstorming, mediators seek to elicit ideas from the parties, along with other information and statements that can help move the discussion forward. This phase also allows mediators to re-examine party interests and needs, as well as assess party dynamics. Traditionally, brainstorming in the physical world required face-to-face meetings and the use of flip charts and markers. Brainstorming was selected as the focus for enhancing NMB's use of ODR because of the centrality of the process and because of the potential of technology to improve it.

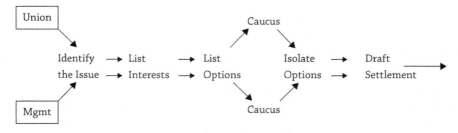

Figure 6.1 National Mediation Board Interest-Based Mediation Process.

The testing of STORM in the NMB mediation context generated important insights on the shift from face-to-face dispute resolution to the online medium. The online brainstorming tool not only added real efficiencies in terms of time, costs, and the administration of the process from the mediators' viewpoint, it also improved the process by empowering parties (especially on the employee side) to voice their opinions—anonymously if they chose. Anonymous input can help to level the playing field among speakers by preventing "group think" dynamics; however, it also comes at a cost to the other functions performed by mediators while brainstorming face to face, namely, the ability to gauge participation levels and address group dynamics and power imbalances within and among groups of stakeholders. The anonymous channel also undercut efforts to present a unified front (problematic in particular for labor unions) by allowing for fragmentation and individual preferences to be voiced. STORM therefore reinforced the understanding that ODR does not merely transplant existing processes into the online context. By changing the medium through which dispute resolution processes are performed, these processes—and their goals and values—are inevitably transformed as well.

The STORM project was also a vivid demonstration of the ways in which online-offline distinctions are constantly being challenged over time—which types of disputes are appropriate for ODR and which are not, given the difficulty of conveying certain types of information online, such as group dynamics. What was clear, though, was that traditional, offline disputes could be handled through digital means, and that those means offered efficiency-related and other qualitative benefits through documentation and the possibility of anonymous, asynchronous input.

Despite these advantages, the NMB's use of ODR remains the exception in the traditional workplace setting. While digital communication is employed widely in traditional workplaces and internal dispute resolution processes have been adopted in both public and private workplaces, there has been only occasional experimentation with ODR by ombudspersons or other workplace conflict management units.[56]

Even the digital work environments discussed in this chapter have been deficient in terms of providing effective avenues for raising and addressing disputes. Amazon Mechanical Turk (AMT), for example, generates many disputes but does not offer any dispute resolution services. Indeed, in responding to complaints by taskers, it has stated: "Our policy is not to interfere in disputes between Workers and Requesters, and as stated on our site, all approvals and rejections are at the sole discretion of the Requester. If you feel a Requester has unfairly rejected a HIT, I would suggest you contact them to see if you can work something out."[57] When AMT workers were asked how they would improve the AMT system if they were the CEO of Amazon, many of them referred to the need for effective avenues of addressing disputes. "I would create a conflict resolution center and have requesters who do not know what they are doing at least spend some time as a worker to get a feel of the system," commented one user. Another contributed: "I have heard HORROR stories about how worker accounts have been closed (and funds tied up) and there isn't a phone number to call or an actual email address to use that is reliable. A few hard blocks from crappy requesters can ruin a turker, yet a turker is powerless to find out what the problem is, make it right, etc." And yet another: "I would allow the users more control over disputes, Amazon is really horrible with users that get blocked by requesters that really don't have a reason. They have no dispute or resolution thing set up for mTurk. And not allowing requesters that continually make new names to scam workers."[58]

Uber, the leading ride-ordering service app, has also offered its drivers very little in terms of their ability to address problems such as disputed rankings by customers. Indeed, Uber has earned a reputation as a company that fails to seriously address any of the disputes that arise out of its services relating to its drivers and clients[59]—disputes which, according to one source, amount to millions of monthly complaints.[60] One explanation given for this state of affairs has to do with the manner in which Uber has dealt with customer service representatives who are tasked with addressing disputes that arise on both the driver and customer end.[61] These workers are often former Uber employees but are now employed through a human resources agency; some of these freelancers reside in the United States, but there has been increasing reliance on outsourced labor in the Philippines.[62] According to some voices, this has caused what has been viewed as a deficient treatment of complaints (due primarily to a quantitative goal of "closing" a high as possible number of complaints per hour)[63] to further deteriorate, as non-native-speaking customer service representatives fail to properly address urgent complaints and/or deliver insensitive messages to complainants.[64]

Screenshots disclosed from complaints made to Uber's customer service seem to indicate a striking number of complaints filed over rape and sexual assaults,[65] some of which have been filed by Uber drivers themselves.[66] In one case, a Manila-based customer service agent failed to escalate a complaint about a driver who demanded sexual favors from a customer.[67] It may be true that "quality control is a challenge when the supervisor is just software,"[68] but the alleged inaction of Uber in the face of these complaints has compounded due to the fact that traditional bodies handling complaints over business operations outside the United States (such as Consumer Affairs Victoria) have failed to intervene, in light of Uber's illegal status in their region.[69] Uber, however, portrays a different picture altogether; they claim their customer service representatives are well trained,[70] that the allegation of large numbers of rape cases are substantially overblown,[71] that it invests substantial efforts in the safety of its customers and drivers,[72] and that its diverse non-U.S. customer service staff is an important part of being a global company.[73]

One global freelancing site that does offer ODR is Upwork.[74] Upwork is an online global marketplace for freelancers. Those in need of workers for a particular project can post the job online and choose a freelancer to perform the work. Most Upwork freelancers are in technology, writing and translation, arts and graphics, or administrative assistance.[75] Registration is free; a fee is paid to Upwork only after the job is delivered and accepted by the client. Freelancers receive feedback by customers but are also rated by Upwork according to various parameters they define.[76] Work can be performed either for a fixed price or on an hourly basis, depending on the nature of the work needed. In fixed-price assignments, clients are encouraged and coached to provide a clear description of work requirements and milestones. In all types of transactions, both sides are instructed to communicate through the assigned workspace on Upwork so as to document all their agreements, communications, and updates on the freelancer's progress.

While Upwork recognizes the need for some parties to communicate via phone or Skype, it requests that the content of such calls be documented to ensure that both parties are clear about the requirements of the job. The major incentive to do so is that failure to document agreements on the workspace will result in the loss of Upwork protections for parties if a dispute arises in the future.

According to Upwork, parties use the tools provided on the site to resolve the problem on their own in 3 percent of the jobs. Users contact Upwork customer support for assistance in addressing a dispute between the parties in only 1 percent of the jobs.[77] The types of problems that arise usually have to do with nonpayment on the freelancer's end, or payment for an incomplete job on the client's end; the average value of disputes is $200. The source of most problems is miscommunication or, in some cases, a complete lack of communication, with some parties "going dark" (stopping communication altogether). Some problems have to do with feedback, but Upwork tends not to get involved in those unless they are egregious.[78] Upwork has a strong incentive to ensure that disputes get resolved and jobs are completed and paid for, as it is paid a percentage of the fee for completed assignments.

The dispute resolution process offered by Upwork differs for fixed price versus hourly jobs.[79] In the latter case, if the parties choose to use Work View Tracker (a feature allowing users to follow the scope of work performed by the freelancer), the number of hours billed is within the authorized scope of hours, and there is a valid payment method, then Upwork will resolve the dispute in its sole discretion. In general, though, disputes are rare in hourly jobs because the client is monitoring the work all the way along. In the case of fixed-price projects,

Upwork offers a payment mechanism in which money is placed in escrow. After milestones are met and portions of the work are performed satisfactorily (and it is the client's obligation to review and object to payment within a specified time), then money is released.

When a dispute arises over whether milestones were met or whether the job was completed satisfactorily, Upwork offers communication tools to the parties. They file a dispute notice form, then have two business days to reach a resolution on their own. If they fail to do so satisfactorily, Upwork will offer its assistance in facilitating a dispute call using Modria software. If the dispute call fails or cannot be scheduled, either party can request an arbitration to be conducted by the American Arbitration Association, partly funded by Upwork.[80] This last step, however, is extremely rare, with arbitration taking place in only ten to twenty cases a month (out of 130,000 jobs conducted during that time frame).[81] Under the Upwork Terms of Service, if one of the parties fails to participate in the dispute resolution process, the funds in escrow will be released to the other party.[82]

Where these processes fail, discussion of the disputes and unsuccessful dispute resolution efforts can spread to various blogs and sites, which have become a central arena for airing problems and complaints with temporary labor assignments. One blog entry described the plight of a young writer who embarked on a freelancing writing career on Upwork (then Elance), but was taken aback by the negative experiences she had with several clients. Three of her projects were rejected by the clients after she completed the work, without giving her a chance to improve the product, leaving her without pay or redress. In one case, the client allegedly ended up using her work product anyway, with minor changes. In the freelancer's own words: "If my work had actually been unsatisfactory, that would have been perfectly fine. I get rejected all the time when I submit stories and poems to journals . . . [T]hey actually did use my brochure, but did not pay me for the work I had completed for them. All they did was change the titles of the sub-sections. Everything else was word-for-word."[83] Upwork could not do anything; the client's account was no longer valid, and the client unresponsive. In a second case, the freelancer's work was berated (undeservedly, she claimed) and payment again refused, resulting in her receiving a negative review on top of not getting paid. In yet a third case, there was a disagreement over the quality of the product the freelancer delivered. Here, the freelancer ultimately involved Upwork, and a compromise was reached wherein she was paid a quarter of the original amount agreed upon and accepted a negative review.[84]

Reactions to this story on the blog were as intriguing as the post itself, including one from Jon Diller, eLance's (as Upwork was called at the time) own vice president of Customer Success. Diller offered assistance and pointed to various mechanisms introduced by Upwork to prevent such conflicts from arising, such as the escrow payment option for fixed-price jobs and Work View for hourly paid jobs, allowing freelancers to document "every minute worked" and guaranteeing payment for time devoted.[85] This particular post engendered heated discussion of Upwork (called eLance at the time) success and failure stories, a discussion populated by repeated misunderstandings resulting in disappointments, unmet expectations, and financial losses for both clients and freelancers.[86] Reactions by other freelance writers toward Upwork were often fierce and quite negative, citing significant power asymmetry between the freelancers and contractors; exploitative work conditions due to the "race to the bottom" nature of auction sites;[87] and "big brother"-like surveillance mechanisms (e.g., Work View), which provide contractors with a level of supervision typically associated with full-time employment, without having to pay the costs associated with that kind of relationship (benefits, vacation time, etc.).[88] Other commentators, however, praised their experience with Upwork, complimenting the escrow service as a highly effective conflict-prevention mechanism, and lauding the significance of the site for workers in the developing world.[89]

As we can see from the description above, various users have had divergent experiences with Upwork. Whereever one stands on this debate, it is impressive that Upwork has chosen to assume responsibility for freelancer-client disputes and to implement an ODR system in an environment in which freelance workers rarely have channels available for voicing complaints and addressing problems.

Formal ODR processes are rarely used for resolving disputes involving temporary labor assignments and the role of ODR in this context is significantly less central than in the e-commerce context. One explanation for the peripheral role ODR mechanisms have played in the workplace lies in the inherent political and economic weakness of workers in this environment.[90] Power asymmetries are becoming more extreme than in the past, with employers, clients, and mediating platforms finding that they can thrive without attending to workers' needs. Since platforms are typically portrayed as technology companies that merely connect clients with freelancers, they do not see themselves as responsible for disputes that arise as a result of their "matchmaking."[91] This results in those platforms often refusing to recognize rights and ethical obligations toward their users, raising concerns about access to justice in the private sector where the "shadow of the law" is weak or even absent.

A second explanation for the scarcity of ODR processes may have to do with the nature of these platforms, which in fact do not have a vested interest in encouraging direct communication between the parties. Such communication would allow for a long-term relationship to emerge that would remove the platform as an intermediary. While less relevant in the case of endeavors such as Airbnb or Uber, this is an immediate concern for the likes of Upwork and TaskRabbit (described further below). Indeed, TaskRabbit at some point revamped its operation completely, shifting from a bidding market for jobs[92] into an elaborate temp agency model, in which taskers are offered possible work opportunities that match their interests (as opposed to the previous model under which they were able to exercise a high degree of control over their schedule and mix of assignments).[93] This forestalls the possibility of people taking the relationship outside the platform by having the platform play a more central role in the matching of taskers with clients.

Finally, a third possible cause for the dearth of ODR in this setting has to do with the shift in the online arena in emphasis from dispute resolution to prevention activities. As described in the following section, some digital workplaces invest substantial efforts in screening users, structuring transactions, and mentoring participants so that work is delivered in a satisfactory manner from the perspective of both sides. The vast amount of data collected by such entities allows them to learn from past experience and prevent problems from recurring. To the extent they are successful, dispute resolution occupies a less central position.

Dispute Prevention in the Digital Workplace

Upwork's lessons in terms of dispute resolution are mostly about the importance of prevention, effective ongoing communication between the parties, incentivizing good behavior through scoring, and ensuring competence through tests, credential verification, and interviews via video and written chat.[94] For employers, Upwork underscores the need to be able to write a clear job description, treat an online freelancer the same way as in the face-to-face arena, keep all information on the job in the workspace area, and require freelancers to submit weekly status reports there as well. Upwork also offers verification of freelancer qualifications, neutral ranking of freelancers (to which the parties add their own rating), as well as coaching. All of these measures contribute greatly to the prevention of problems, reflecting ongoing learning by Upwork on sources of conflicts.

TaskRabbit, founded in 2008, has adopted a variety of dispute prevention mechanisms. Described as the "Uber for everything" or the "eBay of jobs," TaskRabbit is a marketplace in which people contract over the performance of tasks. Performers of tasks (formerly referred to as "task rabbits") are connected to customers through the online marketplace, and do everything from assembling IKEA furniture to mowing lawns and washing cars.[95]

Stories abound on the significance of the site in the aftermath of the 2007 economic crisis, when it provided much-needed income for a portion of the U.S. workforce. Beyond monetary compensation, such endeavors were hailed for allowing workers more autonomy and flexibility than conventional employment. At the same time, a review of user experiences uncovers a complex picture in which task performers can be exploited in subtle ways. The client has significant power in dictating the terms of employment: posting the task and defining its scope. These descriptions have powerful implications. For example, one task was defined as cleaning a two-bedroom apartment, and described as a one-hour job. This description turned out to be unrealistic. The task performer now found himself in a bind—perform the task for what now proved to be an extremely low wage, or risk a negative review for having failed to complete the task as defined and accepted by him.[96]

TaskRabbit has attempted to deal with some of these problems through prevention. Like other on-demand economy sites, TaskRabbit has a user-reputation-based system. However despite their prominence, reputation rankings are insufficient to generate trust and prevent problems. As explained above, Upwork makes up for this by complementing user rankings with their own, more sophisticated rating—based on data accumulated over time, safe payment mechanisms, and coaching on screening and ensuring that information is reliable and instructions for the job are clear.

For TaskRabbit, professed preventative measures also include prescreening of users. TaskRabbit conducts background checks on its task performers, which include an identity check, a criminal record check, and an app-orientation session.[97] TaskRabbit also lays out safety rules for taskers, emphasizing how to identify and avoid taking on fraudulent tasks that manage to slip through TaskRabbit screening.[98] If taskers find themselves in a dispute with their client over approval of hours worked, TaskRabbit provides advice and tools for addressing the problem, as well as tips for preventing such issues from arising to begin with in future interactions.[99] Insurance for property damage or bodily injury arising out of tasks as well as theft-related damages is another trust-engendering and conflict-prevention mechanism introduced over the years.[100]

Prevention-related activities are generally taking place more often as our work context evolves. The problem, however, with the various prevention-related activities that take place on these platforms, often through automated means, is that there is very little information available on their operation and impact on the parties involved. What is driving such activities, whose interests are served, and to what extent are rights preserved? As explained earlier, dispute prevention activities originated from the workplace setting but were conducted post-resolution, after both parties' concerns and claims were heard and addressed. In the new arena of pre-resolution online dispute prevention (ODP), the platform is the one raising the problem, weighing the interests involved and deciding whether intervention is in order and what its nature and scope should be.

In 1994, professors Stanley Aronowitz and William DiFazio published a book called *The Jobless Future*, in which they foresaw a trend "toward more low-paid, temporary, benefit-free blue and white collar jobs and fewer decent permanent factory and office jobs."[101] This has become a reality with the rise of many of the on-demand economy endeavors which erode the achievements of organized labor, exploit work for free, increase power asymmetries, and render worker-employer relationships less significant. At its most extreme, prevention efforts may even result in the replacement of human workers by robots.

There are efforts to use the law to counter these trends. One of the principal issues being considered by courts is whether on-demand economy task performers are in fact employees of the platform, not freelancers or independent contractors.[102] This decision would impact the two-tier structure these companies have: a thin layer of internal employees, who enjoy all the related benefits, and a large group of freelancers who are entitled to no benefits or job security (and who create most of the value for the company). Not surprisingly, such divisions often echo racial and gender divides.[103]

Conclusion

Technology has improved access to justice in many areas. But the work context is not one of them. Instead, technology in the workplace to date has generated large numbers of disputes without providing adequate online avenues of redress and prevention. Despite the fact that ODR has much to offer for work-related conflicts, the shift toward online, machine-based resolution and prevention avenues has occurred only sporadically.

In those cases in which dispute resolution avenues do exist and prevention activities do take place, the platform rarely discloses to workers (and others) the terms of dispute resolution outcome patterns and what use, if at all, is being made of data for monitoring and improving such activities.

The existence and structure of dispute resolution mechanisms are by no means independent of the broader social, economic, and political structures that surround workplace relations. The digital labor market has, in many ways, become the mirror image of the consumer marketplace. In some instances, advantages gained by consumers ("clients") have come at the expense of the workers ("taskers"). Where there is no concern over long-term interaction and satisfaction, and the "shadow of the law"[104] is absent, it is unrealistic to expect dispute resolution mechanisms to fill the vacuum.

CHAPTER 7

ODR in Courts and Other Public Institutions

Think about the smartphone in your pocket or purse: it navigates an environment that is constantly ratcheting up in terms of complexity. Yet it does so in ways that grow ever simpler, more elegant, and less costly. Why doesn't that happen in our court systems?
—Gillian K. Hadfield, *Innovating to Improve Access: Changing the Ways Courts Regulate Legal Markets*

After seven years of marriage, with two young children, some assets, and some debt, our fictional couple Sara and Joseph decided to divorce. The couple was "traditional," with Sara working part-time and Joseph the breadwinner who handled the family's financial affairs. As she was trying to consider her options, Sara realized that she was in the dark regarding their finances and began to worry about her financial stability postdivorce.

Sara looked up information on family lawyers online and reached out to a lawyer in her area. She went to meet her in her office, where the attorney described the legal process that awaited her, preparing Sara for lengthy and costly proceedings. The lawyer also instructed Sara to restrict her communications with Joseph, cautioning her not to discuss her strategy too openly with him as matters might become contentious. Sara's attempts to inquire about an alternative, more amicable process were brushed aside. Her searches on the internet later that night uncovered options like mediation and collaborative divorce, but she was swayed by her lawyer and was concerned about unknowingly giving up her rights. Sara felt she did not know enough about her options to ignore her lawyer's advice and forego the legal route, despite being intimidated by the legal route and its expected costs, financially and otherwise.

Sara and Joseph filed their court papers online and were assigned a court date several months after the filing date. They arrived at the courthouse only to find that due to the heavy caseload, their hearing was postponed for several more

Digital Justice. Ethan Katsh and Orna Rabinovich-Einy.

months. Sara's lawyer was relieved; this gave them more time to prepare. The process was clearly going to be lengthy and expensive. In the meantime, both Sara and Joseph felt constrained in their ability to start a new phase in their lives.

Sara assumed that this was an inevitable part of dealing with courts and the law but soon discovered she was mistaken. One evening, while conducting additional online research in preparation for the upcoming hearing, she came across a new process introduced in the Netherlands: an online dispute resolution (ODR) system for handling family cases called *Rechtwijzer*. The platform allows parties to negotiate directly in a process called "Separating Together." The software asks each of the parties a series of questions in plain, everyday language and then structures their communication with one another in an attempt to produce an agreement. Parties can communicate with one another online, twenty-four hours a day, seven days a week, from the convenience of their own home, office, or any other place with internet access. If an agreement is reached, a neutral lawyer reviews it to ensure it is legal and fair to both parties. If the parties fail to agree, they can ask for a third party to assist them. The entire process can be completed in a brief period and at much lower cost than the typical court case.

Sara was simultaneously ecstatic and outraged. This was exactly the type of process she would have wanted had she known of it, but the *Rechtwijzer* process was unavailable in her part of the world. It seemed unfathomable that such processes were not widely available in courts. Could they be?

Generating Disputes: New Expectations by Citizens, New Obligations of Public Institutions

This chapter focuses on the use of, and interest in, ODR within the public sector. Until recently, courts and other public institutions, such as regulatory agencies, lagged behind private companies in adopting ODR. This, however, is changing. Courts have been adopting a cluster of ODR systems which are beginning to have impact and which we will focus on in this chapter. There are, as well, already existing uses of ODR in noncourt governmental settings.

The National Mediation Board (NMB)[1], as noted earlier in Chapter 6, collaborated with the National Center for Technology and Dispute Resolution (NCTDR) in developing a novel ODR tool called "STORM" for online brainstorming. The NMB is responsible for handling disputes in the airline and railroad industries, and its board and Chief of Staff Daniel Rainey recognized some years ago that technology could offer significant efficiencies in terms of time, costs, and the administration of their dispute resolution processes.

Property tax appeals in the United States are now being handled in a growing number of counties through interactive, online processes.[2] Procedures vary from one jurisdiction to another but efforts to reduce one's property tax assessment have traditionally been handled through paper filings, informal meetings with the assessor, and a formal appeals process before an independent body, which may ultimately reach state courts. This process can take time, and on average lasts eighteen months. When property owners challenge assessments in localities using ODR tools developed by the internet start-up Modria, there is available online filing, online case management, automatic status notifications, online messaging and "discussions," and the delivery of decisions online.[3] The online process is not only more efficient but empowers citizens in their dealings with public entities, allowing them easier access to appeal mechanisms and increased information about the process.[4]

In British Columbia, consumer disputes can also be handled through ODR as part of a collaboration between the Ministry of Justice and Consumer Protection BC.[5] Consumer Protection BC offers an online negotiation tool for disputants on a voluntary basis. If the parties are unsuccessful in resolving the dispute through their direct dealings with one another, the disputes can be mediated by the organization. While case volumes thus far have been low, resolution and satisfaction rates have been high.[6] This project is part of a broader initiative to transform the B.C. justice system through the introduction of ODR into administrative tribunals, as described later in this chapter.

These efforts, and others described below, are supported by the belief that what works in the private sector can work in the public sector. One concern in the introduction of public uses of ODR has historically been how willing the public would be to resolve disputes online. This has not turned out to be a problem. In spite of many different data breaches over the past few years, the willingness of individuals to rely on machines for many daily tasks and fill their phone with apps has only increased. Indeed, when the choice is between visiting a physical space to conduct a transaction or doing it online, the online option is usually preferred. What this means is that today, citizens will generally be more frustrated by the absence of an online option than surprised by its presence.[7]

Expectations such as these have changed dramatically over the last five to ten years, but institutional change has been slower. In 2007, it was suggested that an online small claims court would allow one to

> [t]ravel to the courthouse with the click of a mouse and gain access to filing forms via the web. One need not take time off from work to have one's case heard, engage in endless dialogue with court clerks or wait for the return of self-addressed envelopes to obtain a complaint form. Nor need one wait, sometimes for an extended period of time, to have a case resolved, as often occurs in Massachusetts.[8]

A little earlier, Peter Damon, an Iraq war veteran, was at risk of losing a case because he couldn't appear in court. At the time he was in Walter Reed Army Medical Center in Washington, D.C., recovering from the loss of both arms in combat. (The case against him was eventually dismissed.) If Damon's case had been the result of dissatisfaction with something he had purchased online, he might have filed an online claim since readily accessible voice-assisted technologies are available for the disabled.[9] Not so in the court system.

In 2016, some small claims court forms in Massachusetts are available online—but not much else. The web first began with the simple presentation of information online. Courts—except for a few exceptions discussed below—are still largely in that stage. Information, however, rather than being an end, should be the first step in an online process that is evolving into a set of ODR processes and systems.

In 2007, which was also the year that the iPhone was introduced, it was not only the technology that was different. People's expectations about how institutions should work were also different. The internet isn't just preferred to physical trips for many today; increasingly, it's also preferred over the telephone. For this reason alone, pressure on the public sector to provide services and processes online will inevitably grow.

Meeting growing citizen expectations about what should be provided online will be a significant challenge for government. The rollout of the healthcare.gov website—intended to bring health insurance to millions who had no health insurance—was, at the beginning, a fiasco.[10] It was not only difficult to use, but rarely worked. The site was fixed and today works quite well. What is remarkable, however, is that so many individuals have the skills, technological resources, and willingness to sign up using the online system.

Part of the reason ODR efforts have developed faster in the private sector is competition. While there are market failures, at least in some cases, online businesses need to provide the three elements of the dispute resolution triangle—trust, convenience, and expertise—or their users will move on to someone else who does. The public sector has been able to resist providing ODR without fear of citizens "moving on" because they have no other place to move on to. But pressure on governments to provide online systems is now increasing, not because of direct competition but because of what has been called "liquid expectations." This occurs when

> consumer experiences seep over from one industry into another, creating an expectations chasm. As customer experiences with any product category affect how customers experience products in other categories previously thought to be unrelated, all businesses need to add new dimensions to how they understand and define their competitive

strategy . . . Increasingly, your most important competitors are those we call perceptual: those competing to shape the expectations customers have for experiences in every category. For example, Uber's checkout, which is as simple and seamless as shutting the car door, will reset consumers' expectations for how convenient checkout can be in every industry, causing consternation as they stand in a queue at a store or wait for a server to bring the check.[11]

In short, citizens used to the eBay or Alibaba resolution centers or the Amazon product return system will eventually start asking why the local small claims court is so inconvenient and inefficient in comparison.[12] At some point, it will seem reasonable to replace the small claims court with a "smartphone court" that a user can engage with on-demand.

A plan by the Internal Revenue Service to allow citizens to interact online with the IRS staff or machines was proposed in 2015. In her yearly report to Congress, the IRS's Taxpayer Advocate wrote about why she thought this was not a good idea:

Even among taxpayers who have Internet access and skills and are comfortable handling financial transactions online, the complexity of tax issues and the amount of money at stake will make online resolution impractical or undesirable from the taxpayer's perspective in many cases. Online resolution will be difficult partly due to the complexity of the transaction and partly due to the difficulty in designing a website that is both easily navigable by first-time users and capable of handling a wide range of transactions. Online accounts work well for "cookie cutter" transactions. For example, a bank website can be easy to use if the account holder is solely seeking to pay bills; an airline website can be easy to use if a passenger is solely seeking to purchase tickets; and a retailer's website can be easy to use if a customer is seeking solely to make a purchase. But if the account holder wishes to dispute an erroneous charge, the passenger is seeking a refund, or the purchaser of retail goods has not received his order by the promised date, a telephone call is often necessary.[13]

Is this truly so? Shouldn't we expect government to provide the same online conveniences that we expect from online stores, where a telephone call is not, in fact, necessary under any of these circumstances? After the healthcare.gov problems, it is reasonable to be concerned about the IRS's ability to build an easy-to-use and trustworthy system. It is less reasonable to object to a system out of fear that citizens will not use it and that it cannot be made sufficiently user friendly to handle a large percentage of taxpayer problems. In fact, the IRS is the perfect government agency to implement an ODR system. Many citizens already use software to prepare their return and submit their tax returns. One tax software program, TurboTax, tells users that "all you need to know is yourself. You don't need any tax knowledge to get your taxes done right because TurboTax translates taxes into simple questions about your life and puts everything on the right forms for you."[14] Designed well, ODR software would certainly be used by those currently frustrated by an inability to communicate with the IRS. The report quoted above noted that the IRS hung up on callers 8.8 million times without making contact.

Would ODR systems as we know them from the private sector change as they were instituted in public settings? How would the introduction of ODR in the public sector change such institutions? As ODR processes migrate from the private to the public realm they can transform the ways in which public institutions have engaged with citizens, as well as imbue ODR with some of the values and goals associated with public dispute resolution-fairness, due process, accountability, and transparency and, potentially, change the way in which we understand and think about these values and goals. When discussing technology in courts thus far, the emphasis has often been on efficiency-related considerations and "access"—less on other qualities of technology that may fall under "justice." As we analyze the introduction of technology and increasing number of novel pilot projects involving ODR in courts, we need to consider whether we should in fact think about the very concepts "access" and "justice" differently than we have in the past.

Dispute Resolution by Public Institutions: A Focus on Courts

For many years, courts have seemed impervious to the impact of digital technology. They have been slow to adopt innovations and always "proceeded cautiously when it comes to adopting new technologies in certain aspects of their own operation."[15] In 1989, it was written that

> [o]n the surface, the law appears to be relatively immune from the effects of the new media compared with . . . other institutions. A judge of 1889 who was transported through time to a modern courtroom would undoubtedly be mystified by many cases brought before him. But he would be far more understanding of what was transpiring than a businessman, an athlete, or a politician who underwent a similar experience. A judge of a century ago who found himself in the Supreme

Court of the United States today would need some orientation, but the process being used would not be totally alien. Imagine, however, how bewildered a business executive of a past age would feel on entering the floor of the New York Stock Exchange.[16]

It isn't the case anymore that there hasn't been any change. Law offices and courtrooms have been computerized, case management has been made more efficient, legal databases are now available online and often for free, emails are now a central means of communication, and courtrooms have been modified to allow for the presentation of visual graphics, videos, and digital evidence.[17] But most of the technology introduced into the courts in the last two decades has been aimed at improving efficiency and dealing with budget reductions, rather than focusing on providing new tools and resources to resolve cases.[18] The fact that physical, geographic, and even psychological boundaries in handling disputes have been overcome in the ODR processes of private companies represents proof of concept in how to provide online access to justice in courts and regulatory agencies.

The penetration of digital technology into courts is occurring in three phases. The first involves efficiencies and case management; the second connects with the growth of e-government, making more governmental information and new tools available to the public; and finally, change is occurring through an "access to justice" prism, under which some legal processes are conducted online and the traditional understanding of both "access" and "justice" is revisited. We are currently witnessing the early signs of the third phase in several jurisdictions, but for the most part, courts are still far from realizing the full potential of digital technology in enhancing access to justice by delivering digital justice.

TECHNOLOGY AS CASE MANAGEMENT

The first contribution of technology toward digitizing court processes was in case management. The aim was to streamline processes and allow work from afar and when the physical court was closed.[19] This was perceived as an important move forward toward making judicial work and court proceedings more efficient.[20]

As courts were computerized, internal processes shifted from paper-based to computer-mediated. Lawyers, court administrators, and individual judges relied less and less on paper and used computers for processing court-related documents, but parties' and lawyers' communication with the courts remained paper-based or required a physical presence, with faxes accepted under certain circumstances.[21] These changes were no different from those experienced by other large organizations who were substituting computers and digital documents for typewriters and paper. Computerization was still an internal and bureaucratic development. This began to change with the infiltration of e-government initiatives into courts' operations.

E-GOVERNMENT AND USE OF TECHNOLOGY BY COURTS

E-government involves the use of information technology to make the workings of the various branches of government more accessible and transparent to citizens.[22] It is also about enhancing public participation in public forums, thereby strengthening democracy.[23] Court digitization could be seen as part of the broader development toward e-government, involving greater access to information, the capability for two-way communication, and the tailoring of information to the specifics of a given claim or potential claim. In 2002 the United States enacted the e-Government Act, which established a federal chief information officer to enhance government provision of information and citizen participation in government through internet communication.[24] In the European Union, e-government-related declarations, action plans, and local initiatives also needed to be supplemented by European-wide measures for making government more accessible and collaborative.[25]

These governmental efforts have spurred the development of court websites, initially through computer access and in recent years with an emphasis on mobile e-government services.[26] These sites provide a broad range of information on the law, on vindicating rights and defending against actions, and on additional resources such as legal aid sites and other organizations that can assist litigants (or would-be litigants) in their interactions with the court system. Initially, court websites offered large quantities of general information. The emphasis was on transparency and opening up access to information that had been unavailable (or difficult to obtain) in the past.[27] This approach proved challenging for individuals, since the application of such information to their case without professional intermediation was a complicated task. The mere provision of information was not necessarily a barrier-reducing step; in certain cases it could even function as a barrier enhancer.[28]

TECHNOLOGY AS A MEANS FOR TRANSFORMING "ACCESS TO JUSTICE"

With advancements in technology and the shift from providing information to processing information in the decade that followed, it was clear that a rethinking of the ways in which technology could be used to enhance access to justice was needed. In 1998 the first governmental summit on the use of technology to improve access to justice took place. The summit gave rise to a "Technology

Initiative Grant," which distributed $40 million to courts, legal services organizations, and nonprofits. The funds also helped finance website development and document assembly applications.[29]

Over time, court websites have improved dramatically, as website design advanced, interactivity increased, and software began to be used more often to tailor legal information to meet individual needs and circumstances.[30] Courts in Illinois, California, and New York partnered with legal aid organizations to provide large and resource-rich self-help sites.[31] Courts have redesigned their sites to allow for search engine optimization, videos, podcasts, and interactive questionnaires that help litigants navigate the system.[32] These changes have dramatically sped up the time it takes courts to process self-represented litigants' applications.[33]

Legal aid organizations have developed a variety of tools to assist self-represented parties. Some sites now allow for remote guidance using various software programs, relying on multilingual staff[34] and even, in some cases, volunteer attorneys.[35] Software has the potential to improve access to justice not only by offering legal aid staff to remote rural areas[36] or to individuals unable to reach legal aid organizations[37] but also by offering assistance on an anonymous basis—a feature that can rarely be ensured when providing aid in person.[38] Technology also lowers training and collaboration costs for legal aid staff with the assistance of new training software, technology for virtual meetings, and free online courses.[39] Some have suggested developing technology that would better allocate much-needed legal services to those most in need of legal services.[40]

One particularly impressive tool for self-represented litigants is A2J Author, designed by the Chicago-Kent College of Law. After many hours of observation, the college created a web-based product that could assist self-represented litigants in divorce proceedings and simplify court procedures.[41] Through a series of plain language questions, the software is able to assess the needs of the party and refer him or her to the appropriate body/process/form. A virtual guide welcomes the litigant and walks him or her toward a graphical virtual courtroom. As the party answers questions, he or she progresses and can always see what stage he or she is at in the process. The prototype was later expanded to include additional guided interviews in a collaboration between the Chicago-Kent College of Law and the Center for Computer-Assisted Legal Instruction. There are now over 1,200 guided interviews available, which have been used over 75,000 times.[42] Like TurboTax, the product is a model for how answering simple questions can make it unnecessary to understand legal intricacies.

I-CAN! (Interactive Community Assistance Network) is another interesting model. I-CAN! was created by the nonprofit Legal Aid Society of Orange County in partnership with the Superior Court of California in Orange County. I-CAN!'s goal is to use technology to assist *pro se* litigants with often complex legal forms. It "utilizes the combination of 5th grade literacy content, interactive questions and answers and a video guide that enable users to answer a multiple choice and fill-in-the-blanks interview."[43] This is followed up with a review of the form by a certified attorney and a telephone consultation if necessary.[44] Other "smart forms" provide data validation, help with calculations, and check for completeness of the form (however, these forms also require significant staff time for assisting users and updating the forms).[45]

Hybrid assistance that relies on both technology-based and human intervention has been particularly helpful for self-represented litigants dealing with such matters as domestic violence or eviction proceedings.[46] By breaking down the process into its components—rather than providing the same general principles and online copies of information available offline—unrepresented parties are better able to ascertain their legal situation. They receive answers and guidance in an easy-to-understand format, including whether they should turn to the courts and, if so, what actions they will have to take and what arguments they will need to prepare. Legal aid organizations have also used document assembly applications to assist their own staff—a staff which is almost always under severe financial limitations and manpower constraints. Even the single tool of Google Translate has had a significant impact on access to justice for non-English speakers.[47]

The more sophisticated uses of technology involve interactive software that not only offers information but solicits relevant information from the parties themselves—information that in turn helps to provide more individualized, accurate, and helpful information for self-represented parties. In some very few cases, we are beginning to even see ODR introduced into this landscape. At the moment, ODR processes have been introduced mainly to address simple, low-value disputes, or to overcome geographical distances, thereby reducing costs for all involved. These processes are conducted online, asynchronously, and at times without legal representation, thereby reducing costs associated with legal representation and physical attendance at court hearings. But the introduction of even very simple, minimal ODR processes into the courts reflects a significant change in understanding the role technology can and should play in the delivery of legal services. By offering ODR in courts, we as a society are beginning to ask whether courts are "a service or a place."[48]

Online Dispute Resolution in Courts

EARLY ODR INITIATIVES

In February 2001, the Federal Court of Australia launched an eCourtroom. The eCourtroom functions through written communication, much like email exchanges on a secure website, along with a message board; it also allowed for the online receipt of submissions, affidavit evidence, and court orders. These changes have made it possible for more information to surface prior to court hearings, for parties to be better prepared, for court hearings to be briefer, and for some decisions to be delivered online without having to convene face to face.[49] The eCourtroom is used to address various types of disputes, including native title claims. In these cases, distance is a significant hurdle for parties and the ability to communicate with the judge online, between hearings, helped identify important information and generate trust in the process. In other cases[50], it is the complexity of the matters at hand—the number of parties or claims involved, the numerous documents relating to the dispute, or the scope of discovery required—that has made online communication appealing.[51]

In the United Kingdom, "Money Claim Online" has been available for over a decade. The process involves initiating monetary claims by filling out an online form, which can be executed online if the defendant does not file a counterclaim or contest the claim. Otherwise, the claim is referred to a traditional court.[52] This process is considered very successful and widely used for certain types of county court claims of up to £100,000, with over 60,000 claims a year.[53]

RECENT ODR INITIATIVES

In some of the more recent ODR programs in the courts, technology is viewed not just as a tool for improving the way courts operated in the past but as an opportunity to reimagine the ways in which disputes can be handled. Some of the more advanced pilot projects involving ODR reflect this transformative approach. One recent example can be found in the upcoming reform in the United Kingdom.

In January 2015, a report by an ODR Advisory Group to the Civil Justice Council, headed by Professor Richard Susskind, recommended the establishment of an online court called "Her Majesty's Online Court" (HMOC).[54] The court would handle civil disputes with a value of up to £25,000 through ODR. The process envisioned would be composed of three stages: online evaluation, online facilitation, and online judgment. The first stage encompasses problem diagnosis and helping the parties to understand their problem and their options. This is done by providing information and assistance on the court website, as well as facilitating access to external resources. The expectation is that better informed litigants will be better able to resolve their difficulties before they escalate into full-fledged legal problems.[55] If problems are not resolved in the first phase, parties are referred to the online facilitation stage, where a mix of skilled facilitators and automated negotiation tools assist in reaching an early resolution through nonadversarial processes.[56] Finally, for those disputants who could not resolve their dispute through facilitation, a third stage of online judgment would be offered. Such decisions would be decided online, and would be binding and enforceable in the same way that traditional court decisions are. The third stage may be an online written process, but could also allow for a trial with hearings (via telephone or video-conference, and, as last resort, face to face).[57] This initiative has since been incorporated into Lord Justice Briggs' Report on the Civil Courts Structure Review for the Judiciary of England and Wales, where it is referred to as an "Online Solutions Court."[58] While the precise name of the online court has yet to be determined, the Ministry of Justice has already allocated the budget (as part of the general £730 million budget to digitize the courts and tribunals) and aims launch in full by April 2020.[59]

The U.K. proposal is similar to another system, already in action: the British Columbia Civil Resolution Tribunal (CRT).[60] While the CRT is an administrative tribunal and not a court, it has civil jusridiction over claims that in the Canadian context would typically be handled by a court. The CRT was established under the Civil Resolution Tribunal Act of 2012 and has authority over small claims of up to Can$25,000, and certain condominium disputes (not including land title). The process is composed of several phases. The first step of the CRT ODR process is the "Solution Explorer."[61] This is a problem diagnosis phase which helps the parties narrow the problem and define it in legal terms. The software is able to provide the users with information based on this categorization that is relevant to their particular circumstances and offer possible solutions. If the problem is not resolved, parties are referred to the CRT, the dispute resolution tool. The shift from problem diagnosis to resolution is seamless for users; the information provided by the users in the previous stage travels with the users to the resolution phase. The parties will often be provided with a brief opportunity to negotiate with the other side through an automated negotiation tool, which structures interactions through templates and pull-down menus.[62] If unsuccessful, the automated negotiation phase is followed by a facilitative stage.[63] If this effort results in a mutually acceptable agreement, it can be turned into a tribunal order. If unsuccessful, either party can move the dispute to a final stage of adjudication, which can be conducted online, via phone, or through videoconferencing. The adjudicatory decision is a traditional order with the same force of a court order.[64] The order is subject to a bifurcated appeal process: small claims orders are subject to a new trial on appeal (but unsuccessful appellants will be subject to costs), and condominium cases are subject to a limited right of appeal based on a narrow set of grounds.[65] The entire process is expected to take, on average, sixty to ninety days; representation by attorneys is restricted to limited circumstances in an attempt to level the playing field for those parties who cannot afford or do not wish to be represented in cases of this scale.[66]

The B.C. system is a good demonstration of the transformative potential of technology in the public justice context, as well as some of the barriers that such projects face. The landscape of data documentation and processing is swiftly changing; currently no data on court cases in British Columbia is widely available. The CRT, however, unlike traditional court proceedings in British Columbia, is designed to capture comprehensive data on cases handled through the system, generating knowledge on various types of disputes—their sources, their course of evolution, the duration of resolution efforts, common resolutions used, and so on. The team in charge of the CRT's development has invested significant resources in refining the categorizations of various claims and defenses raised in order to be able to make meaningful use of the data. The insights drawn from such data can be used to improve the CRT and problem diagnosis phases, and even more important, to *prevent* future problems and claims.

Despite its potential, the new CRT system did raise objections and critiques. Some organizations representing the interests of lawyers have been vocal objectors. In spite of their objections, however, amendments to the legislation were enacted in 2015 which made use of the system mandatory. The launching of the system has progressed and became operational in the summer of 2016.[67]

While the United Kingdom's HMOC report was driven by the courts— and the B.C. initiative emerged from legislation—another innovative example, *Rechtwijzer* (discussed in Sara and Joseph's fictional story related above), was developed by HiiL (The Hague Institute for the Internationalisation of Law) in partnership with the Dutch Legal Aid Board and the Dutch Ministry of Security and Justice. *Rechtwijzer* currently operates alongside the Dutch courts and not yet as part of the formal justice system.[68] The program has initially been focused on family cases, and recently expanded to neighbor and debt disputes. The process assists parties with problem diagnosis and negotiation and makes online mediation and arbitration available on a secure platform. The software helps the parties to better understand their rights, interests, and options through a structured question-and-answer session. This session then evolves, where necessary, into problem-solving tools. When parties fail to reach an agreement through direct negotiation, they can involve an online mediator or arbitrator. If such facilitation results in a resolution, the agreement is brought before an independent lawyer for approval to ensure that it meets legal requirements and is fair to both parties.

So far, over one thousand cases have been processed by the *Rechtwijzer* system, several hundred of which have been finalized.[69] Costs have been dramatically lower than traditional court proceedings, ranging from €500 for simple cases to €1,300 for more complex ones. Even at the higher end, these costs are lower than the costs to the Legal Aid Board for representing both parties to divorce proceedings in court.[70] Aside from reducing the costs associated with separation, the software is designed to overcome another challenging feature associated with traditional court proceedings: their adversarial nature. *Rechtwijzer* frames the goal of the process as "separating together," focusing parties on needs and interests rather than rights and power struggles. By having an objective evaluator review the agreements reached, the program can also help bridge power imbalances and protect against instances in which parties agree to an unfair arrangement.

While most ODR in courts has been devoted to small claim civil matters, nineteen Michigan state courts and one Ohio state court have adopted *Matterhorn*, a software platform that allows litigants, law enforcement, and judicial officers to communicate and resolve outstanding disputes. It primarily substitutes for in-court proceedings in outstanding warrant cases and traffic violations (in addition to some civil infractions). The system was introduced in 2013 at the initiative of University of Michigan Law Professor J.J. Prescott and his former student Ben Gubernick.[71] The online process has been developed and applied across various contexts, each with its own particular nuances, but in all instances allowing for the uploading of statements by parties, law enforcement and court personnel from afar in lieu of a court hearing. These convenient, speedy and asynchronous processes have been found to decrease the length and costs of court proceedings. Data on the system is followed closely, evaluating such measures as cost savings, time frames, and impact on access to justice. Significantly, there is evidence that the availability of online proceedings in this context has been an important factor in stimulating more parties to bring their case before the courts due to many benefits associated with online communication.[72]

Dispute resolution in courts, like dispute resolution out of court, is experiencing three major shifts in technology and approach. The first is the shift from a physical setting to a virtual (or semi-virtual) one. Courts that operate on either all-online platforms or platforms that combine physical, face-to-face presence with online activities undermine the physical boundaries and special spaces that have always been the hallmark of court proceedings. Individuals can access courts, evaluate their legal stance, communicate with the other party, and have a third party decide their dispute, all without having to physically attend the court or be restricted to court operating hours.

The virtues of ODR processes were recognized initially in the small claims arena, but have already expanded to additional settings such as divorce proceedings and neighbor disputes. As use of ODR in courts expands to more complex disputes, it will reduce conceptual distinctions between conflicts arising online and those arising offline, and between alternative dispute resolution (ADR) and ODR. Even the long-held distinction between formal and informal avenues for dispute resolution can be expected to fade, as claims are no longer siphoned off to an alternative forum (as they have been with ADR), but are managed by online processes that are offered on the court's platform and that proceed seamlessly through various forms of ODR to adjudication.

The second is the shift from human intervention and decision making to automated processes. The use of automated processes reduces costs and increases capacity for handling cases. The use of ODR in courts is also introducing algorithms into the judicial decision-making process. As discussed in Chapter 2, algorithms can curb human discretion, increasing consistency and reducing biases, thereby enhancing "justice" as well as "access." At the same time, algorithms may also operate in a biased fashion and challenge our aspirations of justice. This depends, to a large extent, on our ability to rigorously monitor the manner in which such algorithms operate and the values that guide algorithms' design.

Automation will have a strong impact on the legal profession as more and more automated systems support self-help options to negotiate or mediate a resolution. Under these systems, professional boundaries will be redrawn, as the need for lawyers in less complex cases will no longer be required.[73] Lawyers will find new roles, as evidenced in *Rechtwijzer*'s use of lawyers to ensure fairness and legality of agreements negotiated by the parties. The shift from human decision making to automated processes introduces a whole new set of professions (such as programmers and web designers) whose professional expertise and fresh perspective will help reshape the litigation process. In the design of the CRT system in British Columbia, for example, emphasis was placed on "user experiences" when designing the software. This is a new area of focus for designers of court processes. New methodologies were employed to evaluate experiences, including the use of online focus groups and user ratings of various features and information presented to users.[74] Responses were then incorporated into the design and modification of the software.

The third shift is the shift from dispute resolution models that value confidentiality to models focused on collecting, using, and reusing data in order to prevent disputes. As courts increasingly rely on digital technology and ODR systems, they will learn to view data as a central feature in dispute resolution. Since data is automatically captured in online processes, it becomes easier to measure and evaluate dispute resolution processes, whether conducted face to face or virtually. In particular, ODR processes allow for instantaneous collection of feedback from users, making it more appealing to involve user groups in the design and evaluation of such systems. As data collection becomes a key feature in the design and refinement of dispute resolution systems, there will be ongoing evaluation of what type of information is needed and how courts (and other dispute resolution processes) can learn from such data. Data will play a critical role in allowing court systems to operate in a realm that is new to them: dispute prevention through data analysis, and the ongoing improvement of court processes.

The impact of these shifts can be expected to redefine the meaning and understanding of such basic concepts as one's "day in court," "procedural justice," "judicial neutrality," or "legitimacy" of courts.[75] Will parties who participate in these processes feel that they have received their "day in court" and have been "heard"? Will users perceive these processes as fair? Will judges sustain their neutrality and authority, and will courts, relying on algorithms, maintain their legitimacy? These questions have yet to be answered as processes change and users' reactions are studied. One thing, however, seems certain: preferences and values will change.

In the pre-digital era, a day in court required a physical appearance before a judge and, indeed, a whole day. Disputants also often evaluated the fairness of dispute resolution efforts according to procedural elements—namely, whether they had had an opportunity to tell their story to a third party who considered their views, treated them in an even-handed and dignified manner, and remained impartial.[76] This was an era in which most conflicts arose in the physical world and could be handled in a face-to-face setting. Being heard implied convening in a physical space, and information could be better protected and contained, allowing decision makers to remain "detached" and impartial.

As individuals conduct a growing part of their lives online, we can expect the notion of being "heard" to expand. It will begin to include the voicing of one's story online. Already, individuals are sharing a range of intimate, exciting, tragic—and above all, deeply personal—experiences with their friends on social media, often more frequently than they do face to face or over the phone. Individuals and corporations are also choosing to voice apologies online, some of which relate to very delicate matters like bullying[77] or discrimination.[78] These types of changes in preferences can be expected to permeate all kinds of perceptions about procedural justice as well.

In much the same way, we can expect to see the meaning of impartiality and confidentiality change as information becomes more difficult to contain and decision makers are exposed to details previously excluded as inadmissible, irrelevant, or unreliable. As automation increases, the need to guarantee impartiality through software design will increase—to ensure that both sides have input in the process and an equal opportunity to shape its outcome. Increased opportunity for lay involvement could in fact enhance procedural fairness and one's (virtual) "day in court," assigning a crucial role to professionals—perhaps lawyers—in ensuring the fairness of the design of procedures and their outcomes and, consequently, the legitimacy of the body conducting these dispute resolution processes.

Adopting technology in the courtroom opens up new opportunities not only for making our existing processes less expensive and cumbersome and more accessible at all hours. It could also change the very nature of court processes, with software playing an increasingly significant role in streamlining, resolving, and preventing claims. Indeed, there is promise for transforming our very understanding of the meaning of *justice*.

We are in the process of shaping a new type of litigation process: less adversarial, less rigid, more dynamic, more transparent, more efficient, and, hopefully, more balanced. What was appealing to Sara in the story at the start of this chapter was not just the convenience and reduced costs associated with an online process (although those were certainly important to her) but also the opportunity to conduct a more amicable process without sacrificing her legal rights. Courts employing technology in this way strive towards *digital justice*, enhancing both "access" and "justice," efficiency and fairness. Figuring out what exactly would constitute that fair process and successfully generate trust and satisfaction for users is the step we must take now, even as our ways of evaluating such values change themselves.

Dispute Prevention by Courts and Public Institutions

Court processes have traditionally been involved in resolving disputes and clarifying or establishing legal norms. When court decisions are clear and infiltrate the public sphere, potential disputes might be prevented.[79] It has been recognized for some time that the law

> usually works not by exercise of force but by information transfer, by communication of what's expected, what forbidden, what allowable, what are the consequences of acting in certain ways. That is, law entails information about what the rules are, how they are applied, with what costs, consequences, etc. For example, when we speak of deterrence, we are talking about the effect of information about what the law is and how it is administered. Similarly, when we describe "bargaining in the shadow of the law," we refer to regulation accomplished by the flow of information rather than directly by authoritative decision. Again, "legal socialization" is accomplished by the transmission of information. In a vast number of instances the application of law is, so to speak, self-administered—people regulate their conduct (and judge the conduct of others) on the basis of their knowledge about legal standards, possibilities and constraints.[80]

Writing several decades ago, the author of this piece could not have foreseen the potential for data-driven dispute prevention for courts. In fact, the idea of focusing on prevention as well as resolution didn't emerge until the late 1980s, and even then not in the context of the courts but in large organizations and corporations.[81] In these large organizations, in-house dispute resolvers were able to discern dispute sources and patterns over time, and work to prevent similar disputes from arising in the future. Such prevention activities depended on the institutional memory of dispute resolvers themselves. They were typically not grounded in data analysis, as ADR activities often frown upon preserving data due to privacy concerns.[82]

The automatic documentation of all dispute data and party characteristics will change all of this. As numbers of users grow and computing capabilities expand, large digital databases will enable new questions and the identification of large-scale trends and patterns we have never seen before, often through automated means instead of human analysis. Courts routinely release the decisions of judges and some statistical data about categories of cases, but little else. There is almost nothing that can be easily accessed about the lowest level of courts, such as small claims courts. The focus of attention on the written opinions of judges supports the idea and practice of precedent and promotes consistency over time. There remains, however, an enormous amount of data that is currently collected on paper and in files in court clerks' offices. We will, in the future, be able to study this data and learn a great deal about the resolution of disputes in court. Those in control of these large data sets will be able to analyze the data and enable us to learn important lessons about disputants, disputing habits, conditions that generate success and failure in resolution, and how to prevent problems in the future.

Private platforms have largely been the pioneers of the ODR field and the domain in which dispute prevention activities have begun to flourish. However, in recent decades court administrators have begun to recognize the significance of data for the delivery of more effective dispute resolution processes. These insights were first implemented in problem-solving courts that have used data to generate more-effective solutions to persistent social problems. These courts have proven successful in sharing success and failure stories as a resource within specific courthouses as well as among various courts.[83]

In recent decades, many court case files have also moved online, as communications between the parties and the court began to occur electronically. Documenting experience can answer many questions, such as what different types of claims arise, what are the sources of disputes, who are the parties to such disputes, what are the common outcomes, how members of different types of groups of litigants perform in the resolution of such disputes, how different types of litigants perceive the legal process, and so forth. We will also begin to understand the impact of various design choices in dispute resolution systems, allowing court administrators to learn from prior successful and unsuccessful resolution efforts.

Dispute prevention as a means of enhancing access to justice is in a very early stage, but opportunities are already apparent. These types of activities allow the courts to study characteristics of various claims and the effectiveness of resolution efforts, highlighting information or structuring processes that can resolve claims at an early stage. When we have that kind of information, courts can likely prevent at least the escalation of disputes—if not the occurrence of the dispute.[84]

Dispute data can be used to prevent problems from recurring.[85] Darin Thompson, a founder of one of the Canadian ODR systems,[86] has pointed out that disputing data can shed light on patterns of disputes in ways that can obviate the need to litigate and, in a sense, prevent the occurrence of a dispute. One example he offers is that by identifying a sudden spike in specific dispute types—such as the rise in torts claims over dog bites— new regulations of dog owners may be necessary.[87] Prevention can also result from identifying repetitive patterns in certain complaint types. In another example, Thompson suggests that upon seeing many instances of divorced husbands required to provide income tax reports postdivorce in monitoring alimony, courts may require such information without their spouses having to initiate court action.[88]

Perhaps an even more far-reaching way in which disputing data could prevent future disputes would be by requiring companies sued by individual customers or employees to proactively examine whether such problems are applicable to others they have engaged with in a similar capacity. Under these circumstances, attempts might be made to remedy the problem before even waiting for a claim to surface. It may be that we are nearing a point in time where this will be both possible and not overly burdensome.[89] If such a development were to materialize, it could reduce or possibly even eliminate the need for certain legal processes like class actions—a tool whose effectiveness in accomplishing broad compensation and deterrence has been doubtful at best.[90]

Conclusion

Most efforts to move court processes online originate with efficiency considerations and the desire to reduce courts' caseloads and, often, to enhance access to justice. Technology has had a dual impact on access to justice in courts. On the one hand, technology has lowered costs for legal advice through online advice, online legal products, and new marketplaces connecting clients with solo practitioners and small firms.[91] On the other hand, digital technology has also been perceived as creating access barriers to courts because of the need to rely on written communication[92] and the gaps in access to the internet across socioeconomic strata.[93] To a large extent, these barriers have been lowered with the advancement of technology. Some barriers (such as cost of legal assistance or proximity to courts) have remained significant but in certain contexts have been outweighed by the benefits of technology, which include accessibility, structure and the benefits associated with data analysis.

The focus on data that comes with the introduction of online systems is today infiltrating the courts and impacting the ways in which courts function. The study of this kind of data was not feasible for a bureaucratic, underbudgeted institution in the pre-digital era. Where courts have begun to study this new rich and easily available resource seriously, results have been surprising and some-times counterintuitive—revealing, for example, that case management has not made civil litigation faster and cheaper.[94] Data will allow courts to justify new processes, uncover sources of claims, and to cooperate with other public entities to prevent future disputes from arising and reaching the courts again.

These developments raise new kinds of questions alongside the new kinds of data we are seeing. These new questions will begin to guide court policies as well: about party preferences, the nature of the dispute, or other considerations. At first blush, some of these considerations may echo those that guided the adoption of ADR in the courts in the previous century.[95] The adoption of ADR and the criteria that were developed for court referral to these processes changed which cases went to court. But with technology, court processes *themselves* are undergoing transformation, challenging existing assumptions on what is and is not appropriate for online resolution and adjudication as the boundary between online and offline activities becomes more and more porous.

It is important to recognize that despite growth in courts' capacity in hand-ling disputes, the vast majority of disputes will continue to be resolved outside the court system. In a reality in which a growing portion of our interactions will be conducted through digital communication, such disputes will need to be addressed through ODR mechanisms that are not court-connected. Increased access to courts will never obviate the need for alternative fora for addressing disputes, as aptly stated by Lawrence Friedman: "How much access to justice do we really want? Let us imagine a world in which everyone who had any claim whatsoever could get a hearing, had inexpensive and convenient access to coun-sel, and presumably could get his claim resolved in his favor. Would this be a good society? It could be an Orwellian nightmare."[96]

At the moment, the development of systems that can provide access to justice in cyberspace is beginning to accelerate. Given the growing numbers of disputes, there are still far fewer avenues of dispute resolution than needed, and those avenues that do exist are often not transparent enough to determine their degree of fairness and efficiency. As Linda Greenhouse wrote, "[a]cross a shifting land-scape, we assign courts an astonishing range of tasks while lacking consensus on whether alternative mechanisms could do some jobs more efficiently, less expensively, and better than adjudication."[97]

As use of technology in and out of court continues to grow, we expect a consensus over the adoption of ODR in the public sector to continue to grow as well. Richard Susskind has predicted that "ODR will prove to be a disruptive technology that fundamentally challenges the work of traditional litigators (and of judges). In the long run, I expect it to become the dominant way to resolve all but the most complex and high-value disputes."[98] We believe this is likely to occur in the not very distant future.

Conclusion: The Present and Future of Digital Justice and the "Moving Frontier of Injustice"

What moves us, reasonably enough, is not the realization that the world falls short of being completely just—which few of us expect—but that there are clearly remediable injustices around us which we want to eliminate.

—Amartya Sen, *The Idea of Injustice*

Looking Forward

In 1996, an essay about the challenge of predicting the future of law used as an example

> the story of videophones. Of course, there aren't any mass-market videophones, and that is the story. Thirty years ago, people were predicting them, and for thirty years they've been nowhere to be seen. Futurists also predicted "bedmaking machines, home dry-cleaning, showers that clean people with sound waves, robots that cut lawns and fight wars, steam- and electric-driven cars, foam-filled tires, plastic teeth and tooth-decay vaccine." We're still waiting.[1]

That was twenty years ago. Today, of course, we are no longer waiting. We have mass-market mobile devices that do much more than videophones, robots that cut lawns, fight wars and do thousands of other things, electric cars and even self-driving cars, and the means to prevent tooth decay. There are home dry-cleaning and bed-making machines, although there seems to be little demand for such devices. As for the future, one can envision demand for showers that do not use water. Who can tell?

Digital Justice. Ethan Katsh and Orna Rabinovich-Einy.
© Ethan Katsh and Orna Rabinovich-Einy 2017. Published 2017 by Oxford University Press.

What we can tell is that change in technology is rapid, complex, extensive, and ongoing. All of the innovation we are experiencing inevitably brings along with it the ingredients for conflict. When we do not acknowledge this and do not attend to growth in the frequency and nature of disputes, those disputes continue to grow and spread. When we do focus on these ingredients, and the communication and on the processing of information in complex and novel ways, new models for resolving and preventing disputes begin to emerge.

Predicting the pace of change is as difficult as predicting the degree of change. The first 3-D printer, for example, is on display at MIT; it was created in 1994. Whether or not 3-D printers become an inexpensive and ubiquitous mass market item is still an open question. The internet itself existed in the background for more than two decades before it began to have a significant social impact. What we do suggest is that if 3-D printers, drones and robots, self-driving cars, gene therapy, virtual reality, smart everything and anything, the Internet of Things, and inventions simmering just below the surface today do become widespread, dispute resolution and prevention will accompany them in an ongoing challenge. Kevin Kelly, in a recent book called *Inevitable*,[2] identifies twelve technological forces that he believes will inevitably shape the future: whether he is right or wrong about those twelve forces, what is truly inevitable are higher levels of conflict. And although far from inevitable, what is now *possible* are new technology-based forms of conflict resolution and prevention.

As innovation proceeds rapidly and new kinds of disputes emerge, the goal is not—and should not be—to eliminate all conflict. This is neither possible nor desirable. A dispute-free environment might be safer, but it would also be stagnant and less interesting. Innovation is both a product of conflict and a contributor to it. Many laws, the First Amendment being the most prominent, protect and even encourage conflict and controversy in expression, thus enabling us to benefit from a rich marketplace of ideas. Intellectual property and other laws encouraging economic growth also assume that competition is a good thing and necessary for progress.

Marc Galanter has described the inevitability and value of conflict as follows:

> We will not approach a problem-free world, for people are capable of identifying or inventing new problems as quickly as the old ones are solved. This is not a cynical observation about an insatiable appetite for a "risk free world." Rather, it is premised in the notion that the very same human capabilities that create solutions for existing problems— by fulfilling existing needs and wants—discover or create new needs, new wants, and new problems. But in the process, as more things are capable of being done by human institutions, the line between unavoidable misfortune and imposed injustice shifts . . . What was seen as fate

may come to be seen as the product of inappropriate policy. Advances in human capability and rising expectations result in a moving frontier of injustice.[3]

While it is true that some degree of conflict is both desirable and inevitable for an expanding economy and an innovative society, it is also true that too much conflict will interfere with creative endeavors and suppress economic and intellectual growth. A society with too few disputes is unlikely to be highly innovative; one with too much risk, too much uncertainty, and too many disputes will also deter innovation.

In highlighting the five areas that seem to us to be in particular need of online dispute resolution (ODR)—e-commerce, healthcare, social media, labor, and the courts—we have tried to identify examples of conflict that are hindering rather than accelerating innovation. How one addresses disputes once they arise is a key to the realization of digital justice. Although cyberspace echoes some of the more familiar disparities between parties, such as socioeconomic status, gender, race, and so forth, we also see that new technologies give rise to a new power structure in which the most salient distinction may be between individuals and platforms. In a reality in which platforms—particularly megaplatforms—control enormous amounts of data and operate under complete opacity, individual users are at a substantial disadvantage.

Most of the examples we have discussed in which bad data, miscommunication, and misconduct are generating problems provide little that is positive and much that is preventable. When bad data combines with Big Data, the outcome will be more bad data. Much inaccurate data, such as that present in electronic health records, can be reduced with better software design and more reliance on input and review by patients. When inaccurate health data is not corrected at an early stage, however, the network may take it and distribute it to public health authorities and others. As this occurs, the problem is compounded and correction becomes much more difficult. It is not surprising that improving patient identification—a seemingly simple task of matching the right name with the right person—is the number one goal of the National Patient Safety Goal for Hospitals.[4] This is a software-design problem that should have been solved when electronic health records were first introduced.

Large numbers of errors in consumer records could also be prevented by better software design. Many instances of identity theft and intentional misuse of data are preventable. Instances of miscommunication between buyers and sellers, Facebook friends, and Wikipedia editors can also be reduced by changing the structure of the interaction. Even where these problems cannot be prevented, online and often automated processes can be put in place to address these mishaps early on, before they escalate. However, our traditional dispute resolution institutions are not effective in a networked and typically global environment; current rules, regulations, and enforcement processes are insufficient. As William Drayton has written, "[i]n a world of escalating change, the rules cover less and less."[5] Others have observed that "norms scale far better than the law."[6] This suggests that, over time, the influence of courts may grow narrower and, perhaps, less authoritative.

The law will not be irrelevant, but the solutions to many of the problems generated by our expanding technological environment will not come from the courts—or at least not from courts that are situated in physical space. Nor will they come from some form of traditional alternative dispute resolution that relies on face-to-face interactions. Face-to-face alternative dispute resolution models also do not scale and are less accessible, more lengthy and costly, and more easily influenced by the adversarial and legalistic mindset.

At the same time that we struggle to modify old institutions and develop new ones, we are in the midst of a shift from relying principally on conflict *resolution* to a focus on conflict *prevention*. Prevention requires understanding patterns of behavior and practices, something that can only be discovered by following the path of data. And this, unfortunately, is hard for public institutions and researchers to do, since much data is buried behind the walls of privately controlled software and algorithms.

The issue of trust, or lack thereof, also stands in the way of innovative uses of technology by consumers, patients, the government, and others. Largely as a consequence of numerous data breaches during the last few years, trust in any entity controlling large amounts of personal data is limited. Our concern in this book has focused more on the accuracy of data than on the privacy and security of data, but at some point the two intersect. Trust in the use and protection of personal data, as well as in its accuracy, needs to be enhanced in order for the public to benefit from a "sharing economy" in which personal information is accessible, controlled, and empowering for users (not merely exploited by private entities). Anticipating conflict and developing new responses to conflict gives us the opportunity to increase access to justice in an environment where there are currently increasing arenas of injustice.

The Role of Law and Courts

Many of the traits that we associate with law, courts, and lawyers have been with us for centuries. The law is an inherently conservative institution, and, as Supreme Court Chief Justice John Roberts recently wrote, "the courts will often choose to be late to the harvest of American ingenuity. Courts are simply different in important respects when it comes to adopting technology, including information technology."[7] The law, however, risks losing influence over citizens by not recognizing how much the online environment needs new justice models.

In a society where everything is on-demand, this degree of caution by the formal legal system may be difficult to maintain. Roberts's statement may remind readers of the doorkeeper in Kafka's *The Trial* that we discussed in Chapter 2. In the parable, a "man from the country" who believes that the law should be "accessible for everyone at all times"[8] finds that a doorkeeper stands in his way. We are, today, still routinely confronted with obstacles to justice. Anyone wishing to correct errors and resolve disputes is still likely to feel that there are many doorkeepers standing in the way, whether those be financial, logistical inconveniences, complex rules and legalities, or other doorkeepers; technology itself is often an obstacle. At the same time, however, technology also provides new opportunities to open doors. One can imagine a contemporary update to Kafka's parable, where there is not one individual trying to enter and seek redress but large groups supporting an individual trying to enter and where these individuals and groups have tools and resources that can overcome or at least erode the power of some of the doorkeepers standing in the way. Kafka's "man from the country" is alone, sitting, waiting, and hoping but never challenging the doorkeeper. That is not today's context, where social media facilitates the formation of groups and the pursuit of collective activities.

Several Supreme Court Justices during the last hundred years—Justice Breyer being the most recent—have asserted that "[t]he United States Supreme Court is not a court of error correction."[9] These justices viewed the role of the Supreme Court not to be the "remedying of a particular litigant's wrong, but the consideration of cases whose decision involves principles, the application of which are of wide public or governmental interest."[10] While "error correction" may not be the role of the Supreme Court, however, it certainly *can* be the role of an online court or ODR process. Indeed, error correction is a particularly appropriate task for online processes that can monitor the accuracy of data used by companies who own large amounts of personal information. As more and more individuals look at their credit reports, electronic health records, online reputations, and other collections of data about themselves, pressure will inevitably build to challenge some of those doors standing in the way of redress.

In spite of its resistance to being characterized as an error-correction body, the Supreme Court today is involved in a case brought by someone who wishes to correct errors in an online report. The case, *Spokeo v. Robins*, involves an individual, Thomas Robins, and a website called Spokeo.com. Spokeo.com is a "people search engine" where one can go to initiate a search for information about an individual. The results pull data from a variety of online public sources. Mr. Robins discovered that a search for him on Spokeo.com generated a great deal of incorrect information: that he was wealthy, married, had children, and worked in a professional or technical field. In fact, he wasn't married, didn't have children, was out of work, and was looking for a job. Even the picture that Spokeo included in the search results was not a picture of Robins.

Robins claimed that he had a right to sue under the Fair Credit Reporting Act, which requires companies like Spokeo to "follow reasonable procedures to ensure maximum possible accuracy" of the information that it makes available for use in credit reports. Robins's position was that Spokeo had not met that standard.

To get the Supreme Court to hear his case, Robins had to pass through many doors. He lost at the Federal District Court level, won at the Court of Appeals level, and the Supreme Court heard his case. In May 2016, however, it sent the case back to the Court of Appeals to clarify an issue. Once the Court of Appeals does that, whoever loses may once again ask the Supreme Court to issue a ruling.[11]

The Fair Credit Reporting Act was enacted in 1970, when almost no one had heard of the internet and when there were very few opportunities to learn about any misinformation in one's credit report. The oral argument before the Supreme Court in the *Spokeo* case, where lawyers for each side present arguments to the Justices and answer questions, does not suggest who will ultimately win, but it does suggest that the Justices are aware of the problems that can be caused by inaccurate data in a credit report.

Justice Kagan, for example, asked the lawyer for Spokeo,

> The dissemination of false information about a particular person . . . if someone did it to me I'd feel harmed. And I think that if you went out on the street and you did a survey, most people would feel harmed. Most people would feel that they had some interest that had been invaded.[12]

It is difficult to predict how the Court of Appeals will rule when it reconsiders the case and how the Supreme Court will rule if the case comes back to it. Even if the Court rules against Mr. Robins, however, public concern over the issue of poor data quality in records will only increase, as will the need to find ways to resolve disputes over information collected about us.

The fact that this case has made it as far as it has is a strong sign that we are all in a different environment from the "man from the country." Kafka's individual waited for the rest of his life and received no satisfaction or explanation. Future generations will be in a very different place with a very different and much less patient mindset as conflict and data problems grow and the need to build innovative conflict resolution and prevention systems increases. If the on-demand environment is contributing to an increase in disputes, approaches to conflict resolution need to be available on demand as well. They need to be easily accessible, engaging, interactive, efficient, and intelligent enough to understand, as the Supreme Court may or may not, how important data is to our search for justice. The limited availability of dispute resolution and prevention avenues that are appropriate for the digital era is part of what we term the "digital justice gap."

Addressing the Digital Justice Gap

Throughout this book, we have discussed disputes and dispute resolution from a perspective that looks beyond courts and legal causes of action. Our focus is on the problems that individuals face in a technologically advanced and changing environment and how they are (or could be) addressed. Nevertheless, law and courts still have a presence. Lawsuits over claims of libelous online reviews; court orders shutting down file-sharing sites; a class action by Uber drivers over their status as employees; liability for errors in electronic health records; a court decision recognizing the "right to be forgotten"; all these are examples of digital disputes being litigated. Technology is also present in the procedural aspects of these types of litigation, as ODR is introduced into and applied toward the resolution of disputes that arose in those various settings.

The "shadow of the law" will continue to have influence beyond the courtroom. Law can motivate websites to address problems: by promising immunity from legal liability if complaint systems are established (as in the case of intellectual property rights infringement), or providing incentives in the opposite direction if such intervention would expose sites to liability. Law can also shape the type of procedures for dispute resolution provided by online entities, by limiting certain procedural arrangements—as the Consumer Financial Protection Bureau and the Health and Human Services Department are working, each in their own domain, to ban predispute mandatory arbitration clauses.[13] And law will inevitably permeate the procedural and substantive realms of ODR, shaping designers' and users' perceptions of fair procedural arrangements and just substantive outcomes. Indeed, where the law has been silent on questions of procedural design of online redress systems, the avenues that emerged, such as the "notice and takedown" regimes or flagging procedures, have raised serious concerns as to their fairness and degree of due process. Similarly, technology is increasingly permeating the governmental sphere—which could bring about a novel understanding of justice, transcending the deep-rooted distinctions between formal and informal; public and private dispute resolution on the one hand, and the distinction between digital disputes and offline conflicts on the other. Under "digital justice," digital technology is adopted in both private and public settings to enhance access to justice in a broad sense, both in and out of courts, based on the understanding that limiting access to justice to the court setting is neither possible nor desirable.[14]

Despite the potential of digital technology to enhance access to justice, what we call a "digital justice gap" exists. Technology has generated a large number of disputes for which there are currently limited channels of redress. Where such mechanisms do exist, it is difficult to ascertain their fairness and efficiency. This is unfortunate in light of the need for avenues of redress and the unavailability of courts and alternative dispute resolution (ADR) processes for many disputes arising online. Many large platforms, however, have thus far thrived without providing full-fledged avenues for raising and addressing complaints. The public setting has only recently made efforts to implement comprehensive ODR schemes.

Courts and other public entities will inevitably adopt more ODR. Frustration with adversarial proceedings continues to grow, heavy caseloads continue to present a problem, and costs associated with lawyers and litigation continue to be very high—too high for a significant number of individuals. But even if not for these issues, other characteristics associated with the legal process, namely, its rigid, top-down, and adversarial nature, make ODR an attractive tool for improving court procedures. More and more, people expect their interactions with public entities to resemble their dealings with private entities—courts included. This expectation often translates into increased involvement through consultation and feedback, online interaction, and more flexible and tailored options. ODR can, where properly designed, meet these expectations.

There are several reasons we expect ODR to be a growth area in the future. The first is related to a central theme of this book: numbers of conflicts are increasing and generating many new types of disputes that challenge traditional, face-to-face dispute resolution mechanisms. As we explain throughout the book, we can expect the scope of digital disputes to expand in light of the growing reliance on, and familiarity with, digital communication in people's lives in modern-day society. We use digital communication to interact with those closest to us and those at a distance, touching on mundane interactions like ordering toothpaste but also more sensitive and complicated matters like memorializing a lost one. The line between online "space" and physical surroundings is increasingly blurred. Even our understanding of what can be done online is changing, making ODR tools seem more appropriate and appealing over time for a much broader range of disputes, some that arose online but also for offline, potentially more complex and intimate, disputes.[15]

The growth of ODR also has to do with the potential of technology to remedy some of the persistent problems with our justice system. As we mention earlier, a major driver for the adoption of ADR processes was the search for a remedy for an expensive, slow, complex, inaccessible, and overburdened court system.[16] These considerations were reinforced by calls for dispute resolution approaches that would go beyond rights to address interests, needs, and feelings, resulting in more satisfactory processes and imaginative outcomes.[17] We also saw, however, that the institutionalization of ADR was accompanied by fierce critiques, ranging from the dangers posed to parties belonging to disadvantaged groups[18] to the curtailment of law development and precedent-setting.[19] To a large extent, this criticism has reflected the understanding that there is an inherent trade-off between the enhanced efficiency through flexible and tailored processes of ADR on the one hand, and formal court processes' fairness through due process protection on the other hand.

Technology may be able to overcome the seemingly inherent trade-off between efficiency and fairness by enhancing both the efficiency of courts as well as the quality of these processes. In this regard, various features of ODR that were initially viewed as shortcomings, such as documentation, are now seen as potentially advantageous by facilitating better monitoring, quality control, consistency, and a higher degree of transparency in informal dispute resolution.[20] Technology also provides opportunities for users' interests and preferences to shape the design of new processes. It will make courts and others offering dispute resolution services more attuned to data and the need to analyze it, measure user satisfaction and trust, evaluate court procedures, and direct attention toward the prevention of disputes.

Another reason we can expect to see expanded use of ODR involves the growing reliance on algorithms. Problems can be resolved quickly and efficiently with machines guiding decisions based on the data provided by users or the company. Unfortunately, algorithms can also seriously damage the level of trust users have in a system. As a recent study found,

> With the realistic possibility of machine learning-based systems controlling industrial processes, health-related systems, and other mission-critical technology, small-scale accidents seem like a very concrete threat, and are critical to prevent both intrinsically and because such accidents could cause a justified loss of trust in automated systems. The risk of larger accidents is more difficult to gauge, but we believe it is worthwhile and prudent to develop a principled and forward-looking approach to safety that continues to remain relevant as autonomous systems become more powerful. While many current-day safety problems can and have been handled with ad hoc fixes or case-by-case rules, we believe that the increasing trend towards end-to-end, fully autonomous systems points towards the need for a unified approach to prevent these systems from causing unintended harm.[21]

Decision making by machines is only likely to grow and also likely to increasingly challenge ODR systems. As algorithms shape more and more aspects of our lives, we will need to design systems that will help citizens to understand how they are being affected and how problems may be resolved. Given the pace and scale at which such problems can be expected to occur, traditional, face-to-face dispute resolution mechanisms, whether private or public, will not be the primary source for addressing such issues. ODR systems will need to be put in place to address algorithm-related problems and prevent them from recurring in the future.

As ODR is institutionalized in public settings, local and international, its appeal and legitimacy can be expected to rise, resulting in increased adoption of ODR systems and tools. Courts in various parts of the world are already in different phases of introducing ODR schemes. The European Union has even passed legislation requiring that member states take part in an ODR platform that can address local and cross-border e-commerce disputes between consumers and businesses of member states. The United Nations Commission on International Trade Law (UNCITRAL) was responsible for an extensive effort to generate an international ODR system for cross-border consumer disputes.

And finally, expansion of ODR systems will accompany the growth of mega-platforms. In the not-too-distant past, there were very few platforms that handled millions, even billions of users. The number of these large platforms, many of which deliver products and services for which there is no real alternative, is fast growing. Even for those platforms claiming to occupy an intermediary role and "merely" connecting users with one another, it is no longer tenable to keep from addressing problems and complaints. Several of the large platforms have learned over time that they must address such problems if they are to keep their status as market leaders. Whether they do so in a manner that truly enhances access to digital justice is a key question for the future.

Digital justice must enhance both "access" and "justice" through the use of technology. Access is enhanced through the wide availability of online redress and prevention mechanisms, as well as by algorithms that can handle large numbers of disputes and employ easy-to-use, plain language, and tailored processes. Justice can be enhanced where algorithms impact parties in an even-handed manner, and are subject to quality control. Dispute data aimed at dispute prevention is a recent development and needs to be used fairly, targeting problems related to a variety of stakeholders, while respecting individual privacy and legal restrictions on use of private information.

To be effective, digital justice will require extensive monitoring of the impact of design choices on both efficiency and fairness. This is no simple task. Despite challenges, however, this new dispute resolution and prevention landscape holds the promise of many important improvements, including our basic understanding of how justice works. No longer will it be dependent on a physical, face-to-face environment, or even subject to the limitations of human decision making.

NOTES

Introduction

1. Tom Ferguson and e-Patient Scholars Working Group, *e-Patients: How They Can Help Us Heal Healthcare* (2007), http://e-patients.net/e-Patients_White_Paper.pdf.
2. *See About e-Patient Dave*, E-PATIENT DAVE, http://e-patients.net/archives/author/dave-debronkart.
3. *Founders Circle*, SOC'Y FOR PARTICIPATORY MED., http://participatorymedicine.org/about/board-of-directors/founders-circle/.
4. *Beth Israel Deaconess Medical Center*, PATIENT SITE, http://www.patientsite.org.
5. *Google Health*, WIKIPEDIA, http://en.wikipedia.org/wiki/Google_Health (last modified June 24, 2016).
6. Dave deBronkart, *Imagine Someone Had Been Managing Your Data, And Then You Looked*, E-PATIENTS.NET (Apr. 1, 2009), http://e-patients.net/archives/2009/04/imagine-if-someone-had-been-managing-your-data-and-then-you-looked.html [hereinafter deBronkart, *Imagine Someone Had Been Managing Your Data*].
7. DeBronkart wrote:

   > Imagine that for all your life, and your parents' lives, your money had been managed by other people who had extensive training and licensing. Imagine that all your records were in their possession, and you could occasionally see parts of them, but you just figured the pros had it under control.
   >
   > Imagine that you knew you weren't a financial planner but you wanted to take as much responsibility as you could—to participate. Imagine that some money managers (not all, but many) attacked people who wanted to make their own decisions, saying "Who's the financial planner here?"
   >
   > Then imagine that one day you were allowed to see the records, and you found out there were a whole lot of errors, and the people carefully guarding your data were not as on top of things as everyone thought. *See* deBronkart, *Imagine Someone Had Been Managing Your Data, supra* note 6.

8. Lisa Wansgness, *Electronic Health Records Raise Doubt*, BOSTON.COM (Apr. 13, 2009), http://www.boston.com/news/nation/washington/articles/2009/04/13/electronic_health_records_raise_doubt/.
9. Dave deBronkart, *Should Patient Engagement Be Regulated?*, BETTER HEALTH (Oct. 11, 2010), http://getbetterhealth.com/should-patient-engagement-be-regulated/2010.10.11.
10. Chris Fleming, *February Health Affairs Issue: New Era of Patient Engagement*, HEALTH AFFAIRS BLOG (Feb. 4, 2013), http://healthaffairs.org/blog/2013/02/04/february-health-affairs-issue-new-era-of-patient-engagement/.

Digital Justice. Ethan Katsh and Orna Rabinovich-Einy.
© Ethan Katsh and Orna Rabinovich-Einy 2017. Published 2017 by Oxford University Press.

11. Lee Aase, *Mayo Chiefs Name a Patient as 2015 Visiting Professor*, MAYO CLINIC (Oct. 22, 2014), http://socialmedia.mayoclinic.org/discussion/mayo-chiefs-name-a-patient-as-2015-visiting-professor/.

12. http://www.youtube.com/watch?v=Ekmok6iSS6g.

13. Richard J. Ross, *Communications Revolutions and Legal Culture: An Elusive Relationship*, 27 L. & SOC. INQUIRY 637, 637–38 (2002).

14. VIKTOR MAYER-SCHONBERGER & KENNETH CUKIER, BIG DATA: A REVOLUTION THAT WILL TRANSFORM HOW WE LIVE, WORK, AND THINK (2013).

15. Sanjana Hattotuwa, *Conversation with Colin Rule, Director of Online Dispute Resolution for eBay and PayPal*, ICT FOR PEACEBUILDING (Sept. 21, 2006), https://ict4peace.wordpress.com/2006/09/21/conversation-with-colin-rule-director-of-online-dispute-resolution-for-ebay-and-paypal/.

16. *See WIPO Domain Name Dispute Resolution Statistics*, WIPO, http://www.wipo.int/amc/en/domains/statistics/; *Domain Name Disputes*, FORUM, http://www.adrforum.com/Domains.

17. Marc Galanter, *Reading the Landscape of Disputes: What We Know and Don't Know (and Think We Know) about Our Allegedly Contentious and Litigious Society*, 31 UCLA L. REV. 4, 12 (1983).

18. Leon Wieseltier, *Among the Disrupted*, N.Y. TIMES SUNDAY BOOK REVIEW (Jan. 7, 2015), http://www.nytimes.com/2015/01/18/books/review/among-the-disrupted.html.

19. John Halamka, Social Media Guidelines for Our Clinicians (September 28, 2016) http://geekdoctor.blogspot.com/2016/09/social-media-guidelines-for-our.html.

20. ROGER FISHER & WILLIAM L. URY, GETTING TO YES: NEGOTIATING AGREEMENT WITHOUT GIVING IN (Bruce Patton ed., Houghton Mifflin Harcourt, 2d ed. 1993).

21. *Factsheet on the "Right to be Forgotten" Ruling (c-131/12)*, EUR. COMMISSION (June 3, 2014), http://ec.europa.eu/justice/data-protection/files/factsheets/factsheet_data_protection_en.pdf.

22. "The Wikipedia edit war on hummus has raged for various reasons for years—and simultaneously mocked by onlookers and even participants. It became so controversial, the article is categorized under The Arab-Israeli Conflict and subject to the rule that only one revert can occur in a 24-hour period. The primary controversy has been whether hummus was first Israeli or Arab. The current terminology is 'Middle Eastern'—no one can disagree about that. People were especially offended by using the term 'Palestine' in discussing its origins. In my studies, Palestine is a perfectly legitimate geographic area term, but it has been so politicized, it can no longer go uncensored . . . and then it drags hummus down with it." *See User: RM395/course/Edit wars/Hummus*, WIKIPEDIA (2013), http://en.wikipedia.org/wiki/User:RM395/Course/Edit_wars/Hummus (last modified Mar. 18, 2013).

23. Kashmir Hill, *Facebook Asks Federal Court to Respect a First Amendment Right to "Like,"* FORBES (Aug. 7, 2012), http://www.forbes.com/sites/kashmirhill/2012/08/07/facebook-asks-federal-court-to-respect-a-first-amendment-right-to-like.

24. F. Gregory Lastowka & Dan Hunter, *The Laws of the Virtual Worlds*, 92 CALIF. L. REV. 1, 71 n.381 (2003).

25. Geeta Dayal, *Man Orders TV through Amazon, Gets Assault Rifle*, WIRED (Aug. 8, 2012), http://www.wired.com/2012/08/tv-amazon-assault-rifle/.

26. *See* Hattotuwa, *supra* note 15.

27. Conversation with Colin Rule, June 22, 2016.

28. In the commercial context, if value is likely to erode quickly, as is often the case with technology products and services, pressure to protect and aggressively extend its value increases. "In the 21st century, technological change just happens too fast, eroding the value of patents once intended to last for years. Innovation life cycles are now measured in months, not years. Innovation is happening around business methods and processes as much as around specific products. As a result, simply stockpiling patents for the long haul doesn't always work out as planned. By the time you try to use those patents, the market may have decisively shifted

away from you." *See* Dominic Basulto, *Patents Are a Terrible Way to Measure Innovation*, Wash. Post (July 14, 2015), http://www.washingtonpost.com/blogs/innovations/wp/2015/07/14/patents-are-a-terrible-way-to-measure-innovation/?wpisrc=nl_innov&wpmm=1.

29. "The furor over Sacco's tweet had become not just an ideological crusade against her perceived bigotry but also a form of idle entertainment. Her complete ignorance of her predicament for those 11 hours lent the episode both dramatic irony and a pleasing narrative arc. As Sacco's flight traversed the length of Africa, a hashtag began to trend worldwide: #HasJustineLandedYet. 'Seriously. I just want to go home to go to bed, but everyone at the bar is SO into #HasJustineLandedYet. Can't look away. Can't leave' and 'Right, is there no one in Cape Town going to the airport to tweet her arrival? Come on, Twitter! I'd like pictures #HasJustineLandedYet.' " *See* Jon Ronson, *How One Stupid Tweet Blew Up Justine Sacco's Life*, N.Y. Times (Feb. 12, 2015), http://www.nytimes.com/2015/02/15/magazine/how-one-stupid-tweet-ruined-justine-saccos-life.html?_r=0.

30. Kashmira Gander, *Heinz Forced to Apologise after QR Code on Ketchup Bottle Linked to Hardcore Porn Site*, The Indep. (June 22, 2015), http://www.independent.co.uk/life-style/food-and-drink/news/heinz-forced-to-apologise-after-qr-code-on-ketchup-bottle-linked-to-hardcore-porn-site-10327313.html.

31. *See* John Markoff, *Killing the Computer to Save It*, N.Y. Times (Oct. 29, 2012), http://www.nytimes.com/2012/10/30/science/rethinking-the-computer-at-80.html?_r=0 (quoting Peter G. Neumann).

32. Eric A. Meyer, *Inadvertent Algorithmic Cruelty*, Eric's Archived Thoughts (Dec. 24, 2014), http://meyerweb.com/eric/thoughts/2014/12/24/inadvertent-algorithmic-cruelty/.

33. Molly Mulshine, *A Major Flaw in Google's Algorithm Allegedly Tagged Two Black People's Faces with the Word "Gorillas,"* Bus. Insider (July 1, 2015), http://www.businessinsider.com/google-tags-black-people-as-gorillas-2015-7.

34. *The Internet in 1990: Domain Registration, E-mail and Networks*, Institute Advanced Prof. Stud., http://www.iaps.com/internet-history-october-1990.html#email.

35. *History of gTLD Domain Name Growth*, ZookNIC, http://www.zooknic.com/Domains/counts.html.

36. *See* discussion on domain names in Chapter 3.

37. Blake T. Bilstad, *Obscenity and Indecency on the Usenet: The Legal and Political Future of Alt.Sex. Stories*, 2 J. Computer-Mediated Comm. (Sept. 1996).

38. *See* Markoff, *supra* note 31.

39. Henry H. Perritt, Law and the Information Superhighway: Privacy, Access, Intellectual Property, Commerce, Liability (1996).

40. Alok Kumar, *101 Ways to Hook Up to the Internet*, Wayback Machine (Apr. 24, 1995), https://web.archive.org/web/20020307173812/.

41. Jay P. Kesan & Rajiv C. Shah, *Fool Us Once Shame on You—Fool Us Twice Shame on Us: What We Can Learn from the Privatizations of the Internet Backbone Network and the Domain Name System*, 79 Wash. U. L. Q. 89 (2001).

42. As noted in Chapter 1, an interesting example of informal dispute resolution in the pre-web time period involved the development and use of the emoticon. *See* Scott E. Fahlman, *Smiley Lore:-)*, Carnegie Mellon U. Sch. of Computer Sci., http://www-2.cs.cmu.edu/~sef/sefSmiley.htm.

43. *See* Lastowka & Hunter, *supra* note 24.

44. John Perry Barlow, *A Declaration of the Independence of Cyberspace*, Electronic Frontier Foundation (Feb. 8, 1996), https://projects.eff.org/~barlow/Declaration-Final.html.

45. Mitchell Kapor, *Where Is the Digital Highway Really Heading?*, Wired (Mar. 1, 1993), http://archive.wired.com/wired/archive/1.03/kapor.on.nii.html.

46. Ethan Katsh & Leah Wing, *Ten Years of Online Dispute Resolution (ODR): Looking at the Past and Constructing the Future*, 38 Tol. L. Rev. 19, 23 (2006).

47. *See* Emily Bazelon, *How to Stop the Bullies*, The Atlantic (Mar. 2013), http://www.theatlantic.com/magazine/archive/2013/03/how-to-stop-the-bullies/309217/.

48. Ethan Katsh et al., *E-Commerce, E-Disputes, and E-Dispute Resolution: In the Shadow of "eBay Law,"* 15 Ohio St. J. on Disp. Resol. 705, 708–12 (2000).

49. SquareTrade handled eBay disputes until 2004. It has since transitioned into a site for consumer warranties. SquareTrade, https://www.squaretrade.com/.

50. Ethan Katsh & Janet Rifkin, Online Dispute Resolution: Resolving Conflicts in Cyberspace 93 (2001).

51. *What Is the Smart Grid?,* Smartgrid.gov, https://www.smartgrid.gov/the_smart_grid/.

52. *Research and Advisory for Companies Challenged by Business Disruptions,* Altimeter, http://www.altimetergroup.com/.

53. Mark Anderson, *Vulnerable "Smart" Devices Make an Internet of Insecure Things,* IEEE Spectrum (Sept. 3, 2014), http://spectrum.ieee.org/riskfactor/computing/networks/vulnerable-smart-devices-make-an-internet-of-insecure-things.

54. John Tagliabue, *Swiss Cows Send Texts to Announce They're in Heat,* N.Y. Times (Oct. 1, 2012), http://www.nytimes.com/2012/10/02/world/europe/device-sends-message-to-swiss-farmer-when-cow-is-in-heat.html?pagewanted=all&_r=0.

55. Jaclyn Trop, *A Black Box for Car Crashes,* N.Y. Times (July 21, 2013), http://www.nytimes.com/2013/07/22/business/black-boxes-in-cars-a-question-of-privacy.html?pagewanted=all&_r=0.

56. Bruce Schneir, *We Need to Save the Internet from the Internet of Things,* (October 6, 2016) https://motherboard.vice.com/read/we-need-to-save-the-internet-from-the-internet-of-things.

57. David Brooks, *The Outsourced Brain,* N.Y. Times (Oct. 26, 2007), http://www.nytimes.com/2007/10/26/opinion/26brooks.html.

58. Karl N. Llewellyn, The Bramble Bush 2 (1st ed. 1930).

59. Marc Galanter, *The Vanishing Trial: An Examination of Trials and Related Matters in Federal and State Courts,* 1 J. Empirical Legal Stud. 459, 495 (2004).While trials in courts are in decline, "trial-like events" outside the courts are on the rise. *See* Marc Galanter & Angela M. Frozena, *A Grin without a Cat: The Continuing Decline & Displacement of Trials in American Courts,* 143 Daedalus 115, 126 (2014).

60. The Administrative Dispute Resolution Act of 1996, Pub. L. No. 104-320, 110 Stat. 3870 (1996) (amending 5 U.S.C. §§ 571–83).

61. "It is a settled and invariable principle in the laws of England, that every right when with-held must have a remedy, and every injury it's [*sic*] proper redress." *See* 4 William Blackstone, Commentaries *109.

62. *See* Chapter 7 on courts.

63. Paul Schiff Berman, *From International Law to Law and Globalization,* 43 Colum. J. Transnat'l L. 485, 498 (2005).

64. "[I]t cannot be helped, it is as it should be, that the law is behind the times." *See* Oliver Wendell Holmes, Speeches 102 (1934).

65. Susan S. Silbey & Sally E. Merry, *Mediator Settlement Strategies,* 8 L. & Pol. 7, 14 (1986).

66. Lawrence Lessig, Code: And Other Laws of Cyberspace 6, 241 n.7 (1999) (citing William J. Mitchell, City of Bits: Space, Place, and the Infobahn 111 (1996)).

67. Frank E. A. Sander & Stephen B. Goldberg, *Fitting the Forum to the Fuss: A User-Friendly Guide to Selecting an ADR Procedure,* 10 Negot. J. 49, 49 (1994).

68. William L. Ury et al., Getting Disputes Resolved: Designing Systems to Cut the Costs of Conflict (1st ed. 1988); *see also* Cathy A. Costantino & Christina Sickles Merchant, Designing Conflict Management Systems: A Guide to Creating Productive and Healthy Organizations (1st ed. 1995).

69. William L.F. Felstiner et al., *The Emergence and Transformation of Disputes: Naming, Blaming, Claiming . . . ,* 15 L. & Soc'y Rev. 631 (1980).

70. Tom Vanderbilt, *Let the Robot Drive: The Autonomous Car of the Future Is Here,* Wired (Jan. 20, 2012, http://www.wired.com/magazine/2012/01/ff_autonomouscars/.

71. Patrick Boehler, *Australian Police Says Apple Maps Can Be "Life Threatening,"* Time (Dec. 11, 2012), http://newsfeed.time.com/2012/12/11/australian-police-says-apple-maps-can-be-life-threatening/.

72. David Pogue, *Maps App for iPhone Steers Right*, N.Y. Times (Dec. 12, 2012), http://www. nytimes.com/2012/12/13/technology/personaltech/google-maps-app-for-iphone-goes-in-the-right-direction-review.html.

73. deBronkart, *Imagine Someone Had Been Managing Your Data, supra* note 6.

74. Markle Foundation, The Connecting for Health Common Framework: Background Issues on Data Quality 2 (2006), https://www.google.co.il/url?sa= t&rct=j&q=&esrc=s&source=web&cd=2&ved=0ahUKEwjEyrPi9q3JAhWKsxQKH QRGCLkQFggiMAE&url=http%3A%2F%2Fresearch.policyarchive.org%2F15515. pdf&usg=AFQjCNFnzepphoQA6tlGBX_BlvG9doZXuQ&sig2=D5a0VrZnILvS3UTdBqZ uxQ&cad=rja.

75. Joseph L. Bower & Clayton M. Christensen, *Disruptive Technologies: Catching the Wave*, 73 Harv. Bus. Rev. 43 (1995). Susskind & Susskind prefer the term "liberating" over "disruptive" in this context, because of the more positive feel associated with the former term. *See* Richard Susskind & Daniel Susskind, The Future of the Professions: How Technology Will Transform the Work of Human Experts 110 (2015).

76. *See* Costantino & Merchant, *supra* note 68.

77. Jonathan M. Hyman & Lela P. Love, *If Portia Were a Mediator: An Inquiry into Justice in Mediation*, 9 Clinical L. Rev. 157 (2002).

78. Marshall McLuhan, Understanding Media: The Extensions of Man 223 (1965).

Chapter 1

1. Keith Houston, *Smile! A History of Emoticons*, Wall St. J. (Sept. 27, 2013), http://www. wsj.com/articles/SB10001424052702304213904579093661814158946; Brita, *Sept. 19, 1982: Can't you take a joke?:-)*, Wired (Sept. 19, 2011, 6:30 AM), http://www.wired. com/2011/09/0919fahlman-proposes-emoticons/. *See* Scott E. Fahlman, *Smiley Lore:-)*, Carnegie Mellon U. Sch. of Computer Sci., http://www-2.cs.cmu.edu/~sef/sefSmiley. htm.

2. Ironically, the first domain name registered in 1984 was by a company, Symbolics.com. Alyson Shontell, *Guess What the First Domain Name Ever Registered Was*, Bus. Insider (May 4, 2011), http://www.businessinsider.com/this-is-the-first-domain-name-ever-registed-2011-5.

3. Christopher C. Stacy, *Getting Started Computing at the AI Lab* 9 (Mass. Inst. of Tech. Artificial Intelligence Laboratory, Working Paper No. 235, Sept. 7, 1982).

4. *The NSFNET Backbone Services Acceptable Use Policy*, Cyber Telecom (1995), http://www. cybertelecom.org/notes/nsfnet.htm#aup.

5. Milo Medin, *What I Saw at the Revolution (or) An Abridged History of the Internet*, NANOG (June 16, 2011), https://www.nanog.org/meetings/nanog52/presentations/Monday/ Medin-nanog-6-15.pdf.

6. AOL bought CompuServe in 1998. *See* Caitlin Dewey, *A Complete History of the Rise and Fall—and Reincarnation!—of the Beloved '90s Chatroom*, Wash. Post (Oct. 30, 2014), https://www.washingtonpost.com/news/the-intersect/wp/2014/10/30/a-complete-history-of-the-rise-and-fall-and-reincarnation-of-the-beloved-90s-chatroom/.

7. Lindsy Van Gelder, *The Strange Case of the Electronic Lover*, Ms. Mag. (Oct. 1985), http:// lindsyvangelder.com/sites/default/files/Plinkers.org%20-%20Electronic%20Lover. htm_.pdf.

8. *Id.*

9. "No provider or user of an interactive computer service shall be treated as the publisher or speaker of any information provided by another information content provider." Communications Decency Act of 1996, 47 U.S.C. § 230(c)(1) (2012).

10. Van Gelder, *supra* note 7.

11. Short for "system operator." *SYSOP*, NetLingo, http://www.netlingo.com/word/sysop.php.

12. Andrew Anderson, *What Is Usenet, Anyway?*, TLDP (Mar. 7, 1996), http://www.tldp.org/ LDP/nag/node257.html.

13. *Giganews' Usenet History*, GIGANEWS, http://www.giganews.com/usenet-history/.

14. Jonathan Zittrain, *The Rise and Fall of Sysopdom*, 10 HARV. J. L. & TECH. 495, 499 (1997).

15. *Id.*

16. Timothy B. Lee, *How a Grad Student Trying to Build the First Botnet Brought the Internet to Its Knees*, WASH. POST (Nov. 1, 2013), https://www.washingtonpost.com/news/the-switch/ wp/2013/11/01/how-a-grad-student-trying-to-build-the-first-botnet-brought-the-internet-to-its-knees/.

17. John Markoff, *Author of Computer "Virus" Is Son of N.S.A. Expert on Data Security*, N.Y. TIMES (Nov. 5, 1988), http://www.nytimes.com/1988/11/05/us/author-of-computer-virus-is-son-of-nsa-expert-on-data-security.html?pagewanted=all. It should be noted that editions of the *Times* in the late 1850s also used the word *internet*, but it is not clear what the meaning of the word was then.

18. Medin, *supra* note 5, at 10.

19. *Newsgroup Spam*, WIKIPEDIA, https://en.wikipedia.org/wiki/Newsgroup_spam (last modified Feb. 17, 2016, 03:33); Brad Templeton, *Origin of the Term "Spam" to Mean Net Abuse*, TEMPLETONS, http://www.templetons.com/brad/spamterm.html.

20. Michael D. Shear, *Free Speech Gets Tangled in the 'Net; Colleges Try to Balance Rights, Cybersensitivity*, WASH. POST (Oct. 23, 1995), https://www.highbeam.com/doc/1P2-861701.html.

21. Amy Rya, *Cornell Students Sexist E-Mail Spreads*, BROWN DAILY HERALD (Feb. 5, 1996), http://idnc.library.illinois.edu/cgi-bin/illinois?a=d&d=AUE19960205.2.46.

22. *Cornell Charges 4 Students in E-Mail Prank*, N.Y. TIMES (Nov. 15, 1995), http://www.nytimes.com/1995/11/15/us/cornell-charges-4-students-in-e-mail-prank.html.

23. Richard T. Griffiths, *Chapter Three: History of Electronic Mail, in History of the Internet, Interest for Historians (and just about everyone else)*, LEIDEN U. (Oct. 2002), http://www.let.leidenuniv.nl/history/ivh/chap3.htm.

24. Mike Godwin, *Meme, Counter-Meme*, WIRED (Oct. 1, 1994), http://www.wired.com/1994/10/godwin-if-2/.

25. Pierre Omidyar, eBay's founder.

26. ADAM COHEN, THE PERFECT STORE: INSIDE EBAY 27 (2003).

27. *Id.*

28. *Id.* at 36.

29. DISPUTE RESOLUTION CONFERENCE (May 22, 1996), http://www.umass.edu/dispute/ncair/.

30. Robert Gellman, *A Brief History of the Virtual Magistrate Project: The Early Months*, THE ON-LINE DISP. RESOL. CONF. (May 22, 1996), http://www.umass.edu/dispute/ncair/gellman.htm.

31. *Id.*

32. Ethan Katsh, *The Online Ombuds Office: Adapting Dispute Resolution to Cyberspace*, THE ON-LINE DISP. RESOL. CONF. (May 22, 1996), http://www.umass.edu/dispute/ncair/katsh.htm.

33. Richard S. Granat, *Creating an Environment for Mediating Disputes on the Internet*, THE ON-LINE DISP. RESOL. CONF. (May 22, 1996), http://www.umass.edu/dispute/ncair/granat.htm.

34. Ethan Katsh et al., *E-Commerce, E-Disputes, and E-Dispute Resolution: In the Shadow of "eBay Law,"* 15 OHIO ST. J. DISP. RESOL. 705 (2000) [hereinafter Katsh et al., *E-commerce, E-Disputes*].

35. *The Internet in 1990: Domain Registration, E-mail and Networks*, IAPS, http://www.iaps.com/internet-history-october-1990.html#email.

36. *History of gTLD Domain Name Growth*, ZOOKNIC, http://www.zooknic.com/Domains/counts.html.

37. Joshua Quittner, *Billions Registered*, WIRED (Oct. 1, 1994), http://archive.wired.com/wired/archive/2.10/mcdonalds.html.

38. David R. Johnson, *Dispute Resolution in Cyberspace*, ELECTRONIC FRONTIER FOUND. (Feb. 10, 1994), http://w2.eff.org/legal/online_dispute_resolution_johnson.article.txt.

39. Daniel Rainey & Ethan Katsh, *ODR and Government, in* ONLINE DISPUTE RESOLUTION: THEORY AND PRACTICE: A TREATISE ON TECHNOLOGY AND DISPUTE RESOLUTION 248 (M. S. Wahab et al. eds., 2012).

40. Colin Rule & Mark Wilson, *Online Resolution and Citizen Empowerment: Property Tax Appeals in North America, in* REVOLUTIONIZING THE INTERACTION BETWEEN STATE AND CITIZENS THROUGH DIGITAL COMMUNICATIONS 185 (Sam B. Edwards III & Diogo Santos eds., 2015).

41. *About Community Member Spotlight*, EBAY, http://community.ebay.com/.

42. Steve Abernethy, *Trusted Access to the Global Digital Economy/Square Trade International ODR Case Study*, UNECE FORUM ON ONLINE DISP. RESOL. (June 6–7, 2002).

43. *Id.*

44. Ethan Katsh et al., *Process Technology for Achieving Government Online Dispute Resolution, in* PROCEEDINGS OF THE 2004 ANNUAL NATIONAL CONFERENCE ON DIGITAL GOVERNMENT RESEARCH 1–2 (dg.o '04 ed. 2004).

45. Katsh et al., *E-Commerce, E-Disputes, supra* note 34, at 90–116; David A. Larson, *Technology Mediated Dispute Resolution (TMDR): A New Paradigm for ADR*, 38 U. OF TOL. L. REV. 213, 215–17 (2006); ARNO R. LODDER & JOHN ZELEZNIKOW, ENHANCED DISPUTE RESOLUTION THROUGH THE USE OF INFORMATION TECHNOLOGY (Cambridge University Press 2010).

46. For example, the use of software for an online brainstorming process. *See* Ethan Katsh & Leah Wing, *Ten Years of Online Dispute Resolution: Looking at the Past and Constructing the Future*, 38 TOL. L. REV 101 (2006). *See also* DEBATEGRAPH, http://debategraph.org (DebateGraph's visualization tools are used for exploring various aspects of a problem and potential solutions).

47. THE MEDIATION ROOM, http://www.themediationroom.com/.

48. BENOAM, http://www.benoam.co.il/.

49. Paul Kirgis, *Cybersettle and the Value of Online Dispute Resolution*, INDISPUTABLY (July 7, 2010), http://www.indisputably.org/?p=1456.

50. *See* ROBERT H. MNOOKIN ET AL., BEYOND WINNING: NEGOTIATING TO CREATE VALUE IN DEALS AND DISPUTES 18–22 (2000); LODDER & ZELEZNIKOW, *supra* note 45, at 40, n.3.

51. Ernest M. Thiessen & Joseph P. McMahon, *Beyond Win-Win in Cyberspace*, 15 OHIO ST. J. ON DISP. RESOL. 643, 647–48 (2000).

52. *Id.* at 648.

53. ETHAN KATSH & JANET RIFKIN, ONLINE DISPUTE RESOLUTION: RESOLVING CONFLICTS IN CYBERSPACE 73–92 (1st ed. 2001).

54. LODDER & ZELEZNIKOW, *supra* note 45, at 79 (introducing the "Fifth Party," which represents the provider of the technology).

55. YOUSTICE, http://www.youstice.com/en/.

56. MODRIA, http://modria.com/.

57. PICTURE IT SETTLED, http://pictureitsettled.com/.

Chapter 2

1. FRANZ KAFKA, THE TRIAL 267 (E. M. Butler ed., Willa Muir & Edwin Muir trans., Alfred A. Knopf, Inc. 1956).

2. Frank E. A. Sander, *Varieties of Dispute Processing, in* THE POUND CONFERENCE: PERSPECTIVES ON JUSTICE IN THE FUTURE (A. Levin & R. Wheelers eds., 1979). The vision of a "multidoor courthouse" was presented by Professor Sander at the Pound Conference as part of an effort to reduce courts' caseload and improve access to courts.

3. DEBORAH L. RHODE, ACCESS TO JUSTICE (2004) [hereinafter RHODE, ACCESS TO JUSTICE]; Benjamin P. Cooper, *Access to Justice without Lawyers*, 47 AKRON L. REV. 205, 207 (2014); Marc Galanter, *Access to Justice in a World of Expanding Social Capability*, 37 FORDHAM URB. L.J. 115, 115 & n.1, 122 (2010); William C. Vickrey et al., *Access to Justice: A Broader*

Perspective, 42 Loy. L.A. L. Rev. 1147, 1154 (2009). For a broader perspective, *see* Rebecca L. Sandefur, *The Fulcrum Point of Equal Access to Justice: Legal and Non-Legal Institutions of Remedy*, 42 Loy. L.A. L. Rev. 949 (2009); William Davis & Helga Turku, *Access to Justice and Alternative Dispute Resolution*, 2011 J. Disp. Resol. 47 (2011); Lawrence M. Friedman, *Access to Justice: Some Historical Comments*, 37 Fordham Urb. L.J. 3 (2010); Steven H. Hobbs, *Shout from Taller Rooftops: A Response to Deborah L. Rhode's* Access to Justice, 73 Fordham L. Rev. 935 (2004).

4. On the changes in the legal and political environment that allowed such a movement to emerge in the United States, *see* Rhode, Access to Justice, *supra* note 3, at 62–69.

5. Deborah L. Rhode, *Symposium: The Constitution of and the Good Society: Access to Justice*, 69 Fordham L. Rev. 1785, 1785 (2001) (stating, "[m]illions of Americans lack any access to the system, let alone equal access").

6. Richard E. Miller & Austin Sarat, *Grievances, Claims, and Disputes: Assessing the Adversary Culture*, 15 Law & Soc'y Rev. 52 (1980–81). While the dispute resolution pyramid has been widely used, there have also been alternative conceptions of the evolution of disputes, as evidenced in the dispute resolution tree. See Catherine R., Albiston, Lauren B. Edelman, and Joy Milligan. *The Dispute Tree and the Legal Forest*. 10 Annual Review of Law and Social Science 105 (2014).

7. Miller & Sarat, *supra* note 6, at 61 (stating, "[t]he overall picture is of a remedy system that minimizes formal conflict but uses the courts when necessary in those relatively rare cases in which conflict is unavoidable").

8. Rebecca L. Sandefur, *Accessing Justice in the Contemporary USA: Findings from the Community Needs and Services Study*, Am. B. Found. 16 (2014), http://www.americanbarfoundation. org/uploads/cms/documents/sandefur_accessing_justice_in_the_contemporary_usa._ aug._2014.pdf.

9. Marc Galanter, *Justice in Many Rooms: Courts, Private Ordering, and Indigenous Law*, 13 J. Legal Pluralism & Unofficial L. 1 (1981) [hereinafter Galanter, *Justice in Many Rooms*].

10. Marc Galanter, *Why the "Haves" Come Out Ahead: Speculations on the Limits of Legal Change*, 9 Law & Soc'y Rev. 95 (1974).

11. 3 Mauro Cappelletti & Bryant G. Garth, Access to Justice: Emerging Issues and Perspectives 9–10 (Mauro Cappelletti & Bryant G. Garth eds., 1978) [hereinafter 3 Cappelletti & Garth]. It is interesting to note that this has not always been the case with courts: "In colonial America, local courts were 'on the whole, cheap, informal and accessible.' Today they are, on the whole, expensive, highly formalized, and effectively unavailable to all but wealthy individuals and businesses." *See* Gillian K. Hadfield, *Innovating to Improve Access: Changing the Way Courts Regulate Legal Markets*, 143 Daedalus 83, 84 (2014).

12. Mark Blacksell, *Social Justice and Access to Legal Services: A Geographical Perspective*, 21 Geoforum 489 (1990).

13. David A. Larson, *Access to Justice for Persons with Disabilities: An Emerging Strategy*, 3 Laws 220 (2014).

14. 3 Cappelletti & Garth, *supra* note 11, at 10.

15. *Id.*

16. William L. F. Felstiner et al., *The Emergence and Transformation of Disputes: Naming, Blaming, Claiming . . .* , 15 Law & Soc'y Rev. 631 (1980).

17. *See* Konstantina Vagenas, *Table of Contents, A National Call to Action: Access to Justice for Limited English Proficient Litigants: Creating Solutions to Language Barriers in State Courts*, Nat'l Ctr. St. Cts. (2013), http://www.ncsc.org/services-and-experts/areas-of-expertise/language-access/~/media/files/pdf/services%20and%20experts/areas%20of%20expertise/ language%20access/call-to-action.ashx.

18. Charles M. Grabau & Llewellyn Joseph Gibbons, *Protecting the Rights of Linguistic Minorities: Challenges to Court Interpretation*, 30 New Eng. L. Rev. 227, 255–60. (1996).

19. 1 Mauro Cappelletti & Bryant Garth, Access to Justice: A World Survey (Mauro Cappelletti ed., 1978) [hereinafter 1 Cappelletti & Garth].

20. 3 Cappelletti & Garth, *supra* note 11, at 401–03.

21. 1 CAPPELLETTI & GARTH, *supra* note 19, at 21.

22. 3 CAPPELLETTI & GARTH, *supra* note 11, at 173.

23. Mauro Cappalletti & Bryant Garth, *Access to Justice: The Newest Wave in the Worldwide Movement to Make Rights Effective*, 27 BUFF. L. REV. 181, 225 (1978).

24. Galanter, *Justice in Many Rooms, supra* note 9.

25. Sandefur, *supra* note 3.

26. For the distinction between "quantitative" and "qualitative" advantages, *see* Carrie Menkel-Meadow, *Pursuing Settlement in an Adversary Culture: A Tale of Innovation Co-Opted or "The Law of ADR,"* 19 FLA. ST. U. L. REV. 1, 6 (1991) [hereinafter Menkel-Meadow, *Pursuing Settlement*]. For a critique of courts' "limited remedial imagination," *see id.* at 3.

27. Carrie Menkel-Meadow, *When Litigation Is Not the Only Way: Consensus Building and Mediation as Public Interest Lawyering*, 10 WASH. U. J. L. & POL'Y 37, 42 (2002).

28. Nancy Welsh et al., *The Application of Procedural Justice Research to Judicial Actions and Techniques in Settlement Sessions*, in THE MULTI-TASKING JUDGE: COMPARATIVE JUDICIAL DISPUTE RESOLUTION (Tania Sourdin & Archie Zariski eds., 2013); TOM R. TYLER, PSYCHOLOGY AND THE DESIGN OF LEGAL INSTITUTIONS (2007). On procedural justice in mediation, *see* Nancy A. Welsh, *Making Deals in Court-Connected Mediation: What's Justice Got to Do with It?*, 79 WASH. U. L. Q. 787, 817 (2001).

29. Carrie Menkel-Meadow, *When Dispute Resolution Begets Disputes of Its Own: Conflicts Among Dispute Professionals*, 44 UCLA L. REV. 1871, 1872–73 (1997) [hereinafter Menkel-Meadow, *When Dispute Resolution Begets Disputes of Its Own*]; RHODE, ACCESS TO JUSTICE, *supra* note 3, at 87.

30. For literature providing various justifications for the formation of an alternative dispute resolution system, *see* DAVID B. LIPSKY ET AL., EMERGING SYSTEMS FOR MANAGING WORKPLACE CONFLICT: LESSONS FROM AMERICAN CORPORATIONS FOR MANAGERS AND DISPUTE RESOLUTION PROFESSIONALS 76–78 (2003) [hereinafter LIPSKY, EMERGING SYSTEMS]; CARRIE MENKEL-MEADOW ET AL., DISPUTE RESOLUTION: BEYOND THE ADVERSARIAL MODEL 6–13 (2d ed. 2010) [hereinafter MENKEL-MEADOW, DISPUTE RESOLUTION]; ROBERT H. MNOOKIN ET AL., BEYOND WINNING: NEGOTIATING TO CREATE VALUE IN DEALS AND DISPUTES 100–01 (2000); Deborah R. Hensler, *Our Courts, Ourselves: How the Alternative Dispute Resolution Movement Is Re-Shaping Our Legal System*, 108 PENN. ST. L. REV. 165, 171 (2003); Menkel-Meadow, *When Dispute Resolution Begets Disputes of Its Own, supra* note 29, at 1872–75; Jacqueline M. Nolan-Haley, *Court Mediation and the Search for Justice through Law*, 74 WASH. U. L. Q. 47, 54–55 (1996).

31. Nancy A. Welsh, *Look Before You Leap and Keep on Looking: Lessons from the Institutionalization of Court-Connected Mediation*, 5 NEV. L.J. 399, 407–08 (2004); Nancy A. Welsh, *The Current Transitional State of Court-Connected ADR*, 95 MARQ. L. REV. 873, 874 (2012); MENKEL-MEADOW, DISPUTE RESOLUTION, *supra* note 30, at 406–09; Menkel-Meadow, *Pursuing Settlement, supra* note 26, at 6; Jacqueline Nolan-Haley, *Mediation as the "New Arbitration,"* 17 HARV. NEGOT. L. REV. 61, 73–89 (2012).

32. Carrie Menkel-Meadow, *Regulation of Dispute Resolution in the United States of America: From the Formal to the Informal to the "Semi-Formal,"* in REGULATING DISPUTE RESOLUTION: ADR AND ACCESS TO JUSTICE AT THE CROSSROADS 419 (Felix Steffek et al. eds., 2013).

33. TANIA SOURDIN & ARCHIE ZARISKI, THE MULTI-TASKING JUDGE: COMPARATIVE JUDICIAL DISPUTE RESOLUTION (2013).

34. Menkel-Meadow, *Pursuing Settlement, supra* note 26, at 3.

35. Owen M. Fiss, *Against Settlement*, 93 YALE L. J. 1073, 1075 (1984).

36. LIPSKY, EMERGING SYSTEMS, *supra* note 30. (Drawing on a wide-scale empirical study of Fortune 1000 companies' corporate conflict strategies conducted by the authors that analyzed, among other things, the proliferation of internal dispute resolution systems, the sources of such growth and future developments).

37. RHODE, ACCESS TO JUSTICE, *supra* note 3, at 87.

38. Lauren B. Edelman et al., *Internal Dispute Resolution: The Transformation of Civil Rights in the Workplace*, 27 Law & Soc'y Rev. 497 (1993).

39. Only in recent decades have certain problem solving courts engaged in dispute prevention activities in an attempt to reduce recidivism and address the "revolving door" phenomenon. *See* Greg Berman & John Feinblatt, *Problem-Solving Courts: A Brief Primer*, 23 Law & Pol'y 125, 126 (2001); Bruce J. Winick, *Therapeutic Jurisprudence and Problem-Solving Courts*, 30 Fordham Urb. L.J. 1055, 1056 (2003).

40. Anjanette H. Raymond, *Yeah, But Did You See the Gorilla? Creating and Protecting an Informed Consumer in Cross-Border Online Dispute Resolution*, 19 Harv. Neg. L. Rev. 129 (2014).

41. Richard Susskind, Tomorrow's Lawyers: An Introduction to Your Future 85–86 (2013) (conveying a broad understanding of access to justice in the digital age, one which includes not only dispute resolution but also dispute containment, avoidance, and "legal health promotion").

42. Frank Pasquale & Glyn Cashwell, *Four Futures of Legal Automation*, 63 UCLA L. Rev. Discourse 26, 39 (2015); Maayan Perel & Niva Elkin-Koren, *Accountability in Algorithmic Copyright Enforcement*, 19 Stanford Tech. L. Rev. (forthcoming, 2016) (on the challenges presented by algorithms to transparency); Tal Zarsky, *The Trouble with Algorithmic Decisions: An Analytic Road Map to Examine Efficiency and Fairness in Automated and Opaque Decision Making*, 41 Sci., Tech. & Hum. Values 118, 122–23 (2015) [hereinafter Zarsky, *The Trouble with Algorithmic Decisions*]; Tal Z. Zarsky, *Automated Prediction: Perception, Law, and Policy*, 55 Comm. of the ACM, Sept. 2012, at 33, 35 [hereinafter Zarsky, *Automated Prediction*].

43. Judith Resnik, *Diffusing Disputes: The Public in the Private of Arbitration, the Private in Courts, and the Erasure of Rights*, 124 Yale L.J. 2804 (2015).

44. Pablo Cortes, Online Dispute Resolution for Consumers in the European Union 107–09 (2010); Julia Hornle, *Legal Controls on the Use of Arbitration Clause in B2C E-Commerce Contracts*, 2 Masaryk U. J. L. & Tech. 23, 28–33 (2008).

45. Colin Rule, Online Dispute Resolution for Business: B2B, E-Commerce, Consumer Employment, Insurance, and Other Commercial Conflicts 61–71, 77 (2002).

46. Richard E. Susskind & Daniel Susskind, The Future of the Professions: How Technology Will Transform the Work of Human Experts 101–02 (2015).

47. For other definitions, *see* Danielle Keats Citron, *Technological Due Process*, 85 Wash. U. L. Rev. 1249, 1257 n.45 (2008) (referencing a definition of an algorithm as a "mechanical or recursive computational procedure"); Michael L. Rich, *Machine Learning, Automated Suspicion Algorithms, and the Fourth Amendment* 164 U. Pa. L. Rev. 871, 876 (2016) (referencing a definition of algorithms as "sequences of instructions to convert some input into an output").

48. 2005 Annual Report, Amazon.com (2005), http://library.corporate-ir.net/library/97/976/97664/items/193688/AMZN2005AnnualReport.pdf.

49. *See* Susskind, *supra* note 41, at 89 (stating that with software, the "rules are embedded in the system. Failure to comply is not an option."); Anupam Chander, *The Racist Algorithm?*, 115 Mich. L. Rev. (forthcoming, 2017); Citron, *supra* note 47, at 1253; Orna Rabinovich-Einy, *Technology's Impact: The Quest for a New Paradigm for Accountability in Mediation*, 11 Harv. Negot. L. Rev. 253, 264 (2006) [hereinafter Rabinovich-Einy, *Technology's Impact*].

50. Rabinovich-Einy, *Technology's Impact, supra* note 49, at 276–78; Anjanette H. Raymond & Scott J. Shackelford, *Technology, Ethics and Access to Justice: Should an Algorithm Be Deciding Your Case?*, 35 Mich. J. Int'l L. 485, 522 (2014) [hereinafter Raymond & Shackelford, *Technology, Ethics and Access to Justice*]; Zarsky, *Automated Prediction, supra* note 42, at 35.

51. Rule, *supra* note 45.

52. *See* discussion in Chapter 7 on courts and how software programs like A2J and ODR sites in courts can help translate legal rules and options to plain English tailored advice to disputants and potential disputants.

53. Trina Grillo, *The Mediation Alternative: Process Dangers for Women*, 100 YALE L.J. 1545, 1567–69 (1991); Zarsky, *Automated Prediction, supra* note 42, at 35.

54. Rabinovich-Einy, *Technology's Impact, supra* note 49, at 263–64.

55. *Id.* at 266, 273, 289–90.

56. Citron, *supra* note 47, at 1249; Zarsky, *The Trouble with Algorithmic Decisions, supra* note 42, at 121.

57. Zarsky, *The Trouble with Algorithmic Decisions, supra* note 42, at 126; Tal Z. Zarsky, *Understanding Discrimination in the Scored Society*, 89 WASH. L. REV. 1375 (2014).

58. Pasquale & Cashwell, *supra* note 42, at 38.

59. Citron, *supra* note 47, at 1261–62.

60. Citron, *supra* note 47; Zarsky, *The Trouble with Algorithmic Decisions, supra* note 42 at 123–30.

61. *What Is Chat Bot?*, WEBOPEDIA, http://www.webopedia.com/TERM/C/chat_bot.html.

62. *Microsoft "Deeply Sorry" for Racist and Sexist Tweets by AI Chatbot*, THE GUARDIAN (Mar. 26, 2016), http://www.theguardian.com/technology/2016/mar/26/microsoft-deeply-sorry-for-offensive-tweets-by-ai-chatbot.

63. Sarah Jeong, *How to Make a Bot that Isn't Racist*, MOTHERBOARD (Mar. 25, 2016), http://motherboard.vice.com/read/how-to-make-a-not-racist-bot.

64. "Computerized medical devices can fail in many ways, including through programming errors, incorrect calibration, and exposure to malicious intrusions, as well as physical or medical errors. Over a thousand recalls were issued on software-based medical devices from 1999 to 2005. Hundreds of deaths have been attributed to software failure in medical devices." Long Comment Regarding a Proposed Exemption Comment of a Coalition of Medical Device Researchers in Support of Proposed Class 27: Software—Networked Medical Devices, at 2, U.S. COPYRIGHT OFF. LIBR. CONGRESS, http://copyright.gov/1201/2015/comments-020615/InitialComments_longform_Coalition_of_Medical_Device_Researchers_Class27.pdf.

65. Zarsky, *The Trouble with Algorithmic Decisions, supra* note 42, at 122.

66. *Id.* at 130. *See also* Amy J. Schmitz, *Secret Consumer Scores and Segmentations: Separating "Haves" from "Have-Nots,"* 2014 MICH. ST. L. REV. 1411, 1469 (2014) (stating, in the consumer rating context, that auditing procedures need to be put in place to supervise use of data and to ensure the legitimacy of automated decision-making systems).

67. Citron, *supra* note 47, at 1309.

68. Rich, *supra* note 47, at 66.

69. Citron, *supra* note 47; Julia Angwin, *Make Algorithms Accountable*, N.Y. TIMES (Aug. 1, 2016), http://www.nytimes.com/2016/08/01/opinion/make-algorithms-accountable.html?_r=0

70. Citron, *supra* note 47; Kate Crawford & Jason Schultz, *Big Data and Due Process: Toward A Framework to Redress Predictive Privacy Harms*, 55 BC L. Rev. 93 (2014).

71. Anjanette H. Raymond & Scott J. Shackelford, *Jury Glasses: Wearable Technology and Its Role in Crowdsourcing Justice*, 17 CARDOZO J. CONFLICT RESOL. 115, 129 (2015); Zarsky, *The Trouble with Algorithmic Decisions, supra* note 42, at 120, 122. In many respects, this criticism is reminiscent of that of "litigation romanticists" against ADR enthusiasts in that the former tended to dismiss the problematic aspects of courts' operation while thoroughly criticizing ADR (*see* Carrie Menkel-Meadow, *Whose Dispute Is It Anyway?*, 83 GEO. L.J. 2663, 2669 (1995)).

72. RHODE, ACCESS TO JUSTICE, *supra* note 3, at 86. Indeed, the trade-off conception is so strong that it continues to color the discussion on ODR. *See* Raymond & Shackelford, *Technology, Ethics and Access to Justice, supra* note 50, at 487. The writing on ODR has also assumed the existence of a trade-off. JULIA HORNLE, CROSS-BORDER INTERNET DISPUTE RESOLUTION (2009) 17; ARNO R. LODDER & JOHN ZELEZNIKOW, ENHANCED DISPUTE RESOLUTION THROUGH THE USE OF INFORMATION TECHNOLOGY 21 (2010).

73. For a definition of fairness that builds on due process and general theories of procedural fairness, *see* HORNLE, *supra* note 72. We complement this approach by looking at the disparate effects of procedural arrangements on outcomes.

74. Orna Rabinovich-Einy, *Deconstructing Dispute Classifications: Avoiding the Shadow of the Law in Dispute System Design in Healthcare*, 12 Cardozo J. Disp. Resol. 55, 78–80 (2010).

75. *Id.*

76. Some readers may question the desirability of expanding the number of complaints that are redressed out of a fear of over-litigiousness. In this vein, Lawrence Friedman stated that "we cannot have a system that provides unlimited access to justice; the pyramid must remain a pyramid rather than become a square." *See* Friedman, *supra* note 3 (our view is different). We share Prof. Rhode's view that the focus should not be on over litigiousness, but rather on "inaccessible rights and remedies." Rhode, Access to Justice, *supra* note 3, at 5. Unlike Rhode, though, we look beyond courts and rights to nonlegal institutions and problems.

77. Felstiner et al., *supra* note 16, at 636.

78. Joseph Cox & Jason Koebler, *Facebook Decides Which Killings We're Allowed to See*, Motherboard (July 7, 2016), http://motherboard.vice.com/read/philando-castile-facebook-live; Kalev Leetaru, *Is the Internet Evolving Away from Freedom of Speech?*, Forbes (Jan. 15, 2016), http://www.forbes.com/sites/kalevleetaru/2016/01/15/is-the-internet-evolving-away-from-freedom-of-speech/.

79. Adrienne LaFrance, *Even the Editor of Facebook's Mood Study Thought It Was Creepy*, The Atlantic (June 28, 2014), http://www.theatlantic.com/technology/archive/2014/06/even-the-editor-of-facebooks-mood-study-thought-it-was-creepy/373649/; Galen Panger, *Reassessing the Facebook Experiment: Critical Thinking about the Validity of Big Data Research*, *in* Information, Communication & Society 1 (2015).

80. The Muse, *The Facebook Experiment: What It Means for You*, Forbes (Aug. 4, 2014), http://www.forbes.com/sites/dailymuse/2014/08/04/the-facebook-experiment-what-it-means-for-you/.

81. *See* Jonathan Zittrain, *Facebook Could Decide an Election without Anyone Ever Finding Out*, New Republic (June 1, 2014), https://newrepublic.com/article/117878/information-fiduciary-solution-facebook-digital-gerrymandering. Jonathan Zittrain discussed the possibility of digital gerrymandering by Facebook or Twitter, supporting the concept of these platforms as "information fiduciaries" as a potential constraint on their power.

82. *Id.*; Zeynep Tufekci, *Engineering the Public: Big Data, Surveillance and Computational Politics*, 19 First Monday (July 15, 2014), http://firstmonday.org/article/view/4901/4097 (describing the dangers of computational politics in the age of Big Data).

83. Peter Lee, *Learning from Tay's Introduction, Official Microsoft Blog*, Microsoft (Mar. 25, 2016), http://blogs.microsoft.com/blog/2016/03/25/learning-tays-introduction/#sm.0000fbizbacc7e7ay492gmco4gmct.

84. Jeong, *supra* note 63.

85. Genève Campbell, *Security Testing for Trolls*, Medium (Mar. 24, 2016), https://medium.com/@geneve/security-testing-for-trolls-a80784be8b01#.k9mx9qc6o.

86. Citron, *supra* note 47, at 1271–72 (revealing the failures of automated systems and the significance of human involvement in the decision-making process, especially in light of the "automation bias," which "effectively turns a computer program's suggested answer into a trusted final decision"); *id.* at 1303–04 (stating that "[a]utomation is more attractive where the risks associated with human bias outweigh that of automation bias. It is advantageous when an issue does not require the exercise of situation-specific discretion. Decisions best addressed with standards should not be automated"); Raymond & Shackelford, *Technology, Ethics and Access to Justice, supra* note 50, at 517.

87. Robert Klara, *How Big a Problem Is It for Google and Facebook That Consumers Don't Trust Them?*, *Advertising & Branding*, AdWeek (Jan. 21, 2016), http://www.adweek.com/news/advertising-branding/how-big-problem-it-google-and-facebook-consumers-don-t-trust-them-169108.

88. Amy J. Schmitz & Colin Rule, The New Handshake: Online Dispute Resolution and the Future of Consumer Protection 69 (forthcoming, on file with authors). *See also id.* at 78–79 (stating, "independent evaluatorsshould play a role in ensuring the fairness if these privately created processes"); Orly Lobel, *The Law of the Platform*, 101 Minn. L. Rev. (forthcoming, 2016) (discussing the need to require platforms to disclose data and assist in its analysis).

Chapter 3

1. The "sharing economy" is known by many other names, including the "new economy," "collaborative consumption," "access economy," "peer-to-peer (or P2P) economy," "cooperative economy," and "relationship economy," among others. *See* Heather Scheiwe Kulp & Amanda L. Kool, *You Help Me, He Helps You: Dispute Systems Design in the Sharing Economy*, 48 WASH. U. J. L. & POL'Y 179, 181 (2015).

2. "It is considered illegal to use the ARPANet for anything which is not in direct support of Government business . . . personal messages to other ARPANet subscribers (for example, to arrange a get-together or check and say a friendly hello) are generally not considered harmful . . . Sending electronic mail over the ARPANet for commercial profit or political purposes is both anti-social and illegal. By sending such messages, you can offend many people, and it is possible to get MIT in serious trouble with the Government agencies which manage the ARPANet." *See* Christopher C. Stacy, *Getting Started Computing at the AI Lab* 9 (Massachusetts Institute Of Technology Artificial Intelligence Laboratory, Working Paper No. 235, Sept. 7, 1982), https://www.academia.edu/1416892/Getting_Started_Computing_at_the_AI_Lab.

3. JOHN MARKOFF, WHAT THE DORMOUSE SAID: HOW THE 60'S COUNTERCULTURE SHAPED THE PERSONAL COMPUTER INDUSTRY 109 (2006).

4. Thomas Claburn, *Modria's Fairness Engine: Justice on Demand*, INFO. WEEK (Nov. 16, 2012), http://www.informationweek.com/cloud/platform-as-a-service/modrias-fairness-engine-justice-on-demand/d/d-id/1107435?.

5. Brad Templeton, *Reflections on the 25th Anniversary of Spam*, TEMPLETONS, http://www.templetons.com/brad/spam/spam25.html.

6. Brad Templeton, *The Insidious Evil of Spam*, TEMPLETONS, http://www.templetons.com/brad/spam/evil.html.

7. Brad Templeton, *Origin of the Term "Spam" to Mean Net Abuse*, TEMPLETONS, http://www.templetons.com/brad/spamterm.html.

8. SHANE GREENSTEIN, HOW THE INTERNET BECAME COMMERCIAL: INNOVATION, PRIVATIZATION, AND THE BIRTH OF A NEW NETWORK (2016).

9. *Green Card through the Diversity Immigrant Visa Program*, U.S CITIZENSHIP & IMMIGR. SERVICES (Feb. 14, 2014), http://www.uscis.gov/green-card/other-ways-get-green-card/green-card-through-diversity-immigration-visa-program/green-card-through-diversity-immigrant-visa-program.

10. Ray Everett-Church, *The Spam That Started It All*, WIRED (Apr. 13, 1999), http://www.wired.com/1999/04/the-spam-that-started-it-all/.

11. Philip Elmer-Dewitt, *Battle for the Soul of the Internet*, TIME MAG. (Mar. 18, 2005), http://content.time.com/time/magazine/article/0,9171,981132,00.html.

12. *Malware Definition*, TECHTERMS, http://techterms.com/definition/malware.

13. Brad Templeton, *Best Way to End Spam*, TEMPLETONS, http://www.templetons.com/brad/spam/endspam.html.

14. Robert Deis, *"Eternal Vigilance Is the Price of Liberty,"* THIS DAY IN QUOTES (2009), http://www.thisdayinquotes.com/2011/01/eternal-vigilance-is-price-of-liberty.html.

15. Robin Sidel et al., *Target Hit by Credit-Card Breach*, WALL ST. J. (Dec. 19, 2013), http://www.wsj.com/articles/SB10001424052702304773104579266743230242538.

16. Electronic Fund Transfer Act, 15 U.S.C. §§ 1693–1693r (2012).

17. *See What Is a Chargeback, Chargeback Management Guidelines for Visa Merchants* 5, VISA (2015), https://usa.visa.com/dam/VCOM/download/merchants/chargeback-management-guidelines-for-visa-merchants.pdf.

18. Arnold S. Rosenberg, *Better than Cash? Global Proliferation of Payment Cards and Consumer Protection Policy*, 44 COLUM. J. TRANSNAT'L L. 520, 537 (2006).

19. *See User Agreement for PayPal Services* ¶ 7, PAYPAL, https://www.paypal.com/il/webapps/mpp/ua/useragreement-full.

20. Internet communication is creating a growth in conflicts because of its "borderless, ubiquitous nature, the difficulty of establishing a user's location and the fact that it allows direct, multimedia communications and transactions between individuals on a global basis." JULIA HORNLE, CROSS-BORDER INTERNET DISPUTE RESOLUTION 25 (2009).

21. Raouf Ben Aissa, *Forget Bitcoin—What Is Blockchain and Why Should You Care?*, LINKEDIN (Apr. 18, 2016), https://www.linkedin.com/pulse/forget-bitcoin-what-blockchain-why-should-you-care-source-ben-aissa (quoting Mike Gault, *Forget Bitcoin—What Is the Blockchain and Why Should You Care?*, RE/CODE (July 5, 2015)).

22. A. Michael Froomkin, *Wrong Turn in Cyberspace: Using ICANN to Route Around the APA and the Constitution*, 50 DUKE L.J. 17, 37–38 (2000) [hereinafter Froomkin, *Wrong Turn in Cyberspace*].

23. *The Internet in 1990: Domain Registration, E-mail and Networks*, IAPS, http://www.iaps.com/internet-history-october-1990.html#email.

24. *History of gTLD Domain Name Growth*, ZOOKNIC, http://www.zooknic.com/Domains/counts.html.

25. "Domain Name Industry Brief," https://www.verisign.com/en_US/innovation/dnib/index.xhtml.

26. A form of cybersquatting. For a definition of "cybersquatting," *see* Tenesa S. Scaturro, *The Anticybersquatting Consumer Protection Act and the Uniform Domain Name Dispute Resolution Policy, The First Decade: Looking Back and Adapting Forward*, 11 NEV. L.J. 877, 880 (2011).

27. Michal Koščík, *"Sucks Cases" in Wipo Domain Name Decisions*, 1 MASARYK U. J. L. & TECH. 229, 230–32 (2007).

28. *See Official Worldwide Scrabble Home Page*, SCRABBLE.COM, http://www.scrabble.com/.

29. *See Consensus Policy ¶ 5(b)(iv)*, ICANN (2016), http://www.icann.org/en/resources/registrars/consensus-policies.

30. *Consensus Policy*, ICANN (2016), http://www.icann.org/en/resources/registrars/consensus-policies.

31. Jude A. Thomas, *Fifteen Years of Fame: The Declining Relevance of Domain Names in the Enduring Conflict between Trademark and Free Speech Rights*, 11 J. MARSHALL REV. INTELL. PROP. L. 1, 24 (2011).

32. *See generally Uniform Domain Name Dispute Resolution Policy*, ICANN (2016), http://www.icann.org/en/help/dndr/udrp/policy [hereinafter UDRP Rules]; Thomas, *supra* note 31, at 22.

33. UDRP Rules, *supra* note 32, at ¶ 4(b)(iv).

34. Doug Isenberg, *Why Trademark Owners Need Not Fret over Every Domain Name That "Sucks*,*"* GIGALAW (11, 2015), http://www.gigalaw.com/2015/05/11/why-trademark-owners-need-not-fret-over-a-domain-name-that-sucks/.

35. *See* discussion of dispute resolution triangle in Chapter 1.

36. Michael Geist, *Fair.com?: An Examination of the Allegations of Systemic Unfairness in the ICANN UDRP*, 27 BROOK. J. INT'L L. 903 (2002).

37. *Archived Statistical Summary of Proceedings under Uniform Domain Name Dispute Resolution Policy*, ICANN (May 10, 2004), http://archive.icann.org/en/udrp/proceedings-stat.htm (UDRP statistics up to 2004). For French provider statistics referring also to general statistics, *see UDRP Statistics 2012: One Year of French Touch*, SKETCHLEX INFOGRAPHIES JURIDIQUES (Feb. 3, 2013), http://sketchlex.com/03/02/2013/infographies/udrp-statistics-2012-year-of-french-touch/.

38. *Geist, supra* note 36, at 911.

39. Thomas, *supra* note 31, at 23 (citing a WIPO report according to which in 2008 85 percent of complaints were decided in favor of the complainant); A. Michael Froomkin, *ICANN'S "Uniform Dispute Resolution Policy"—Causes and (Partial) Cures*, 67 BROOK. L. REV. 605, 718 (2002) [hereinafter Froomkin, *ICANN'S UDRP*]; Froomkin, *Wrong Turn in Cyberspace*, *supra* note 22, at 99–100 (noting that the UDRP does not require actual notice, as well as the short time-frame for respondents to respond).

40. Thomas, *supra* note 31, at 23.

41. For an analysis of the UDRP system and its critiques, *see* Pablo Cortés, Online Dispute Resolution for Consumers in the European Union 69–70, 114–35 (2010).

42. *Alibaba Presentation Notes*, International Conference on Online Dispute Resolution (Beijing, China, September 19-20, 2016) [on file with authors].

43. *Id.*

44. Melanie Lee, *Alibaba Allows Users to Play Judge in E-Commerce Disputes*, Alizila (Jan. 2, 2014), http://www2.alizila.com/alibaba-allows-users-play-judge-e-commerce-disputes.

45. *Alibaba Presentation Notes, supra* note 42.

46. Neil Gough, *Snooping in the Bathroom to Assess Credit Risk in China*, N.Y. Times (Oct. 10, 2016), http://www.nytimes.com/2016/10/11/business/international/snooping-in-the-bathroom-to-assess-credit-risk-in-china.html?ref=business&_r=1.

47. Danielle Keats Citron and Frank Pasquale, *The Scored Society: Due Process for Automated Predictions*, 89 Wash. L. Rev. 1 (2014). For the implications of scoring on discrimination, *see* Tal Z. Zarsky, *Understanding Discrimination in the Scored Society*, 89 Wash. L. Rev. 1375 (2014).

48. *Alibaba Presentation Notes, supra* note 42.

49. Gough, *supra* note 46.

50. *Alibaba Presentation Notes, supra* note 42.

51. *Id*; email from Alibaba Representative to Angela Zhu (October 24, 2016) (on file with authors).

52. *Alibaba Presentation Notes, supra* note 42.

53. Justin Fox, *The Rise of the 1099 Economy*, Bloomberg View (Dec. 11, 2015), http://www.bloombergview.com/articles/2015-12-11/the-gig-economy-is-showing-up-in-irs-s-1099-forms.

54. "This sharing economy is based on people coming together to create their own markets (Airbnb), their own products (Etsy) and their own currency (TimeBanks). It relies on shared needs, trust and the belief that the group is stronger than the individual." Sara Horowitz, *Occupy Big Business: The Sharing Economy's Quiet Revolution*, The Atlantic (Dec. 6, 2011), http://www.theatlantic.com/business/archive/2011/12/occupy-big-business-the-sharing-economys-quiet-revolution/249582/. "[T]his whole marketplace is based on trust." Russ Roberts, *Nathan Blecharczyk on Airbnb and the Sharing Economy*, EconTalk–Libr. Econ. & Liberty (Sept. 1, 2014), http://www.econtalk.org/archives/2014/09/nathan_blecharc.html (quoting Nathan Blecharczyk, co-founder and chief technology officer of Airbnb).

55. "Cities can't screen as well as technologies can screen." Tom Slee, *Sharing and Caring*, Jacobin (Jan. 24, 2014), https://www.jacobinmag.com/2014/01/sharing-and-caring (quoting Brian Chesky, CEO of Airbnb).

56. Some of the labels are most relevant to this chapter on e-commerce, and some, because of the nature of what is being bought and sold, will be explored later in Chapter 6. Uber, for example, raises questions about the status of drivers and whether they are employees or independent contractors. The "1099 economy" label refers to a tax form that independent contractors receive, one different from what employees receive. Independent contractors also do not receive health and other benefits.

57. Email from Colin Rule, to Ethan Katsh (July 24, 2015) (on file with authors).

58. *Id.*

59. *How Design Thinking Transformed Airbnb from a Failing Startup to a Billion Dollar Business*, First Round Rev., http://firstround.com/review/How-design-thinking-transformed-Airbnb-from-failing-startup-to-billion-dollar-business/.

60. *Airbnb Host Guarantee*, Airbnb, https://www.airbnb.com/guarantee.

61. Tom Slee, What's Yours Is Mine 108 (2015).

62. Benjamin G. Edelman et al., *Digital Discrimination: The Case of Airbnb* (Harvard Business Sch. NOM Unit Working Paper No. 14-054, 2014).

63. Slee, *supra* note 61, at 61.

64. Laura W. Murphy, *Airbnb's Work to Fight Discrimination and Build Inclusion: A Report Submitted to Airbnb*, AIRBNB (Sept. 8, 2016), http://blog.airbnb.com/wp-content/uploads/2016/09/REPORT_Airbnbs-Work-to-Fight-Discrimination-and-Build-Inclusion.pdf?3c10be.

65. Tom Gardner, *To Read, or Not to Read … The Terms and Conditions: PayPal Agreement Is Longer than Hamlet, While iTunes Beats Macbeth*, DAILY MAIL (Mar. 22, 2012), http://www.dailymail.co.uk/news/article-2118688/PayPal-agreement-longer-Hamlet-iTunes-beats-Macbeth.html.

66. *Airbnb Terms of Service*, AIRBNB (Mar. 29, 2016), https://www.airbnb.com/terms.

67. *Id.*

68. *What Is the Resolution Center?*, *Airbnb Help Center*, AIRBNB, https://www.airbnb.com/help/article/435/what-happens-when-i-involve-airbnb-in-my-resolution-center-request.

69. *Host Protection Insurance*, AIRBNB, https://www.airbnb.com/host-protection-insurance.

70. Colin Rule & Chittu Narjaran, *Leveraging the Wisdom of the Crowds: The eBay Community Court and the Future of Online Dispute Resolution* at 5, AC RESOL. (Winter 2010).

71. HAZEL GENN ET AL., REGULATING DISPUTE RESOLUTION: ADR AND ACCESS TO JUSTICE AT THE CROSSROADS 437, n.113 (Felix Steffek & Hannes Unberath eds., 2013).

72. Julie Bort, *Airbnb Banned from Condo Complex after Guest Caused $10,000 of Damage*, BUS. INSIDER (Oct. 9, 2014), http://www.businessinsider.com/airbnb-guest-caused-10000-of-damage-2014-10.

73. Colin Rule, *Quantifying the Economic Benefits of Effective Redress: Large E-Commerce Data Sets and the Cost-Benefit Case for Investing in Dispute Resolution*, 34 U. ARK. LITTLE ROCK L. REV. 767, 775 (2012).

74. Russ Juskalian, *Bosch's Survival Plan*, MIT TECH. REV. (June 21, 2016), https://www.technologyreview.com/s/601502/boschs-survival-plan/.

75. *Id.*

76. Inessa Love, *Settling Out of Court: How Effective Is Alternative Dispute Resolution?*, THE WORLD BANK GROUP at 2 (Note. No. 329, Oct. 2011), http://siteresources.worldbank.org/FINANCIALSECTOR/Resources/282044-1307652042357/VP329-Setting-out-of-court.pdf.

77. Rule, *supra* note 73.

78. AMY J. SCHMITZ & COLIN RULE, THE NEW HANDSHAKE: ONLINE DISPUTE RESOLUTION AND THE FUTURE OF CONSUMER PROTECTION 25 (forthcoming, on file with authors).

79. *Id.*

80. B. TRAVEN, THE NIGHT VISITOR AND OTHER STORIES (American Century Series ed. 1966).

81. Kathy Rebello, *Inside Microsoft: The Untold Story of How the Internet Forced Bill Gates to Reverse Course*, BLOOMBERG (July 15, 1996), http://www.bloomberg.com/news/articles/1996-07-14/inside-microsoft.

82. *PayPal Global—All Countries and Markets*, PAYPAL, https://www.paypal.com/webapps/mpp/country-worldwide.

83. "When selling internationally, read our international trading policy. Although certain items may be legal to sell in your country, they might be illegal elsewhere." *Prohibited and Restricted Items—Overview*, EBAY, http://pages.ebay.com/help/policies/items-ov.html.

84. Julian Dibbell, *On the Nature of the Intangible: A Dialogue*, PLAY MONEY (Oct. 17, 2003), http://www.juliandibbell.com/playmoney/2003_10_01_playmoney_archive.html.

85. *See* Directive on Consumer ADR, 2013 O.J. (L 165/63), EUR. COMMISSION, http://eur-lex.europa.eu/LexUriServ/LexUriServ.do?uri=OJ:L:2013:165:0063:0079:EN:PDF; Regulation on Consumer ODR, 2013 O.J. (L 165/1), EUR. COMMISSION, http://eur-lex.europa.eu/LexUriServ/LexUriServ.do?uri=OJ:L:2013:165:0001:0012:EN:PDF [hereinafter European ADR/ODR].

86. *UNCITRAL Arbitration Rules*, U.N. (Jan. 10, 2016), http://www.uncitral.org/uncitral/en/uncitral_texts/arbitration/2010Arbitration_rules.html.

87. European ADR/ODR, *supra* note 85.

88. *UNCITRAL Arbitration Rule (as revised in 2010)* (2011), https://www.uncitral.org/pdf/english/texts/arbitration/arb-rules-revised/arb-rules-revised-2010-e.pdf.

89. Leslie Bailey, *The Enforceability of Pre-Dispute Arbitration Clauses: Are There Any Limits Left?*, N.D. CAL. 2014 JUD. CONF. 2014, http://events.whitecase.com/ndca-2014/materials/ Bailey-Enforceability-of-Pre-Dispute-Arbitration-Clauses.pdf.

90. Amy J. Schmitz, *American Exceptionalism in Consumer Arbitration*, 10 LOY. U. CHICAGO INT'L L. REV. 81, 95–98 (2016).

91. *Airbnb Terms of Service, supra* note 66.

92. Few consumers actually read the terms of these online agreements. *See* SCHMITZ & RULE, *supra* note 78, at 11.

93. Amy J. Schmitz, *Secret Consumer Scores and Segmentations: Separating "Haves" from "Have-Nots,"* 2014 MICH. ST. L. REV. 1411 (2014).

Chapter 4

1. OPENNOTES, http://www.opennotes.org/.

2. Michael Hiltzik, *Anthem Is Warning Consumers about Its Huge Data Breach. Here's a Translation*, L.A. TIMES (Mar. 6, 2015), http://www.latimes.com/business/la-fi-mh-anthem-is-warning-consumers-20150306-column.html.

3. Niam Yaraghi & Joshua Bleiberg, *The Anthem Hack Shows There Is No Such Thing as Privacy in the Health Care Industry*, BROOKINGS (Feb. 12, 2015), http://www.brookings.edu/blogs/ techtank/posts/2015/02/12-anthem-hack-health-privacy. For a view that it would not have helped if Anthem had encrypted the files, *see* Ken Westin, *Encryption Wouldn't Have Stopped Anthem's Data Breach*, TECH. REV. (Feb. 10, 2015), https://www.technologyreview.com/s/ 535111/encryption-wouldnt-have-stopped-anthems-data-breach/.

4. Robert Lowes, *Physician's Stolen Laptop Leads to $1.5 Million Settlement*, MEDSCAPE (Sept. 21, 2012), http://www.medscape.com/viewarticle/771348; Jack Newsham, *Beth Israel Fined $100,000 for Patient Data Breach*, BOS. GLOBE (Nov. 21, 2014), https://www. bostonglobe.com/business/2014/11/21/beth-israel-fined-for-patient-data-breach/ W8LT4a0gN6NMT93KtEDq7H/story.html.

5. Barbara Starfield, *Is US Health Really the Best in the World?*, 284 JAMA 483, 484 (2000).

6. John T. James, *A New, Evidence-Based Estimate of Patient Harms Associated with Hospital Care*, 9 J. PATIENT SAFETY 122 (2013).

7. Abigail Zuger, *The Importance of Getting Sick in the Right Place*, N.Y. TIMES (May 11, 2015), http://well.blogs.nytimes.com/2015/05/11/the-importance-of-getting-sick-in-the-right-place/?ref=health&_r=1&mtrref=undefined&gwh=62F88DB5546D6D2DB1F99A86194F 0DF0&gwt=pay.

8. *See* Charles Ornstein, *Small Violations of Medical Privacy Can Hurt Patients and Erode Trust*, NPR (Dec. 10, 2015), http://www.npr.org/sections/health-shots/2015/12/10/ 459091273/small-violations-of-medical-privacy-can-hurt-patients-and-corrode-trust?utm_ campaign=KHN%3A+First+Edition&utm_source=hs_email&utm_medium=email&utm_ content=24472997&_hsenc=p2ANqtz-86-o8122DCjwGIYWGNo9oUCDGf8FhXX7 8GajqNnvWlcYa1VkCvZYFiKyXHt2V9PSokJcHGTa0KtQNQZCJp38NPxkOoaw&_ hsmi=24472997.

9. DAVE DEBRONKART ET AL., LET PATIENTS HELP!: A PATIENT ENGAGEMENT HANDBOOK (2013); Suzanne Allard Levingston, *Does Your Doctor Listen When You Talk?*, WASH. POST (Nov. 30, 2015), https://www.washingtonpost.com/national/health-science/does-your-doctor-listen-when-you-talk/2015/11/30/a148a88a-6ad2-11e5-b31c-d80d62b53e28_ story.html. AHRQ defines patient engagement as "a set of behaviors by patients, family members, and health professionals and a set of organizational policies and procedures that foster both the inclusion of patients and family members as active members of the health care team and collaborative partnerships with providers and provider organizations." Maureen Maurer et al., *Guide to Patient and Family Engagement: Environmental Scan Report*, AHRQ (AHRQ Pub. No. 12-0042-EF, May 2012), http://www.ahrq.gov/sites/default/files/ publications/files/ptfamilyscan.pdf.

10. Fazal Khan, *The "Uberization" of Healthcare: The Forthcoming Legal Storm over Mobile Health Technology's Impact on the Medical Profession,* 26 Health Matrix 123 (2016).

11. *Transcript of Clinton's 1997 State of the Union,* CNN (Jan. 31, 2005), http://www.cnn.com/ 2005/ALLPOLITICS/01/31/sotu.clinton1997.3/index.html.

12. *George W. Bush: Address Before a Joint Session of the Congress on the State of the Union,* Am. Presidency Project (Feb. 2, 2005), http://www.presidency.ucsb.edu/ws/index. php?pid=58746.

13. *President Bush's State of the Union Address,* Wash. Post (Jan. 31, 2006), http://www. washingtonpost.com/wp-dyn/content/article/2006/01/31/AR2006013101468.html.

14. *Remarks of President Barack Obama—Address to Joint Session of Congress,* The White House (Feb. 24, 2009), https://www.whitehouse.gov/the-press-office/remarks-president-barack-obama-address-joint-session-congress.

15. American Recovery and Reinvestment Act of 2009, Pub. L. No. 111–5, 123 Stat. 115 (2009).

16. Priyanka Dayal McCluskey, *New $1.2b Partners Computer System Brings Prescription for Frustration,* Bos. Globe (May 17, 2016), https://www.bostonglobe.com/business/ 2016/05/16/partners-healthcare-new-computer-challenges-some-doctors-nurses/ 1I4QsWGjCJ97xFmUbcDbaJ/story.html.

17. John Palfrey and Urs Gasser, Interop 194 (2012).

18. David Blumenthal, *Launching HITECH,* 362 New Eng. J. Med. 382, 385 (2010), http:// www.nejm.org/doi/pdf/10.1056/NEJMp0912825.

19. *Catalyze Breakthroughs for National Priorities,* The White House, http://www.whitehouse. gov/issues/economy/innovation/breakthroughs. *See also Benefits of Electronic Health Records (EHRs),* HealthIT (July 30, 2015), https://www.healthit.gov/providers-professionals/ benefits-electronic-health-records-ehrs.

20. http://www.doctorsaccess.com/emr-electronic-health-record.html

21. Without HIT "neither individual physicians nor health care institutions can perform at their best or deliver the highest-quality care, any more than an Olympian could excel with a failing heart. . . . The provisions of the HITECH Act are best understood not as investments in technology per se but as efforts to improve the health of Americans and the performance of their health care system." Blumenthal, *supra* note 18.

22. Rebeccca Robins, *Insurers Want to Nudge You to Better Health. So They're Data Mining Your Shopping Lists,* STAT News (Dec. 15, 2015), https://www.statnews.com/2015/12/15/ insurance-big-data/.

23. Laura Landro, *Health-Care Providers Want Patients to Read Medical Records, Spot Errors,* Wall St. J. (June 9, 2014), http://www.wsj.com/articles/health-care-providers-want-patients-to-read-medical-records-spot-errors-1402354902#livefyre-comment.

24. *Top Health Industry Issues of 2016: Thriving in the New Health Economy,* PWC (Dec. 2015), https://www.pwc.com/us/en/health-industries/top-health-industry-issues/assets/2016-us-hri-top-issues.pdf.

25. *Id.*

26. *See* Robert Weisman, *Patients Push Back,* Bos. Globe, Dec. 4, 2015, at C1; *see also* Nicolas Terry, Health Affairs Blog, http://healthaffairs.org/blog/author/nterry/.

27. Ashley Gold, *Despite FDA Moves, Push Continues for Congress to Act on Mobile Health,* Politico (Feb. 11, 2015), http://www.politico.com/story/2015/02/fda-digital-health-companies-115113.

28. Marla Durben Hirsch, *ABA 15: Telemedicine Movement Gaining Steam,* FierceHealthcare (Dec. 8, 2015) (quoting Nathaniel Lacktman), http://www.fierceemr.com/story/ aba-15-telemedicine-movement-gaining-steam/2015-12-08?utm_medium=nl&utm_ source=internal&mkt_tok=3RkMMJWWfF9wsRonvKnMdO%252FhmjTEU5z17ukrUK KwgIkz2EFye%252BLIHETpodcMTsNrMbDYDBceEJhqyQJxPr3HJdQN18R7RhHnDg %253D%253D [hereinafter Durben Hirsch, *ABA 15*].

29. Greg Slabodkin, *App for Kids to ID Asthma Attack Triggers,* Health Data Mgmt. (Dec. 7, 2015), http://www.healthdatamanagement.com/news/app-for-kids-to-id-asthma-attack-triggers.

30. LuAnn E. White et al., *Technology Meets Healthcare: Distance Learning and Telehealth*, 3 OCHSNER J. 22 (2001).

31. Iowa and Minnesota allow "telemed" abortions. Women confer with a doctor through a video connection and can then be prescribed two drugs, mifepristone and misoprostol, which when taken in sequence induce an abortion. Women who opt for a medication abortion can be no more than nine weeks into their pregnancy. A 2011 study published in *Obstetrics & Gynecology*, compared the results for patients who received medication abortions telemedically in Iowa versus those who were in the room with the doctor. The results were almost identical: 99 percent of telemedicine patients had a successful abortion compared with 97 percent of those who were face to face with the doctor. Daniel Grossman et al., *Effectiveness and Acceptability of Medical Abortion Provided through Telemedicine*, 118 OBSTETRICS & GYNECOLOGY 296 (2011).

32. *OUR OPINION: Need to Keep Telemedicine Strong for State is Real*, DAILY J. (Feb. 9, 2016), http://djournal.com/opinion/our-opinion-need-to-keep-telemedicine-strong-for-state-is-real/.

33. Durben Hirsch, *ABA 15, supra* note 28 (quoting Natasa Sokolovich, Executive Director of Telemedicine at UPMC).

34. Heal, *Heal—Doctor House Calls for Adults and Kids, App Store*, iTUNES, https://itunes.apple.com/us/app/heal-doctor-house-calls-for/id961252579?mt=8.

35. Pager, Inc., *Pager—Talk with Doctors and Nurses Immediately for Urgent Care Needs, App Store*, iTUNES, https://itunes.apple.com/us/app/pager-talk-board-certified/id864058356?mt=8.

36. Tim Moynihan, *Google Takes on the Challenge of Making Robot Surgery Safer*, WIRED (Mar. 30, 2015), http://www.wired.com/2015/03/google-robot-surgery/.

37. John Markoff, *As Aging Population Grows, So Do Robotic Health Aides*, N.Y. TIMES (Dec. 4, 2015), http://www.nytimes.com/2015/12/08/science/as-aging-population-grows-so-do-robotic-health-aides.html.

38. K. G. Fulda & K. Lykens, *Ethical Issues in Predictive Genetic Testing: A Public Health Perspective*, 32 J. MED. ETHICS 143 (2006).

39. Tal Zarsky, "Correlation vs. Causation in Health-Related Big Data Analysis: The Role of Reason and Regulation" (2016) (on file with the authors).

40. Latanya Sweeney, *Policy and Law: Identifiability of De-identified Data*, LATANYA SWEENEY (2009), http://latanyasweeney.org/work/identifiability.html.

41. Greg Slabodkin, *Release of De-Identified Health Data Poses Elevated Risk*, HEALTH DATA MGMT. (Dec. 14, 2015), http://www.healthdatamanagement.com/news/release-of-de-identified-health-data-poses-elevated-risk.

42. I. Glenn Cohen, Ruben Amarasingham, Anand Shah, Bin Xie and Bernard Lo, *The Legal And Ethical Concerns That Arise From Using Complex Predictive Analytics In Health Care*, 33 HEALTH AFFAIRS 1139 (2014) http://content.healthaffairs.org/content/33/7/1139.

43. Donald Voltz, *Ebola Pushing EHRs in New Direction*, HIT CONSULTANT (Oct. 20, 2014), http://hitconsultant.net/2014/10/20/ebola-pushing-ehrs-new-direction/?lang=fr.

44. Among the data-quality elements that make the content of the EHR complex are the following from *HIM Principles in Health Information Exchange*, developed by the American Health Information Management Association.

   - Data Accuracy: Data are the correct values and are valid.
   - Data Accessibility: Data items should be easily obtainable and legal to collect.
   - Data Comprehensiveness: All required data items are included. Ensure that the entire scope of the data is collected and document intentional limitations.
   - Data Consistency: The value of the data should be reliable and the same across applications.
   - Data Currency: The data should be up-to-date. A datum value is up-to-date if it is current for a specific point in time. It is outdated if it was current at some preceding time yet incorrect at a later time.
   - Data Definition: Clear definitions should be provided so that current and future data users will know what the data mean. Each data element should have clear meaning and acceptable values.

- Data Granularity: The attributes and values of data should be defined at the correct level of detail.
- Data Precision: Data values should be just large enough to support the application or process.
- Data Relevancy: The data are meaningful to the performance of the process or application for which they are collected.
- Data Timeliness: Timeliness is determined by how the data are being used and their context.

Ahima e-HIM Workgroup on HIM in Health Information Exchange, *HIM Principles in Health Information Exchange*, app. *Data Quality Attributes Grid*, AHIMA (2007), http://www.umass.edu/eei/2009Workshop/pdfs/HIM%20Principles%20in%20Health%20Information%20Exchange.pdf.

45. Krzysztof Zielinski et al., Information Technology Solutions for Healthcare 143 (1st ed. 2006).
46. *Id.*
47. Keith L. Klein, *Electronic Medical Records May Cast Physicians in Unfavorable Light During Lawsuits*, Doctors Company, http://www.thedoctors.com/KnowledgeCenter/PatientSafety/articles/Electronic-Medical-Records-May-Cast-Physicians-in-Unfavorable-Light-During-Lawsuits.
48. Arthur Allen, *Electronic Record Errors Growing Issue in Lawsuits*, Politico (May 4, 2015), http://www.politico.com/story/2015/05/electronic-record-errors-growing-issue-in-lawsuits-117591.
49. Kim C. Stanger, *Unintended Consequences: Liability for Electronic Health Records*, Mont. Rural Healthcare PIN (July 1, 2014), http://www.mtpin.org/docs/Champions/2014/EHRLiability_Stanger.pdf.
50. Ross Koppel & David Kreda, *Health Care Information Technology Vendors' "Hold Harmless" Clause*, 301 JAMA 1276, 1276 (2009).
51. Office of the National Coordinator for Health Information Technology, *EHR Contracts Untangled: Selecting Wisely, Negotiating Terms, and Understanding The Fine Print* (Sept. 2016) https://www.healthit.gov/sites/default/files/EHR_Contracts_Untangled.pdf.
52. Sharona Hoffman & Andy Podgurski, *Finding a Cure: The Case for Regulation for Oversight of Electronic Health Record Systems*, 22 Harv. J. L. & Tech. 103, 120 (2008).
53. Joan S. Ash et al., *The Extent and Importance of Unintended Consequences Related to Computerized Provider Order Entry*, 14 J. Am. Med. Informatics Ass'n 415, 423 (2007).
54. Peter J. Kaboli et al., *Assessing the Accuracy of Computerized Medication Histories*, 10 Am. J. Managed Care 872 (2004); Sunil Kripalani et al., *Promoting Effective Transitions of Care at Hospital Discharge: A Review of Key Issues for Hospitalists*, 2 J. Hosp. Med. 314 (2007); Maria Staroselsky et al., *An Effort to Improve Electronic Health Record Medication List Accuracy between Visits: Patients' and Physicians' Response*, 77 Int'l J. Med. Informatics 153 (2008); P. Varkey et al., *Improving Medication Reconciliation in the Outpatient Setting*, 33 Joint Commission J. Quality & Patient Safety 286 (2007).
55. Saul N. Weingart et al., *Medication Reconciliation in Ambulatory Oncology*, 33 Joint Commission J. Quality & Patient Safety 750 (2007).
56. P. Varkey et al., *supra* note 54.
57. K. S. Chan et al., *Review: Electronic Health Records and the Reliability and Validity of Quality Measures: A Review of the Literature*, 67 Med. Care Res. & Rev. 503 (2010).
58. Sharon Fisher, *How Complexity Makes Software Bad*, Laserfiche (Oct. 19, 2015), http://quibb.com/links/how-complexity-makes-software-bad/view.
59. David J. Brailer, *They're Your Vital Signs, Not Your Medical Records*, Wall St. J. (Apr. 30, 2015), http://www.wsj.com/articles/theyre-your-vital-signs-not-your-medical-records-1430436971.
60. Eta S. Berner & Mark L. Graber, *Overconfidence as a Cause of Diagnostic Error in Medicine*, 121 A. J. Med. S2, S6 (2008).

61. Andrew Rosenblum, *Your Doctor Doesn't Want to Hear about Your Fitness-Tracker Data*, MIT TECH. REV. (Nov. 24, 2015), https://www.technologyreview.com/s/543716/your-doctor-doesnt-want-to-hear-about-your-fitness-tracker-data/.

62. *Fitness Trackers Don't Count Calories Well, Study Finds* (Mar. 21, 2016), http://www.nbcnews.com/health/diet-fitness/fitness-trackers-don-t-count-calories-well-study-finds-n542826.

63. *Update from 23andMe*, 23ANDMEBLOG (June 8, 2010), http://blog.23andme.com/23andme-and-you/update-from-23andme/.

64. Ed Jones, *Correction Key Privacy/Security Principle of Meaningful Use 2011 Objectives*, HIPAA. COM (June 26, 2009), https://www.hipaa.com/correction-key-privacysecurity-principle-of-meaningful-use-2011-objectives/.

65. *Overview of Health Reform*, THE WHITE HOUSE, https://www.whitehouse.gov/health-care-meeting/proposal/whatsnew/overview.

66. Email from Dave deBronkart to Ethan Katsh (October 26, 2016).

67. *Background Issues on Data Quality*, CONNECTING HEALTH COMMON FRAMEWORK 2 (2006), http://bok.ahima.org/PdfView?oid=63654.

68. Health Information Technology for Economic and Clinical Health Act 2009, Pub. L. 111-5, Div. A, Title XIII, Div. B, Title IV, 123 Stat. 226, 467 (2009).

69. *CMS Finalizes Requirements for the Medicaid Electronic Health Records (EHR) Incentive Program*, CMS.GOV (July 16, 2010), https://www.cms.gov/Newsroom/MediaReleaseDatabase/Fact-sheets/2010-Fact-sheets-items/2010-07-162.html.

70. *Welcome to the Medicare & Medicaid EHR Incentive Program Registration & Attestation System*, EHR INCENTIVE PROGRAM, https://ehrincentives.cms.gov/hitech/login.action.

71. *Meaningful Use*, CDC, http://www.cdc.gov/ehrmeaningfuluse/.

72. *Medicare and Medicaid Programs; Electronic Health Record Incentive Program—Stage 3 and Modifications to Meaningful Use in 2015 through 2017*, FED. REG. (Oct. 16, 2015), https://www.federalregister.gov/articles/2015/10/16/2015-25595/medicare-and-medicaid-programs-electronic-health-record-incentive-program-stage-3-and-modifications.

73. Natasha Singer, *When a Health Plan Knows How You Shop*, NY TIMES, (June 28, 2014).

74. DEBRONKART ET AL., *supra* note 9.

75. Erin A. Mackay, *Patients, Consumers, and Caregivers: The Original Data Stewards*, 3 EGEMs 2 (Mar. 23, 2015), http://repository.edm-forum.org/cgi/viewcontent.cgi?article=1173&context=egems.

76. Koppel & Kreda, *supra* note 50, at 1278 ("[I]n many cases, HIT problems may be caused not by clinicians but by poor software."); Sharona Hoffman & Andy Podgurski, *E-Health Hazards: Provider Liability and Electronic Health Record Systems*, 24 BERKELEY TECH. L.J. 1523 (2009); Marla Durben Hirsch, *5 Unique EHR Contract Stipulations*, FIERCEHEALTHCARE (June 17, 2014), http://www.fierceemr.com/story/5-unique-ehr-contract-stipulations/2014-06-17; Ronald L. Scott, *IT Vendor and Institutional Liability for Electronic Health Records*, U. HOUS. L. CTR. (Aug. 2006), https://www.law.uh.edu/healthlaw/perspectives/2006/(RS)ITVendorLiab.pdf.

77. Anita Soni, *Statistical Brief #331: Top 10 Most Costly Conditions Among Men and Women, 2008: Estimates for the U.S. Civilian Noninstitutionalized Adult Population, Age 18 and Older*, AGENCY HEALTHCARE RES. & QUALITY (July 2011), http://meps.ahrq.gov/mepsweb/data_files/publications/st331/stat331.shtml.

78. *Don't Pay for Mistake, Check your Medical Bills Carefully*, CONSUMERREPORTS (May 14, 2009), http://www.consumerreports.org/cro/news/2009/05/don-t-pay-for-mistakes-check-your-medical-bills-carefully/index.htm; *see* Elisabeth Rosenthal, *The Medical Bill Mystery*, N.Y. TIMES (May 2, 2015), http://www.nytimes.com/2015/05/03/sunday-review/the-medical-bill-mystery.html?_r=0, citing a study showing an error rate of 90 percent.

79. *Medical Billing Errors: What Can Go Wrong? What Can You Do?*, CLEV. PLAIN DEALER (June 24, 2012), http://www.cleveland.com/healthfit/index.ssf/2012/06/medical_billing_errors_what_ca.html.

80. *How It Works*, COPATIENT, https://www.copatient.com/how-it-works/ (explaining how medical and hospital bill correction and reduction works).

81. Jay Hancock, *Radical Approach to Huge Hospital Bills: Set Your Own Price*, KHN (May 13, 2015), http://khn.org/news/radical-approach-to-huge-hospital-bills-set-your-own-price/?utm_campaign=KHN%3A+First+Edition&utm_source=hs_email&utm_medium=email&utm_content=17652308&_hsenc=p2ANqtz-8e2vqhC7vFTJYcrLMJ9g17L1bEo0Qbaa1qxx2CZqR VSOoxYEgBK76FQPXH4qsFZzpPCFCaJ7ttD0jq_BciDgJyuwlaNw&_hsmi=17652308.

82. Greg Slabodkin, *Lack of Accuracy, Health Info Sharing Stymie Benefits of Big Data*, HEALTHDATA MGMT. (June 25, 2014), http://www.healthdatamanagement.com/news/Lack-of-Accuracy-Health-Info-Sharing-Stymie-Benefits-of-Big-Data-48289-1.html?utm_campaign=ehrs-jun%2030%202014&utm_medium=email&utm_source=newsletter&ET=healthdatamana gement%3Ae2784122%3A3890879a%3A&st=email.

83. Andrew F. Sellars, LONG COMMENT REGARDING A PROPOSED EXEMPTION UNDER 17 U.S.C. § 1201, Comment of a Coalition of Medical Device Researchers in Support of Proposed Class 27: Software—Networked Medical Devices, at 2, http://copyright.gov/1201/2015/comments-020615/InitialComments_longform_Coalition_of_Medical_Device_Researchers_Class27.pdf.

84. Andrew Sellars, *Protecting Independent Medical Device Research*, CYBERLAW CLINIC (June 30, 2015), http://cyberlawclinic.berkman.harvard.edu/2015/06/30/dmca/.

85. Andrew Sellars, *DMCA Exemption Granted for Med Device Research, Patient Access to Data*, CYBERLAW CLINIC (Oct. 27, 2015), http://cyberlawclinic.berkman.harvard.edu/2015/10/27/dmca-exception-granted-for-medical-device-research-patient-access-to-data/.

86. *FDA's Role in the Precision Medicine Initiative, What FDA Officials Are Saying*, FDA, http://www.fda.gov/ScienceResearch/SpecialTopics/PrecisionMedicine/default.htm.

87. John T. Wilbanks & Eric J. Topol, *Stop the Privatization of Health Data*, NATURE (July 29, 2016), http://www.nature.com/news/stop-the-privatization-of-health-data-1.20268.

88. Mike Orcutt, *The White House Is Pushing Precision Medicine But It Won't Happen for Years*, MIT TECH. REV. (July 18, 2016), https://www.technologyreview.com/s/601883/the-white-house-is-pushing-precision-medicine-but-it-wont-happen-for-years/.

89. The most famous dispute over genetic data involved Henrietta Lacks. *See* Rebecca Skloot, *The Immortal Life of Henrietta Lacks* (2010).

Chapter 5

1. Nadia Drake, *Help, I'm Trapped in Facebook's Absurd Pseudonym Purgatory*, WIRED (June 19, 2015), http://www.wired.com/2015/06/facebook-real-name-policy-problems.

2. Chris Cox, *Facebook Status Update*, FACEBOOK (Oct. 1, 2014), https://www.facebook.com/chris.cox/posts/10101301777354543.

3. CLAY SHIRKY, HERE COMES EVERYBODY: THE POWER OF ORGANIZING WITHOUT ORGANIZATIONS (2008).

4. *Id.*

5. Chris Crowley, *Follow That Cab!: The Age of the iChase*, NEW YORKER (Oct. 10, 2011), http://www.newyorker.com/magazine/2011/10/10/follow-that-cab-chris-crowley.

6. Nicholas Confessore, *A Cellphone Is Lost, and a Saga Ensues*, N.Y. TIMES (June 20, 2006), http://www.nytimes.com/2006/06/20/nyregion/20cnd-sidekick.html.

7. DAVID KIRKPATRICK, THE FACEBOOK EFFECT: THE INSIDE STORY OF THE COMPANY THAT IS CONNECTING THE WORLD (2010).

8. Ami Sedghi, *Facebook: 10 Years of Social Networking, in Numbers*, GUARDIAN (Feb. 4, 2014), http://www.theguardian.com/news/datablog/2014/feb/04/facebook-in-numbers-statistics.

9. Geoffrey A. Fowler, *Life and Death Online: Who Controls a Digital Legacy?*, WALL ST. J. (Jan. 5, 2013), http://www.wsj.com/articles/SB10001424127887324677204578188220364231346.

10. *Id. See* Emma Glanfield, *Apple Refuses Sons' Request to Unlock Cancer Victim Mother's iPad*, DAILY MAIL (Mar. 6, 2014), http://www.dailymail.co.uk/news/article-2574697/Apple-refuses-grieving-sons-request-unlock-cancer-victim-mothers-iPad-tells-need-dead-womans-written-consent.html.

11. Fowler, *supra* note 9.

12. *Id.*

13. *Id.*

14. Fredrick Kunkle, *Virginia Family, Seeking Clues to Son's Suicide, Wants Easier Access to Facebook*, WASH. POST (Feb. 17, 2013), https://www.washingtonpost.com/local/va-politics/virginia-family-seeking-clues-to-sons-suicide-wants-easier-access-to-facebook/2013/02/17/e1fc728a-7935-11e2-82e8-61a46c2cde3d_story.html.

15. Court of Justice of the European Union Press Release No. 70/14, *Internet Search Engine Operator Is Responsible for Processing of Personal Data* (May 13, 2014), http://curia.europa.eu/jcms/upload/docs/application/pdf/2014-05/cp140070en.pdf.

16. *Search Removal Request under Data Protection Law in Europe*, GOOGLE https://support.google.com/legal/contact/lr_eudpa?product=websearch.

17. *Id.*

18. Sylvia Tippman & Julia Powles, *Google Has Accidentally Revealed Detailed Information of Nearly 220,000 "Right To Be Forgotten" Requests*, BUS. INSIDER (July 14, 2015), http://www.businessinsider.com/google-accidentally-revealed-detailed-information-of-nearly-220000-right-to-be-forgotten-requests-2015-7.

19. *Number of Monthly Active Twitter Users Worldwide from 1st Quarter 2010 to 2nd Quarter 2016 (in Millions)*, STATISTA, http://www.statista.com/statistics/282087/number-of-monthly-active-twitter-users/; *Twitter Usage Statistics*, INTERNET LIVE STATS, http://www.internetlivestats.com/twitter-statistics/#trend.

20. Michael Andor Brodeur, *Signs of Backlash to Internet Trolls Appearing*, BOS. GLOBE (June 12, 2015), https://www.bostonglobe.com/arts/2015/06/12/large/hOqlbvVXsgRjoPuN1qelvI/story.html. Trolling is not limited to individuals or to the private sphere for that matter, as was revealed in Adrian Chenjune's disturbing investigative reporting on Russia's orchestrated trolling campaign. Adrian Chen, *The Agency*, N.Y. TIMES (June 2, 2015), http://www.nytimes.com/2015/06/07/magazine/the-agency.html?_r=0.

21. Jim Edwards, *One Statistic Shows That Twitter Has a Fundamental Problem Facebook Solved Years Ago*, BUS. INSIDER (Apr. 17, 2015), http://www.businessinsider.com/statistics-on-twitter-abuse-rape-death-threats-and-trolls-2015-4.

22. J. Nathan Matias et al., *Reporting, Reviewing, and Responding to Harassment on Twitter*, WAM! (May 13, 2015), https://womenactionmedia.org/cms/assets/uploads/2015/05/wam-twitter-abuse-report.pdf.

23. Kim Zetter, *Parents of Dead Teen Sue School over Sexting Images*, WIRED (Dec. 8, 2009), http://www.wired.com/2009/12/sexting-suit/.

24. Charlie Wells, *Teen Bullying Victim's Family Gets Settlement*, N.Y. DAILY NEWS (Oct. 9, 2012), http://www.nydailynews.com/news/national/teen-bullying-victim-family-settlement-article-1.1178783.

25. Ravi Baichwal & Eric Horng, *Yik Yak Disables App in Chicago Amid Bullying Concerns*, RAVI BAICHWAL, ABC7 CHIC. (Mar. 7, 2014), http://abc7chicago.com/archive/9457339/.

26. Alexandra Svokos, *Yik Yak Threats Lead to Charges for Students*, HUFF. POST (Nov. 25, 2014), http://www.huffingtonpost.com/2014/11/25/yik-yak-threats-college_n_6214794.html.

27. Sam Thielman, *Controversial Anonymous Networking App Secret to Close Down*, GUARDIAN (Apr. 29, 2015), http://www.theguardian.com/technology/2015/apr/29/secret-controversial-anonymous-networking-app-close-down.

28. Maeve Duggan et al., *Online Harassment*, PEW RES. CTR. (Oct. 2014), http://www.pewinternet.org/files/2014/10/PI_OnlineHarassment_102214_pdf1.pdf.

29. Becky Gardiner et al., *The Dark Side of Guardian Comments*, GUARDIAN (Apr. 12, 2016), https://www.theguardian.com/technology/2016/apr/12/the-dark-side-of-guardian-comments.

30. Most people report that they "ignore" harassment as bystanders. *See* Nathaniel Levy et al., *Bullying in a Networked Era: A Literature Review*, Pub. No. 2012–17 BERKMAN CTR. RES. 22–23 (2012).

31. *See id.* at 36–48; Eric Goldman, *Unregulating Online Harassment*, 57 DENVER U. L. REV. ONLINE 59 (2010).

32. In the United Kingdom criminal convictions of "trolling" has increased by eightfold in the last decade. *See* Michael Andor Brodeur, *Signs of Backlash to Internet Trolls Appearing,* Bos. Globe (June 12, 2015), https://www.bostonglobe.com/arts/2015/06/12/large/hOqlbvVXsgRjoPuN1qelvI/story.html.

33. *Id.* (referring to the outing of 63-year-old Brenda Leyland who committed suicide several days after her Reddit troll identity was revealed).

34. *Someone on Twitter Is Engaging in Abusive or Harassing Behavior,* Twitter (2016), https://support.twitter.com/forms/abusiveuser.

35. Matias et al., *supra* note 22, at 3. "The WAM! reporting form asked reporters to categorize the type of harassment they were reporting, drawing on eight preassigned categories. The associated radio buttons of the form allowed reporters to select only one of these eight. This aspect of form design significantly affected the categorization of harassment, as revealed by responses in the free text of the 'Other' category, answers to the subsequent question Please describe in detail the harassment you are receiving, and later correspondence." *Id.* at 15.

36. *Id.*

37. Lindy West, *Twitter Doesn't Think These Rape and Death Threats Are Harassment,* Daily Dot (Dec. 23, 2014), http://www.dailydot.com/opinion/twitter-harassment-rape-death-threat-report/.

38. *Id.*

39. *Id.*

40. Stuart Dredge, *Twitter Has Tripled the Size of Its Team Handling Abuse Reports,* Guardian (Feb. 27, 2015), http://www.theguardian.com/technology/2015/feb/27/twitter-tripled-team-abuse-reports.

41. Matias et al., *supra* note 22, at 1–3.

42. Jim Rutenberg, *On Twitter, Hate Speech Bounded Only by a Character Limit,* N.Y. Times (Oct. 2, 2016), http://www.nytimes.com/2016/10/03/business/media/on-twitter-hate-speech-bounded-only-by-a-character-limit.html?_r=0.

43. David Cohen, *INFOGRAPHIC: Facebook Details Its Reporting Process,* Soc. Times (June 19, 2012), http://www.adweek.com/socialtimes/facebook-reporting-guide/395387.

44. *More Transparency in Reporting,* Facebook (Apr. 26, 2012), https://www.facebook.com/notes/facebook-safety/more-transparency-in-reporting/397890383565083.

45. West, *supra* note 37.

46. David Cohen, *Facebook Engineering Director Arturo Bejar on Conflict Resolution, "Compassion Research,"* Soc. Times (Sept. 14, 2012), http://www.adweek.com/socialtimes/arturo-bejar-qa/402998; James O'Toole, *Facebook's Other User Experiment: Conflict Resolution,* CNN Money (July 1, 2014), http://money.cnn.com/2014/07/01/technology/social/facebook-compassion-research/; Katie Shonk, *Using a Negotiation Approach to Resolve a Conflict: On Facebook, Dispute Resolution Goes Live,* Program Negot. Harv. L. Sch. (Feb. 15, 2016), http://www.pon.harvard.edu/daily/dispute-resolution/on-facebook-dispute-resolution-goes-live/.

47. The Muse, *The Facebook Experiment: What It Means for You,* Forbes (Aug. 4, 2014), http://www.forbes.com/sites/dailymuse/2014/08/04/the-facebook-experiment-what-it-means-for-you/#27baf7741cbc.

48. *See* sources cited *supra* note 46.

49. Adrian Chen, *When the Internet's "Moderators" Are Anything But,* N.Y. Times (July 21, 2015), http://www.nytimes.com/2015/07/26/magazine/when-the-internets-moderators-are-anything-but.html?rref=collection%2Fsectioncollection%2Fmagazine&action=click&contentCollection=magazine&region=stream&module=stream_unit&contentPlacement=7&pgtype=sectionfront&_r=1.

50. Nathan J. Matias, *The Tragedy of the Digital Commons,* Atlantic (June 8, 2015), http://www.theatlantic.com/technology/archive/2015/06/the-tragedy-of-the-digital-commons/395129/ [hereinafter Matias, *Tragedy of Digital Commons*].

51. Drake, *supra* note 1.

52. Josh Constine, *Facebook Launches Verified Accounts and Pseudonyms*, TechCrunch (Feb. 15, 2012), http://techcrunch.com/2012/02/15/facebook-verified-accounts-alternate-names/.

53. *What Names Are Allowed on Facebook?*, Facebook Help Ctr., https://www.facebook.com/help/112146705538576.

54. Drake, *supra* note 1.

55. Cox, *supra* note 2.

56. Benjamin Lowndes, *"Join the Conversation": Why Twitter Should Market Itself as a Technology Mediated Dispute Resolution Tool*, 2 Int'l J. Online Disp. Resol. (2015).

57. Michelle Higgins, *Twitter Comes to the Rescue*, N.Y. Times (July 1, 2009), http://www.nytimes.com/2009/07/05/travel/05prac.html.

58. Mitch Lipka, *Social Media Dispute Resolution Stumps Some Companies*, Reuters (Jan. 18, 2013), http://www.reuters.com/article/net-us-consumer-complaints-socialmedia-idUSBRE90G0XQ20130118.

59. *Wikipedia: Dispute Resolution*, Wikipedia, https://en.wikipedia.org/wiki/Wikipedia:Dispute_resolution (last modified July 17, 2016).

60. *Wikipedia*, Wikipedia, https://en.wikipedia.org/wiki/Wikipedia (last modified Aug. 6, 2016).

61. David A. Hoffman & Salil K. Mehra, *Wikitruth through Wikiorder*, 59 Emory L.J. 151 (2010).

62. James Grimmelmann, *The Virtues of Moderation*, 17 Yale J. L. & Tech. 42, 82 (2015).

63. *Id.*

64. Sara Ross, *Your Day in "Wiki-Court": ADR, Fairness, and Justice in Wikipedia's Global Community*, Osgoode Legal Stud. Res. Paper No. 56/2014 (2014).

65. Grimmelmann, *supra* note 62, at 81–82.

66. Ross, *supra* note 64, at 15.

67. *Id.*; Orna Rabinovich-Einy & Ethan Katsh, *Lessons from Online Dispute Resolution for Dispute Systems Design*, *in* Online Dispute Resolution: Theory and Practice: A Treatise on Technology and Dispute Resolution 51 (M. S. Wahab et al. eds., 2012); Grimmelmann, *supra* note 62, at 86–87.

68. *Wikipedia: Dispute Resolution*, *supra* note 59.

69. *Wikipedia: Requests for Comment*, Wikipedia, https://en.wikipedia.org/wiki/Wikipedia:Requests_for_comment (last modified July 2, 2016).

70. *Wikipedia: Editor Assistance/Assistants*, Wikipedia, https://en.wikipedia.org/wiki/Wikipedia:Editor_assistance/Assistants (last modified Apr. 5, 2007); *Wikipedia: Third Opinion*, Wikipedia, https://en.wikipedia.org/wiki/Wikipedia:Third_opinion (last modified Aug. 6, 2016).

71. *Wikipedia: Mediation*, Wikipedia, https://en.wikipedia.org/wiki/Wikipedia:Mediation (last modified May 6, 2016).

72. Grimmelmann, *supra* note 62, at 86.

73. *Wikipedia: Mediation*, *supra* note 71.

74. *Wikipedia: Arbitration Committee*, Wikipedia, https://en.wikipedia.org/wiki/Wikipedia:Arbitration_Committee#What_happens_to_incoming_ArbCom_email.3F (last modified June 24, 2016).

75. Ross, *supra* note 64, at 11.

76. *Id.* at 12; Grimmelmann, *supra* note 62, at 86–87.

77. *Wikipedia: Dispute Resolution*, *supra* note 59.

78. *Id.*

79. *Id.*

80. Grimmelmann, *supra* note 62, at 83.

81. Alongside these mechanisms for addressing abuse ex post, there are also preventative measures that operate ex ante such as restricting the editing of certain controversial articles to logged-in users, or by banning certain accounts or IP addresses from editing in general or articles on specific topics. *See* Grimmelmann, *supra* note 62, at 84.

82. R. Stuart Geiger & David Ribes, *The Work of Sustaining Order in Wikipedia: The Banning of a Vandal*, *in* Proceedings of the 2010 ACM Conference on Computer Supported Cooperative Work, CSCW 117 (2010).

83. R. Stuart Geiger, *The Lives of Bots*, *in* Critical Point of View: A Wikipedia Reader 79 (Geert Lovnik & Nathaniel Tkacz eds., 2011).

84. *Id.*

85. *Id.*

86. *Id.*

87. *Id.*

88. *Id.*

89. *Id.*

90. *Id.*

91. *Id*

92. *Id.*

93. Matias, *Tragedy of Digital Commons, supra* note 50.

94. Geiger, *supra* note 83, at 85–86.

95. Adrian Chen, *The Laborers Who Keep Dick Pics and Beheadings Out of Your Facebook Feed*, Wired (Oct. 23, 2014), http://www.wired.com/2014/10/content-moderation/ [hereinafter Chen, *Laborers Who Keep Dick Pics*].

96. Grimmelmann, *supra* note 62.

97. Chen, *Laborers Who Keep Dick Pics, supra* note 95.

98. *Id.*

99. *Id.* As Grimmelmann points out, paradoxically by making human content moderation "into assemblyline piecework" it becomes more similar to algorithmic moderation with all of its deficiencies, mainly its need for fixed rules and lack of flexibility. *See* Grimmelmann, *supra* note 62, at 65.

100. *Id.*

101. Brodeur, *supra* note 20.

102. Maayan Perel & Niva Elkin-Koren, *Accountability in Algorithmic Copyright Enforcement*, 19 Stan. Tech. L. Rev. (forthcoming, 2016).

103. *Id.* at 42–43.

104. *Id.* at 57, n.244.

105. *Id.* at 44–48.

106. Kashmir Hill, *How Nextdoor Reduced Racist Posts by 75%*, Fusion (Aug. 25. 2016), http://fusion.net/story/340171/how-nextdoor-reduced-racial-profiling/.

107. Chen, *Laborers Who Keep Dick Pics, supra* note 95.

108. Tarleton Gillespie, *The Dirty Job of Keeping Facebook Clean*, Soc. Media Collective Res. Blog (Feb. 22, 2012), http://socialmediacollective.org/2012/02/22/the-dirty-job-of-keeping-facebook-clean/; *see* Grimmelmann, *supra* note 62, at 64, n.98 (referring to the problems of overzealous censorship by algorithms).

109. Julian Dibbell, *A Rape in Cyberspace*, *in* My Tiny Life (1998), http://www.juliandibbell.com/articles/a-rape-in-cyberspace/.

110. Sherry Turkle, Life on the Screen: Identity in the Age of the Internet 11–14 (Simon & Schuster 1997).

111. Dibbell, *supra* note 109.

112. Kyle Wagner, *The Future of the Culture Wars Is Here, and It's Gamergate*, Deadspin (Oct. 14, 2014), http://deadspin.com/the-future-of-the-culture-wars-is-here-and-its-gamerga-1646145844.

113. *Id.*

114. Matias et al., *supra* note 22, at 1.

115. Wagner, *supra* note 112.

116. Laura Hudson, *Curbing Online Abuse Isn't Impossible. Here's Where We Start*, Wired (May 15, 2014), http://www.wired.com/2014/05/fighting-online-harassment/.

117. Another example is the Sims where a Sims Mafia, "a gang of digital enforcers," was established to "lay down the law inside the Sims Online." *See* Hiawatha Bray, *Justice Has Its Price in Sim World*, Bos. Globe (Jan. 14, 2004), http://archive.boston.com/news/globe/living/articles/2004/01/14/justice_has_its_price_in_sim_world/.

118. Hudson, *supra* note 116.

119. *Id.*

120. *Id.*

121. *See* Grimmelmann, *supra* note 62, at 61, n.88 (citing Jason Kottke, *The Blogger Code*, Kottke. org (Apr. 9, 2007), http://kottke.org/07/04/the-blogger-code).

Chapter 6

1. Tamara Kneese et al., *Understanding Fair Labor Practices in a Networked Age* 4 (Data & Soc'y, Working Paper, Oct. 8, 2014), http://www.datasociety.net/pubs/fow/FairLabor.pdf.

2. E. Jeffrey Hill et al., *Defining and Conceptualizing Workplace Flexibility*, 11 Community, Work & Fam. 149, 152 (2008).

3. The Future of Work Institute, *The Benefits of Flexible Working Arrangements*, Future of Work (Aug. 2012), https://www.bc.edu/content/dam/files/centers/cwf/individuals/pdf/benefitsCEOFlex.pdf.

4. Katie Johnston, *Firms Step Up Employee Monitoring at Work*, Bos. Globe (Feb. 19, 2016), https://www.bostonglobe.com/business/2016/02/18/firms-step-monitoring-employee-activities-work/2l5hoCjsEZWA0bp10BzPrN/story.html.

5. For some of the disadvantages associated flexible work arraignments, *see* Ellen Ernst Kossek & Jesse S. Michel, *Flexible Work Schedules*, *in* 1 Ellen Ernst Kossek & Jesse S. Michel, APA Handbook of Industrial and Organizational Psychology 535, 535–72 (Sheldon Zedeck ed., 2010); Richard E. Susskind & Daniel Susskind, The Future of the Professions: How Technology Will Transform the Work of Human Experts 126 (2016).

6. George Markowsky & Linda Markowsky, *From Air Conditioner to Data Breach* (2014), http://worldcomp-proceedings.com/proc/p2014/SAM4158.pdf.

7. Kneese et al., *supra* note 1, at 3.

8. *Id.* at 3–4.

9. These companies merged in 2015 to form Upwork.

10. Kneese et al., *supra* note 1, at 8.

11. Julian Dibbell, *The Life of the Chinese Gold Farmer*, N.Y. Times (June 17, 2007), http://www.nytimes.com/2007/06/17/magazine/17lootfarmers-t.html?pagewanted=1&_r=1&sq=julian%20dibbell%20gold%20farmer&st=cse&scp=1&

12. *Id.*

13. Denise Cheng, *The Peer Economy Will Transform Work (or at Least How We Think of It)*, Harv. Bus. Rev. (Dec. 18, 2013), https://hbr.org/2013/12/the-peer-economy-will-transform-work-or-at-least-how-we-think-of-it/.

14. Dan Schawbel, *Adam Penenberg: How Gamification Is Going to Change the Workplace*, Forbes (Oct. 7, 2013), http://www.forbes.com/sites/danschawbel/2013/10/07/adam-penenberg-how-gamification-is-going-to-change-the-workplace/#26be124e39e5.

15. *Id.*

16. *Id.*

17. *Id.*

18. Miriam A. Cherry, *The Gamification of Work*, 40 Hofstra L. Rev. 851, 853 (2012). Free unpaid labor also in the form of volunteer crowdsourced labor, Wikipedia, and the like, plus leisure at workplaces like Google. *See* Kneese et al., *supra* note 1, at 7.

19. David Barboza, *Ogre to Slay? Outsource It to Chinese*, N.Y. Times (Dec. 9, 2005), http://www.nytimes.com/2005/12/09/technology/ogre-to-slay-outsource-it-to-chinese.html.

20. Dibbell, *supra* note 11.

21. Heather Chaplin, *I Don't Want to Be a Superhero*, SLATE (Mar. 29, 2011), http://www.slate.com/articles/technology/gaming/2011/03/i_dont_want_to_be_a_superhero.single.html.

22. Dean Takahashi, *Website Builder DevHub Gets Users Hooked by "Gamifying" Its Service*, VENTUREBEAT (Aug. 25, 2010), http://venturebeat.com/2010/08/25/devhub-scores-engagement-increase-by-gamifying-its-web-site-creation-tools/.

23. Erica Swallow, *Can Gamification Make Customer Support Fun?*, FORBES (Sept. 18, 2012), http://www.forbes.com/sites/ericaswallow/2012/09/18/gamified-customer-support-freshdesk-arcade/#556618c14cdb.

24. David Bornstein, *Open Education for a Global Economy*, N.Y. TIMES (July 11, 2012), http://opinionator.blogs.nytimes.com/2012/07/11/open-education-for-a-global-economy/.

25. *Robotic Surgery*, MEDLINEPLUS MED. ENCYCLOPEDIA, https://www.nlm.nih.gov/medlineplus/ency/article/007339.htm.

26. Matt Simon, *This Incredible Hospital Robot Is Saving Lives. Also, I Hate It*, WIRED (Feb. 10, 2015), http://www.wired.com/2015/02/incredible-hospital-robot-saving-lives-also-hate/.

27. Walter Frick, *What Can a Robot Bellhop Do That a Human Can't?*, HARV. BUS. REV. (Aug. 25, 2014), https://hbr.org/2014/08/what-can-a-robot-bellhop-do-that-a-human-cant/.

28. Jessica Hullinger, *7 New Robots Designed to Do Human Jobs*, MENTAL FLOSS (Aug. 12, 2014), http://mentalfloss.com/article/58332/7-new-robots-designed-do-human-jobs.

29. David Rotman, *Who Will Own the Robots?*, MIT TECH. REV. 2 (June 16, 2015), https://www.technologyreview.com/s/538401/who-will-own-the-robots/.

30. *Id.* at 6.

31. *Id.* at 8.

32. *Id.* at 11.

33. *Id.* at 12.

34. *See* LUCILLE M. PONTE & THOMAS D. CAVENAGH, CYBERJUSTICE: ONLINE DISPUTE RESOLUTION (ODR) FOR E-COMMERCE 9–10 (2004) (discussing how employee use of technology may subject employers to liability for sexual harassment).

35. Gregory M. Huckabee & Cherry Kolb, *Privacy in the Workplace, Fact or Fiction, and the Value of an Authorized Use Policy (AUP)*, 59 S.D. L. REV. 35 (2014).

36. Jennifer Mattern, *Another Freelance Marketplace Bites the Dust—Elance Work View*, ALL INDIE WRITERS (Apr. 9, 2010), http://allindiewriters.com/another-freelance-marketplace-bites-the-dust-elance-work-view/.

37. Jonathan D. Glater, *A Company Computer and Questions about E-Mail Privacy*, N.Y. TIMES (June 27, 2008), http://www.nytimes.com/2008/06/27/technology/27mail.html.

38. Memorandum of Decision Granting Defendants' Motion To Compel Arbitration, Scott Sidell v. Structured Settlement Investments, et al., No. 3:08-cv-00710 (VLB) (Jan. 14, 2009), https://ecf.ctd.uscourts.gov/cgi-bin/show_public_doc?2008cv0710-62.

39. Steven Greenhouse, *Company Accused of Firing over Facebook Post*, N.Y. TIMES (Nov. 8, 2010), http://www.nytimes.com/2010/11/09/business/09facebook.html.

40. Nicole J. Nyman, *Risky Business: What Must Employers Do to Shield Against Liability for Employee Wrongdoings in the Internet Age?*, 1 SHIDLER J. L. COM. & TECH. 7 (2005), https://digital.law.washington.edu/dspace-law/bitstream/handle/1773.1/359/vol1_no2_art7.pdf?sequence=1.

41. *See* Simonetti v. Delta Air Lines, Inc., No. 1:05-CV-2321, 2005 WL 2897844 (N.D. Ga. Sept. 7, 2005).

42. Stephanie Clifford, *Video Prank at Domino's Taints Brand*, N.Y. TIMES (Apr. 15, 2009), http://www.nytimes.com/2009/04/16/business/media/16dominos.html?_r=0.

43. *See* Pietrylo v. Hillstone Rest. Grp., No. 06-5754 (FSH) (D.N.J. July 24, 2008), http://employerlawreport.default.wp1.lexblog.com/files/2013/09/PIETRYLO-v-HILLSIDE-RESTAURANT.pdf.

44. Jeremy Gelms, *High-Tech Harassment: Employer Liability under Title VII for Employee Social Media Misconduct*, 87 WASH. L. REV. 249 (2012).

45. Blakey v. Continental Airlines, Inc. 751 A.2d 538 (N.J. 2000).

46. *See* Scott Cox et al., *Workplace Surveillance and Employee Privacy: Implementing an Effective Computer Use Policy*, 5 COMM. IIMA 57 (2005).

47. Ray Lewis, *Employee E-Mail Privacy Still Unemployed: What the United States Can Learn from the United Kingdom*, 67 LA. L. REV. 959, 963, 965 n.35, 36 (2007); S. Elizabeth Wilborn, *Revisiting the Public/Private Distinction: Employee Monitoring in the Workplace*, 32 GA. L. REV. 825, 868 (1997).

48. Brian Van Wyk, *We're Friends, Right? Client List Misappropriation and Online Social Networking in the Workplace*, 11 VAND. J. ENT. & TECH. L. 743, 754–55 (2009). For example, the NFL has banned its players from posting any comments on social media before, during, and after league games.

49. Dave Hawley, *Your Biggest Social Media Risk: Not Doing Anything about Social Employees*, WIRED, http://www.wired.com/insights/2014/11/social-employees/.

50. Saby Ghoshray, *Employer Surveillance versus Employee Privacy: The New Reality of Social Media and Workplace Privacy*, 40 N. KY. L. REV. 593 (2013). *See also* City of Ontario, Cal. v. Quon, 560 U.S. 746 (2010). In *Quon*, the Supreme Court held that searching an employee's work-provided pager while trying to determine if he's been using it for personal and nonwork related uses is permissible and does not constitute a violation of his Fourth Amendment rights.

51. DAVID B. LIPSKY ET AL., EMERGING SYSTEMS FOR MANAGING WORKPLACE CONFLICT: LESSONS FROM AMERICAN CORPORATIONS FOR MANAGERS AND DISPUTE RESOLUTION PROFESSIONALS 156 (2003).

52. A related phenomenon worth noting is the growing use of online employee satisfaction questionnaires, which, among other things, evaluate organizational conflict climate in the physical workplace environment. *See* CONFLICT CLIMATE INVENTORY, http://www.conflictclimate.com.

53. It should be noted, however, that alongside public outcry and consumer outrage regarding abusive employment practices, the internet has also been a source that has allowed for more effective employee organizing and union activity. In attempts to organize, union activists now try to get hold of employee emails. While in a unionized workforce, the communication by email and other social media can allow for a "faster and more efficient dialogue that, in some circumstances, can avoid employer detection." Jeffrey M. Hirsch, *Worker Collective Action in the Digital Age*, 117 W. VA. L. REV. 921, 926 (2015). In a nonunion workplace, the electronic communications provide an even bigger promise: lowering the barriers for collective action and organization, which, in turn, can provide greater benefits for the workers. The opportunities provided by the proliferation of social media to the potential of workers' collective action raised employer awareness to them. At the same time, efforts to organize and protect worker rights have come with risks. In one case where a union president used email to contact employees, the employer who found out about her digital dialogue (since she used the employer-provided email address) ended up punishing her (Hirsch *id.*). But concerns have run deeper than employee privacy, with the viability of the traditional union model in an age in which employees are increasingly self-employed, working part-time for various platforms, and "clients" being questioned. Kneese et al., *supra* note 1, at 11–14.

54. THE NAT'L MEDIATION BOARD, http://www.nmb.gov/.

55. *Process Technology for Achieving Government Online Dispute Resolution*, Award Abstract No. 0429297, NAT'L SCI. FOUND., http://www.nsf.gov/awardsearch/showAward?AWD_ID=0429297.

56. The National Institute of Health's Office of the Ombudsman is one such example.

57. *Thread: Amazon WILL NOT Stick Up for the People Doing HIT's*, MTURK FORUM (Aug. 22, 2012), http://mturkforum.com/showthread.php?3464-Amazon-WILL-NOT-stick-up-for-the-people-doing-HIT-s.

58. JD, *How I Would Improve mTurk If I Was the CEO of Amazon*, TURKFAST (Dec. 1, 2014), http://www.turkfast.com/how-i-would-improve-mturk-if-i-was-the-ceo-of-amazon/.

59. Dara Kerr, *How Risky Is Your Uber Ride? Maybe More Than You Think*, CNET (Oct. 8, 2014), http://www.cnet.com/news/how-risky-is-your-uber-ride-maybe-more-than-you-think/; Dara Kerr, *Uber Disputes Kidnapping Claims*, CNET (Oct. 14, 2014), http://www.cnet.com/news/uber-disputes-kidnapping-claims/; Clark Taylor, *Uber's Attempt to Silence Its Drivers May Have Just Backfired*, IN THESE TIMES (Aug. 19, 2015), http://inthesetimes.com/working/entry/18328/uber-drivers-court-case.

60. Josh Horwitz, *Uber Customer Complaints from the US Are Increasingly Handled in the Philippines*, QUARTZ (July 30, 2015), http://qz.com/465613/uber-customer-complaints-from-the-us-are-increasingly-handled-in-the-philippines/. It should be noted that complaints by customers over detours and inappropriate routes taken by drivers seem to be dealt with effectively. *See* Anonymous, *My Nine Months as an Uber Customer Service Rep*, BILLFOLD (Sept. 15, 2015), https://thebillfold.com/my-nine-months-as-an-uber-customer-service-rep-30875403f267#.ugz1v93a1; Ivana Kottasova, *Uber Refunds Rider Taken on a 20-Mile Detour*, CNN MONEY (Mar. 30, 2016), http://money.cnn.com/2016/03/30/technology/uber-refund-detour-ride/index.html.

61. Johana Bhuiyan, *Contracts and Chaos: Inside Uber's Customer Service Struggles*, BUZZFEED (Mar. 6, 2016), http://www.buzzfeed.com/johanabhuiyan/contracts-and-chaos-inside-ubers-customer-service-struggles#.isYbn9pvj.

62. Horwitz, *supra* note 60.

63. Anonymous, *supra* note 60.

64. Horwitz, *supra* note 60.

65. Rachel Metz, *Does Uber Have a Sexual Assault Problem?*, MIT TECH. REV. (Mar. 7, 2016), https://www.technologyreview.com/s/600959/does-uber-have-a-sexual-assault-problem/.

66. Bhuiyan, *supra* note 61.

67. *Id.*

68. Geoffrey A. Fowler, *There's an Uber for Everything Now*, WALL ST. J. (May 5, 2015), http://www.wsj.com/articles/theres-an-uber-for-everything-now-1430845789.

69. Alana Schetzer, *Uber Customers in Legal Limbo over Complaints*, THE AGE (Dec. 16, 2015), http://www.theage.com.au/victoria/uber-customers-in-legal-limbo-over-complaints-20151216-glp01m.html.

70. Bhuiyan, *supra* note 61.

71. Metz, *supra* note 65.

72. Joe Sullivan et al., *Safety at Uber*, MEDIUM (Mar. 6, 2016), https://medium.com/@UberPubPolicy/safety-at-uber-6e638616bd4a#.4ahq4bfdm.

73. Bhuiyan, *supra* note 61.

74. For 2014 statistics on job postings and earnings on the site, *see Online Work Report: Global, 2014 Full Year Data*, UPWORK (2015), http://elance-odesk.com/online-work-report-global.

75. UPWORK, https://www.upwork.com/.

76. Upwork, *How to Use Upwork as a Freelancer Webinar*, YOUTUBE (Aug. 28, 2015), https://www.youtube.com/watch?v=huRP7qXc2u0.

77. *eLance Presentation Notes*, INTERNATIONAL CONFERENCE ON ONLINE DISPUTE RESOLUTION (San Francisco, Cal., June 2014) [on file with authors].

78. *Id.*

79. *Dispute Resolution Process*, ELANCE HELP CTR., http://help.elance.com/hc/en-us/articles/203735983-Dispute-Resolution-Process.

80. *Id.*

81. *eLance Presentation Notes*, *supra* note 77.

82. Genevieve Coates, *When Clients Attack: An Elance Story*, ALL INDIE WRITERS (Oct. 31, 2012), http://allindiewriters.com/when-clients-attack-an-elance-story/.

83. *Id.*

84. *Id.*

85. *Id.*

86. *Id.* at cmts. 34 & 35.

87. Indeed, the blogger who runs this site commented that she thought the auction model was inappropriate for services (as opposed to goods-related sites). Interestingly, TaskRabbit decided at some point to change its model from an auction-based site to one that operates differently for many of the reasons cited here. *See* Casey Newton, *TaskRabbit Is Blowing Up Its Business Model and Becoming the Uber for Everything*, The Verge (June 17, 2014), http://www.theverge.com/2014/6/17/5816254/taskrabbit-blows-up-its-auction-house-to-offer-services-on-demand.

88. Coates, *supra* note 82.

89. *Id.*

90. "[A]n estimated 34 percent of the American workforce currently in freelance or independent contractor jobs and as many as 40 percent forecast to be in those jobs by 2020." *See* Alison Griswold, *Young Twentysomethings May Have a Leg Up in the 1099 Economy*, Slate (May 22, 2015), http://www.slate.com/blogs/moneybox/2015/05/22/_1099_economy_workforce_report_why_twentysomethings_may_have_a_leg_up.html.

91. There are now several notable exceptions that have emerged, employing the workers who render the services and claiming that customer satisfaction rates are higher despite having to pay higher fees. *See* Kevin Roose, *Does Silicon Valley Have a Contract-Worker Problem?*, N.Y. Mag. (Sept. 18, 2014), http://nymag.com/daily/intelligencer/2014/09/silicon-valleys-contract-worker-problem.html#.

92. Referred to as the "micro entrepreneur economy." Kneese et al., *supra* note 1, at 9.

93. Caleb Garling, *Hunting Task Wabbits*, Medium (Dec. 3, 2014), https://medium.com/matter/hunting-task-wabbits-c60679bad0f6.

94. *eLance Presentation Notes, supra* note 77; *How to Use Upwork, supra* note 76.

95. Matthew Kosinski, *TaskRabbit Moves toward a Less Exploitative Model of On-Demand Labor*, Recruiter (June 18, 2014), http://www.recruiter.com/i/taskrabbit-moves-toward-a-less-exploitative-model-of-on-demand-labor/.

96. Brad Stone, *My Life as a TaskRabbit*, Bloomberg (Sept. 13, 2012), http://www.bloomberg.com/news/articles/2012-09-13/my-life-as-a-taskrabbit.

97. *Compare* Joshua Brustein, *To Ensure Security, Taskrabbit Meets Its Users*, Bits, N.Y. Times (Aug. 3, 2011), http://bits.blogs.nytimes.com/2011/08/03/to-ensure-security-online-taskrabbit-meets-users-in-real-life/?_php=true&_type=blogs&_r=1; *and How It Works*, TaskRabbit, https://www.taskrabbit.com/trust-and-safety; *with* Tracey Lien & Russ Mitchell, *Uber Sued over Unlawful Business Practices; Lyft Settles*, L.A. Times (Dec. 9, 2014), http://www.latimes.com/business/technology/la-fi-tn-uber-lyft-20141209-story.html.

98. TaskRabbit Support, *Tasker Tips on Fraud*, TaskRabbit, https://support.taskrabbit.com/hc/en-us/articles/204409500-Tasker-Safety-Guidelines.

99. TaskRabbit Support, *What If My Client Doesn't Agree with the Hours Spent on My Task?*, TaskRabbit, https://support.taskrabbit.com/hc/en-us/articles/204409660-What-if-my-Client-doesn-t-agree-with-the-hours-spent-on-my-task. For guidelines on calculating number of hours worked on a task, *see How Do I Calculate the Hours Worked on a Task?*, TaskRabbit, https://support.taskrabbit.co.uk/hc/en-gb/articles/204668690-How-do-I-calculate-the-hours-worked-on-a-task-.

100. Joshua Brustein, *TaskRabbit Adds Insurance to Make Trusting Strangers Easier*, Bloomberg (July 10, 2014), http://www.bloomberg.com/news/articles/2014-07-10/taskrabbit-adds-insurance-to-make-trusting-strangers-easier.

101. Sam Biddle, *If TaskRabbit Is the Future of Employment, the Employed Are Fucked*, ValleyWag (July 23, 2014), http://valleywag.gawker.com/if-taskrabbit-is-the-future-of-employment-the-employed-1609221541.

102. Davey Alba, *Judge Rejects Uber's $100 Million Settlement with Drivers*, Wired (Aug. 18, 2016), http://www.wired.com/2016/08/uber-settlement-rejected/; Heather Somerville, *Federal Judge Rejects $12.25 Million Settlement in Lyft Driver Lawsuit*, Reuters (Apr. 7, 2016), http://www.reuters.com/article/us-classaction-lyft-idUSKCN0X42MN; Nick Statt, *Uber Will Pay $10 Million to Settle Lawsuit over Driver Background Checks*, The Verge (Apr. 7,

2016), http://www.theverge.com/2016/4/7/11389822/uber-lawsuit-background-checks-10-million-settlement; *Uber Lawsuit Information*, UBER LAWSUIT, http://uberlawsuit.com/.

103. Kneese et al., *supra* note 1, at 11.

104. Robert H. Mnookin & Lewis Kornhauser, *Bargaining in the Shadow of the Law: The Case of Divorce*, 88 YALE L. J. 950 (1979).

Chapter 7

1. Orna Rabinovich-Einy & Ethan Katsh, *Technology and the Future of Dispute Systems Design*, 17 HARV. NEGOT. L. REV. 151, 190–94 (2012).

2. Colin Rule & Mark Wilson, *Online Resolution and Citizen Empowerment: Property Tax Appeals in North America*, in REVOLUTIONIZING THE INTERACTION BETWEEN STATE AND CITIZENS THROUGH DIGITAL COMMUNICATIONS 185, 197 (Sam B. Edwards III & Diogo Santos eds., 2015).

3. *Id.* at 195–96.

4. *Id.* at 199.

5. *Consumer Protection BC Tests Online Dispute Resolution Tool for Debt Collection Complaints*, CONSUMER PROTECTION BC (July 17, 2015), http://www.consumerprotectionbc.ca/debt-collection/1252-consumer-protection-bc-tests-online-dispute-resolution-tool-for-debt-collection-complaints.

6. Darin Thompson, *The Growth of Online Dispute Resolution and Its Use in British Columbia*, CIV. LITIG. CONF. (2014), https://www.cle.bc.ca/PracticePoints/LIT/14-GrowthODR.pdf.

7. Jennifer Beese, *Social Media & Government: Cutting Red Tape for Increased Citizen Engagement*, SPROUT SOC. (Aug. 31, 2015), http://sproutsocial.com/insights/social-media-and-government/ (stating that "14% of Americans use social media to find information about a federal agency, while 30% use social either to ask the government a direct question or to resolve an offline issue").

8. Ethan Katsh & Jeff Aresty, *A New Face for Small Claims Courts*, BOS. GLOBE (Sept. 29, 2007), http://www.boston.com/news/globe/editorial_opinion/oped/articles/2007/09/29/a_new_face_for_small_claims_courts/.

9. *Debtors' Hell*, BOSTON.COM, http://archive.boston.com/news/specials/debt/.

10. Eric Lipton et al., *Tension and Flaws Before Health Website Crash*, N.Y. TIMES (Nov. 22, 2013), http://www.nytimes.com/2013/11/23/us/politics/tension-and-woes-before-health-website-crash.html?pagewanted=all&_r=0.

11. Baiju Shah & John Greene, *Liquid Expectations*, ECONOMIST GROUP: MARKETING UNBOUND (May 19, 2015), http://www.economistgroup.com/leanback/consumers/accenture-liquid-expectations/.

12. AMY J. SCHMITZ & COLIN RULE, THE NEW HANDSHAKE: ONLINE DISPUTE RESOLUTION AND THE FUTURE OF CONSUMER PROTECTION 21 (forthcoming, on file with authors).

13. *2015 Annual Report to Congress—Most Serious Problems*, NAT'L TAXPAYER ADVOC., http://www.taxpayeradvocate.irs.gov/Media/Default/Documents/2015ARC/ARC15_Volume1_MSP_01_Taxpayer-Service.pdf.

14. *Get Started with TurboTax Today!*, COM. BANK, https://www.commercebank.com/turbotax/?ref=homePage.

15. *2014 Year-End Report on the Federal Judiciary*, SUP. CT. (Dec. 31, 2014), http://www.supremecourt.gov/publicinfo/year-end/2014year-endreport.pdf [hereinafter *2014 Year-End Report*].

16. ETHAN KATSH, THE ELECTRONIC MEDIA AND THE TRANSFORMATION OF LAW 5–6 (1989).

17. *2014 Year-End Report*, supra note 15, at 4–5; *Fiscal Year 2015 Update: Long Range Plan for Information Technology in the Federal Judiciary*, U.S. CTS., http://www.uscourts.gov/statistics-reports/publications/long-range-plan-information-technology.

18. RICHARD SUSSKIND, TOMORROW'S LAWYERS: AN INTRODUCTION TO YOUR FUTURE 84–91 (2013) [hereinafter SUSSKIND, TOMORROW'S LAWYERS].

19. Also referred to as "e-working." *See id.* at 94–95.
20. Orna Rabinovich-Einy, *Beyond Efficiency: The Transformation of Courts through Technology*, 12 UCLA J. L. & Tech. 1, 34–35 (2008).
21. *Id.* at 45.
22. Beth Simone Noveck, *The Future of Citizen Participation in the Electronic State: Modeling Communicative Action in E-Rulemaking Practice*, 1 ISJLP 1 (2005).
23. *Id.* at 7.
24. The E-Government Act of 2002, Pub. L. No. 107-347, 116 Stat. 289.
25. *See European eGovernment Action Plan 2011–2015*, Eur. Commission, https://ec.europa.eu/digital-single-market/european-egovernment-action-plan-2011-2015.
26. Shin-Yuan Hung et al., *User Acceptance of Mobile E-Government Services: An Empirical Study*, 30 Gov't Info. Q. 33, 33–34 (2013).
27. Donald F. Norris & Christopher G. Reddick, *Local E-Government in the United States: Transformation or Incremental Change?*, 73 Pub. Admin. Rev. 165 (2013).
28. Schmitz & Rule, *supra* note 12.
29. James E. Cabral et al., *Using Technology to Enhance Access to Justice*, 26 Harv. J. L. & Tech. 241, 278 (2012).
30. *Id.* at 248.
31. *Id.* at 247.
32. *Id.* at 248.
33. *Id.* at 260.
34. *Id.* at 249.
35. *Id.* at 249.
36. *Id.* at 261–62.
37. *Id.* at 262–63.
38. *Id.* at 249.
39. *Id.* at 255–56.
40. *Id.* at 292–305.
41. Ronald W. Staudt, *All the Wild Possibilities: Technology That Attacks Barriers to Access to Justice*, 42 Loy. L.A. L. Rev. 1117, 1129–30 (2009).
42. *Id.* at 1133–34.
43. *About I-CAN! Legal*, i-can! Legal, http://www.legalican.com/about.
44. Cabral et al., *supra* note 29, at 251–52.
45. *Id.* at 252.
46. *Id.* at 260. A combination of "limited scope representation" and use of technology could be another solution for self-represented litigants. *See id.* at 307.
47. Cabral et al., *supra* note 29, at 253–54.
48. Susskind, Tomorrow's Lawyers, *supra* note 18, at 99.
49. *Id.*
50. Brian Tamberlin, *Online Dispute Resolution and the Courts*, Third Ann. UN F. Online Disp. Resol. (July 2004).
51. Some Singapore courts also offer an email-based online mediation process ("e-Alternative Dispute Resolution"), specifically for e-commerce-related disputes wherein court action has not yet been initiated. The service is offered free of charge, and the courts appoint a mediator to the case if the parties choose to participate. Aside from this description, very little information on the service and its achievements is available. Nicolas W. Vermeys & Karim Benyekhlef, *ODR and the Courts*, in Online Dispute Resolution: Theory and Practice: A Treatise on Technology and Dispute Resolution 307, 316–18 (M. S. Wahab et al. eds., 2012).
52. *Id.* at 314–15.
53. *Id.*; Susskind, Tomorrow's Lawyers, *supra* note 18, at 102.
54. Richard Susskind, *Online Dispute Resolution: For Low Value Civil Claims: Online Dispute Resolution Advisory Group*, Civ. Just. Council (Feb. 2015), https://www.judiciary.gov.

uk/wp-content/uploads/2015/02/Online-Dispute-Resolution-Final-Web-Version1.pdf [hereinafter Susskind Report].

55. *Id.*
56. *Id.*
57. *Id.*
58. Lord Justice Briggs, *Civil Courts Structure Review: Annual Report*, JUDICIARY ENGLAND & WALES (July 2016), https://www.judiciary.gov.uk/wp-content/uploads/2016/07/civil-courts-structure-review-final-report-jul-16-final-1.pdf.
59. Pablo Cortes & Rafal Manko, *Developments in European Civil Procedures*, in THE NEW REGULATORY FRAMEWORK FOR CONSUMER DISPUTE RESOLUTION 51, 55 (Cortes ed., Oxford U. Press, forthcoming).
60. CIVIL RESOLUTION TRIBUNAL, https://www.civilresolutionbc.ca.
61. Interview with Darin Thompson, British Columbia Ministry of Justice and Shannon Salter, Chair of the Civil Resolution Tribunal (Sept. 10, 2015) (on file with authors) [hereinafter Thompson and Salter Interview].
62. *Id.*
63. *Id.*
64. Susskind Report, *supra* note 54, at 12–13.
65. Thompson and Salter Interview, *supra* note 61.
66. *Id.*
67. *9 Things to Know about the Civil Resolution Tribunal Act (CRTA) Changes*, CIV. RESOL. TRIBUNAL (Mar. 11, 2015), http://www.civilresolutionbc.ca/9-things-to-know-about-the-civil-resolution-tribunal-act-crta-changes/.
68. Interview with Maurits Barendrecht, Research Director at HiiL Innovating Justice (Aug. 11, 2015) (on file with authors).
69. Notes from the 15th ODR Conference (Hague May 24, 2016) (on file with authors).
70. *Id.*
71. Maximilian A. Bulinski & J.J. Prescott, *Online Case Resolution Systems: Enhancing Access, Fairness, Accuracy, and Efficiency*, 21 MICH. J. RACE & L. 205 (2016).
72. Lorelei Laird, *J.J. Prescott: Go to Court Without Leaving Home*, ABA J. (Sept. 7, 2016), http://www.abajournal.com/legalrebels/article/jj_prescott_profile.
73. *Compare* RICHARD E. SUSSKIND & DANIEL SUSSKIND, THE FUTURE OF THE PROFESSIONS: HOW TECHNOLOGY WILL TRANSFORM THE WORK OF HUMAN EXPERTS (2015) (reflecting a view that automation will have a very deep and broad impact on the work of lawyers and the need for them), *with* Dana Remus & Frank S. Levy, *Can Robots Be Lawyers? Computers, Lawyers, and the Practice of Law*, SSRN (Dec. 30, 2015) (conveying a much more reserved view of the impact of automation on lawyering and lawyers). For a similar skeptical view of the extent of impact of automation, *see also* Frank Pasquale, *Automating the Professions: Utopian Pipe Dream or Dystopian Nightmare?*, L.A. REV. BOOKS (Mar. 15, 2016), https://lareviewofbooks.org/article/automating-the-professions-utopian-pipe-dream-or-dystopian-nightmare/#!.
74. Thompson and Salter Interview, *supra* note 61.
75. *See* SUSSKIND, TOMORROW'S LAWYERS, *supra* note 18, at 102–05 (discussing what would constitute a fair trial).
76. TOM R. TYLER, PSYCHOLOGY AND THE DESIGN OF LEGAL INSTITUTIONS (2007); Nancy Welsh et al., *The Application of Procedural Justice Research to Judicial Actions and Techniques in Settlement Sessions*, in THE MULTI-TASKING JUDGE: COMPARATIVE JUDICIAL DISPUTE RESOLUTION (Tania Sourdin & Archie Zariski eds., 2013).
77. *See* Lindsey Robertson, *Former High School Bully Sends a Sweet Facebook Apology 20 Years Later*, MASHABLE (May 18, 2015), http://mashable.com/2015/05/18/facebook-apology-bullying/#qZ8RwFsRnPqc.
78. *See* Chris Cox, *I Want to Apologize to the Affected Community (Facebook Status Update)*, FACEBOOK (Oct. 1, 2014), https://www.facebook.com/chris.cox/posts/10101301777354543.

79. Assuming such messages by the court were effective in reaching individuals and being understood by them, they could enhance access to justice by promoting what Richard Susskind refers to as "legal health promotion." *See* Susskind, Tomorrow's Lawyers, *supra* note 18, at 86.

80. Marc Galanter, *The Legal Malaise; Or, Justice Observed*, 19 L. & Soc'y Rev. 537, 545 (1985).

81. Cathy A. Costantino & Christina Sickles Merchant, Designing Conflict Management Systems: A Guide to Creating Productive and Healthy Organizations 4 (1st ed. 1995); William L. Ury et al., Getting Disputes Resolved: Designing Systems to Cut the Costs of Conflict (1988).

82. Orna Rabinovich-Einy, *Deconstructing Dispute Classifications: Avoiding the Shadow of the Law in Dispute System Design in Healthcare*, 12 Cardozo J. Conflict Resol. 55, 78–80 (2010).

83. Michael C. Dorf & Charles F. Sabel, *Drug Treatment Courts and Emergent Experimentalist Government*, 53 Vand. L. Rev. 831, 866–67 (2000); Michael C. Dorf & Jeffrey A. Fagan, *Problem-Solving Courts: From Innovation to Institutionalization*, 40 Am. Crim. L. Rev. 1501, 1506 (2003).

84. This falls under what Richard Susskind refers to as "dispute containment." *See* Susskind, Tomorrow's Lawyers, *supra* note 18, at 86.

85. This falls under what Richard Susskind refers to as "dispute avoidance." *See* Susskind, Tomorrow's Lawyers, *supra* note 18, at 86.

86. Our thoughts on this area were enriched by our discussions with Darin Thompson, of the CRT of British Columbia. *See* Darin Thompson, *Dispute Prevention and Management in Online Dispute Resolution Systems* (draft) (on file with authors).

87. *Id.*

88. *Id.*

89. We thank Professor Alon Klement of Tel Aviv University for this idea.

90. Daniel A. Crane, *Optimizing Private Antitrust Enforcement*, 63 Vand. L. Rev. 675, 678–702 (2010); Orna Rabinovich-Einy & Yair Sagy, *Courts as Organizations: The Drive for Efficiency and the Regulation of Class Action Settlements*, 4 Stan. J. Complex Litig. 1, 22–25 (2016).

91. Richard Granat, *Avvo—Uber for Legal Services*, eLawyering Blog (Feb. 19, 2016), http://www.elawyeringredux.com/2016/02/articles/competition/avvo-uber-for-legal-services/?utm_source=Richard+Granat+-+eLawyering+Blog&utm_campaign=495cdc99a7-RSS_EMAIL_CAMPAIGN&utm_medium=email&utm_term=0_3591394754-495cdc99a7-70617813.

92. Cabral et al., *supra* note 29.

93. *Id.* at 246.

94. Stephen C. Yeazell, *Courting Ignorance: Why We Know So Little about Our Most Important Courts*, 143 Daedalus 129, 133 (2014).

95. Robert A. Baruch Bush, *Mediation and Adjudication, Dispute Resolution and Ideology: An Imaginary Conversation*, 3 J. Contemp. Legal Issues 1 (1989); Frank E. A. Sander & Stephen B. Goldberg, *Fitting the Forum to the Fuss: A User-Friendly Guide to Selecting an ADR Procedure*, 10 Negot. J. 49 (1994); Andrea K. Schneider, *Building a Pedagogy of Problem-Solving: Learning to Choose Among ADR Processes*, 5 Harv. Neg. L. Rev. 113 (2000).

96. Lawrence M. Friedman, *Access to Justice: Some Historical Comments*, 37 Fordham Urb. L.J. 3 (2010).

97. Linda Greenhouse, *Introduction: The Invention of Courts*, 142 Daedelus 5, 5–6 (2016).

98. Susskind, Tomorrow's Lawyers, *supra* note 18, at 102.

Conclusion

1. Eugene Volokh, *Technology and the Future of Law*, 47 Stan. L. Rev. 1375, 1376 (1995).

2. Kevin Kelly, The Inevitable: Understanding the 12 Technological Forces That Will Shape Our Future (2016).

3. Marc Galanter, *Access to Justice in a World of Expanding Social Capability*, 37 FORDHAM URB. L.J. 115, 125 (2010).

4. *2015 National Patient Safety Goals:* HOSPITAL *Accreditation Program*, JOINT COMMISSION (2015), http://www.jointcommission.org/assets/1/6/2015_NPSG_HAP.pdf; *Patient Identification*, 1 PATIENT SAFETY SOLUTIONS (2007), http://www.who.int/patientsafety/solutions/patientsafety/PS-Solution2.pdf.

5. William Drayton, *A Team of Teams World*, STAN. SOC. INNOVATION REV. (2013), http://ssir.org/articles/entry/a_team_of_teams_world?__hstc=218810630.42efd03e30f63728b03a0a7d7651e6c1.1471312664046.1471312664046.1471312664046.1&__hssc=218810630.1.1471312664048&__hsfp=203841643.

6. Ethan Zuckerman, *John Wilbanks on Science Commons, and Generativity in Science*, ETHAN ZUCKERMAN.COM (Mar. 9, 2010), http://www.ethanzuckerman.com/blog/page/48/.

7. *2014 Year-End Report on the Federal Judiciary*, SUP. CT. (2014), http://www.supremecourt.gov/publicinfo/year-end/2014year-endreport.pdf.

8. FRANZ KAFKA, THE TRIAL 267 (Willa Muir & Edwin Muir trans., Alfred A. Knopf, Inc., revised, with additional chapters and notes by E. M. Butler ed., 1956).

9. Stephen G. Breyer, *Reflections on the Role of Appellate Courts: A View from the Supreme Court*, 8 J. APP. PRAC. & PROCESS 91, 92 (2006).

10. *Id.* at n.1.

11. While the request to correct errors is quite simple, the legal questions, as is typical in any Supreme Court case, are complex. A simplified summary of the legal issue is that while the Fair Credit Reporting Act gives individuals a right to sue, courts may only consider cases in which the plaintiff has "standing." One can only have standing if there is a "case or controversy." This means that courts cannot be asked to respond to hypothetical questions. Someone, therefore, must be suffering some harm. The Supreme Court has held that one needs to show that the harm is "concrete and particularized." The distinction between the two is subtle. "Particularized" means that the plaintiff was affected in a "personal and individual way." The "concrete" standard means that the injury must actually exist, that it be real and not abstract. The District Court ruled that Robins was not actually harmed and, therefore, did not have standing. The Court of Appeals found that he *was* harmed, in that a report showing him to be wealthy would hurt his chances of securing a job, since a potential employer might wonder why he was applying for a relatively low-paying job. Six members of the Supreme Court felt that the Court of Appeals only looked at the "particularized" issue but had not considered whether Robins met the "concrete" standard, namely, that he suffered actual harm. Justices Ginsburg and Sotomayor dissented and felt that Robins met both standards for suffering harm.

12. Justice Kagan, Transcript of Oral Argument at 6, Spokeo, Inc. v. Robins, 135 S. Ct. 1892 (2015).

13. *See* Richard Cordray, BUREAU CONSUMER FIN. PROTECTION, 12 CFR Part 1040, Docket No. CFPB-2016-0020 (May 3, 2016), http://files.consumerfinance.gov/f/documents/CFPB_Arbitration_Agreements_Notice_of_Proposed_Rulemaking.pdf; Jessica Silver-Greenberg & Micahel Corkery, *U.S. Just Made it a lot Less Difficult to Sue Nursing Homes*, N.Y. TIMES (Sept. 28, 2016), http://www.nytimes.com/2016/09/29/business/dealbook/arbitration-nursing-homes-elder-abuse-harassment-claims.html?emc=edit_tnt_20160928&nlid=57146577&tntemail0=y&_r=1.

14. Marc Galanter, *Justice in Many Rooms: Courts, Private Ordering, and Indigenous Law*, 19 J. LEGAL PLURALISM 1, 4–5 (1981) (as aptly stated by Galanter, "Is the utopia of access to justice a condition in which all disputes are fully adjudicated? Surely not . . . We know enough about the work of American courts to suspect that such a condition would be equally monstrous in its own way.").

15. ETHAN KATSH & JANET RIFKIN, ONLINE DISPUTE RESOLUTION: RESOLVING CONFLICTS IN CYBERSPACE 93 (1st ed. 2001).

16. MICHAL ALBERSTEIN, JURISPRUDENCE OF MEDIATION (2007) (in Hebrew); Carrie Menkel-Meadow, *Pursuing Settlement in an Adversary Culture: A Tale of Innovation Co-Opted or "The Law of ADR,"* 19 FLA. ST. U. L. REV. 1 (1991); Mary P. Rowe, *The Ombudsman's Role in a Dispute Resolution System,* 7 NEGOT. J. 353 (1991).

17. ROGER FISHER & WILLIAM L. URY, GETTING TO YES: NEGOTIATING AGREEMENT WITHOUT GIVING IN (2d ed. 1993); ROBERT H. MNOOKIN ET AL., BEYOND WINNING: NEGOTIATING TO CREATE VALUE IN DEALS AND DISPUTES (2000); Carrie Menkel-Meadow, *Toward Another View of Legal Negotiation: The Structure of Problem Solving,* 31 UCLA L. REV. 754 (1984); Carrie Menkel-Meadow, *When Dispute Resolution Begets Disputes of Its Own: Conflicts Among Dispute Professionals,* 44 UCLA L. REV. 1871 (1997).

18. Richard Delgado et al., *Fairness and Formality: Minimizing the Risk of Prejudice in Alternative Dispute Resolution,* 1985 WIS. L. REV. 1359 (1985); Trina Grillo, *The Mediation Alternative: Process Dangers for Women,* 100 YALE L.J. 1545 (1991); Laura Nader & Harry F. Todd, *The Disputing Process: Law in Ten Societies,* 82 AM. ANTHROPOLOGIST 160 (1980).

19. ALBERSTEIN, *supra* note 16; Owen M. Fiss, *Against Settlement,* 93 YALE L.J. 1073 (1984); David Luban, *Settlements and the Erosion of the Public Realm,* 83 GEO. L.J. 2619 (1995).

20. Orna Rabinovich-Einy, *Technology's Impact: The Quest for a New Paradigm for Accountability in Mediation,* 11 HARV. NEGOT. L. REV. 253 (2006).

21. Dario Amodei et al., *Concrete Problems in AI Safety,* ARXIV:1606.06565 (June 21, 2016), https://arxiv.org/pdf/1606.06565v1.pdf.

BIBLIOGRAPHY

Abel, Richard. *Politics of Informal Justice*. Academic Press, 1982.

Abel, Richard. "A Comparative Theory of Dispute Institutions in Society." 8 *Law and Society Review* 217 (1973).

Abt, Clark. *Serious Games*. University Press of America, 1972.

Alberstein, Michal. *Jurisprudence of Mediation*. Jerusalem: The Hebrew University Magnes Press, 2007.

Albiston, Catherine R., Lauren B. Edelman, and Joy Milligan. "The Dispute Tree and the Legal Forest." *Annual Review of Law and Social Science* 10 (2014): 105–131.

Amsler, Lisa Blomgren, Janet Martinez, and Stephanie Smith. *Dispute Systems Design*. Palo Alto: Stanford University Press (Forthcoming 2017).

Auerbach, Jerold. *Justice without Law?* New York: Oxford University Press, 1984.

Balkin, Jack, and Beth Simone Noveck, eds. *The State of Play: Law, Games, and Virtual Worlds*. New York: NYU Press, 2006.

Barabasi, Albert-László. *Linked: How Everything Is Connected to Everything Else and What It Means for Business, Science, and Everyday Life*. Cambridge, MA: Perseus Publishing, 2003.

Barrett, F. J. "Generative Metaphor Intervention: A New Approach for Working with Systems Divided by Conflict and Caught in Defensive Perception." 26 *The Journal of Applied Behavioral Science* 219 (1990).

Benedikt, Michael. *Cyberspace*. Cambridge, MA: MIT Press, 1992.

Benkler, Yochai. "Peer Production and Cooperation." In *Handbook on the Economics of the Internet*, edited by J. M. Bauer and M. Latzer. Cheltenham and Northampton: Edward Elgar Publishing, 2016.

Benkler, Yochai. "Sharing Nicely: On Shareable Goods and the Emergence of Sharing as a Modality of Economic Production." 114 *Yale Law Journal* 273 (2004).

Benkler, Yochai. *The Wealth of Networks: How Social Production Transforms Markets and Freedom*. New Haven, CT: Yale University Press, 2006.

Digital Justice. Ethan Katsh and Orna Rabinovich-Einy.
© Ethan Katsh and Orna Rabinovich-Einy 2017. Published 2017 by Oxford University Press.

Berman, Greg, and John Feinblatt. "Problem-Solving Courts: A Brief Primer." 23 *Law and Policy* 125 (April 2001).

Berman, Paul Schiff. "From International Law to Law and Globalization." 43 *Columbia Journal of Transnational Law* 485 (2005).

Berner, Eta S., and Mark L. Graber. "Overconfidence as a Cause of Diagnostic Error in Medicine." 121 *The American Journal of Medicine* S2 (May 2008).

Bilstad, Blake T. "Obscenity and Indecency on the Usenet: The Legal and Political Future of Alt.Sex.Stories." 2 *Journal of Computer-Mediated Communication* 321 (September 1996).

Bingham, Lisa B. "Self-Determination in Dispute System Design and Employment Arbitration." 56 *University of Miami Law Review* 873 (2002).

Blacksell, Mark. "Social Justice and Access to Legal Services: A Geographical Perspective." 21 *Geoforum* 489 (January 1990).

Blumenthal, David. "Launching HITECH." 362 *New England Journal of Medicine* 382 (February 4, 2010).

Boulton, Jean G., Peter M. Allen, and Cliff Bowman. *Embracing Complexity: Strategic Perspectives for an Age of Turbulence.* New York: Oxford University Press, 2015.

Bower, Joseph L., and Clayton M. Christensen. "Disruptive Technologies: Catching the Wave." 713 *Harvard Business Review* 43 (January–February 1995).

Brenner, Susan. *Law in an Era of Smart Technologies.* New York: Oxford University Press, 2007.

Brynjolfsson, Eric, and Andrew McAfee. *The Second Machine Age: Work, Progress, and Prosperity in a Time of Brilliant Technologies.* New York: W. W. Norton & Company, 2016.

Bulinski, Maximilian A. and J.J. Prescott, "Online Case Resolution Systems: Enhancing Access, Fairness, Accuracy, and Efficiency." 21 *Michigan Journal of Race and Law* 2015 (2016).

Bush, Robert A. Baruch. "Mediation and Adjudication, Dispute Resolution and Ideology: An Imaginary Conversation." 3 *Journal of Contemporary Legal Issues* 1 (1989).

Cabral, James E., Abhijeet Chavan, Thomas M. Clarke, John Greacen, Bonnie Rose Hough, Linda Rexer, Jane Ribadeneyra, and Richard Zorza. "Using Technology to Enhance Access to Justice." 26 *Harvard Journal of Law & Technology* 241 (2012).

Cahn, Edmund. *Confronting Injustice.* Boston, MA: Little Brown, 1962.

Cappalletti, Mauro, and Bryant Garth. "Access to Justice: The Newest Wave in the Worldwide Movement to Make Rights Effective." 27 *Buffalo Law Review* 181 (1978).

Cappelletti, Mauro, and Bryant Garth. *Access to Justice: A World Survey*, edited by Mauro Cappelletti. Vol. 1. Netherlands, Giuffrè Editore, 1978.

Cappelletti, Mauro, and Bryant Garth. *Access to Justice: Emerging Issues and Perspectives,* edited by Mauro Cappelletti. Vol. 3. Netherlands: Giuffrè Editore, 1978.

Carneiro, David, Paulo Novais, and Jose Neves. *Conflict Resolution and Its Contexts.* New York: Springer, 2014.

Chan, K. S., J. B. Fowles, and J. P. Weiner. "Review: Electronic Health Records and the Reliability and Validity of Quality Measures: A Review of the Literature." 67 *Medical Care Research and Review* 503 (February 11, 2010).

Chander, Anupam. "The Racist Algorithm." 115 *Michigan Law Review* (Forthcoming 2017).

Cherry, Miriam A. "The Gamification of Work." 40 *Hofstra Law Review* 851 (2012).

Christie, Nils. "Conflicts and Property." 17 *British Journal of Criminology* 1 (1977).

Citron, Danielle Keats. *Hate Crimes.* Cambridge, MA: Harvard University Press, 2014.

Citron, Danielle Keats. "Technological Due Process." 85 *Washington University Law Review* 1248 (2008).

Citron, Danielle Keats, and Mary Anne Franks. "Criminalizing Revenge Porn," 49 *Wake Forest Law Review* 345 (2014).

Citron, Danielle Keats, and Frank A. Pasquale. "The Scored Society: Due Process for Automated Predictions." *Washington Law Review* 89 (2014).

Cohen, Adam. *The Perfect Store.* Boston: Little, Brown, 2002.

Cohen, I. Glenn, Ruben Amarasingham, Anand Shah, Bin Xie, and Bernard Lo. "The Legal and Ethical Concerns that Arise from Using Complex Predictive Analytics in Health Care." 33 *Health affairs* 1139 (2014).

Conbere, John P. "Theory Building for Conflict Management System Design." 19 *Conflict Resolution Quarterly* 215 (2001).

Cooper, Benjamin P. "Access to Justice without Lawyers." 47 *Akron Law Review* 207 (2014).

Cortés, Pablo. *Online Dispute Resolution for Consumers in the European Union.* London: Routledge, 2010.

Cortés, Pablo (ed.) *The New Regulatory Framework for Consumer Dispute Resolution.* Oxford University Press, 2017.

Costantino, Cathy A. "Using Interest-Based Techniques to Design Conflict Management Systems." 12 *Negotiation Journal* 207 (1996).

Costantino, Cathy A., and Christina Sickles S. Merchant. *Designing Conflict Management Systems: A Guide to Creating Productive and Healthy Organizations.* San Francisco: Jossey-Bass, Publishers, 1996.

Cox, Scott, Tanya Goette, and Dale Young. "Workplace Surveillance and Employee Privacy: Implementing an Effective Computer Use Policy." 5 *Communications of the IIMA* 57 (2005).

Crane, Daniel A. "Optimizing Private Antitrust Enforcement." 63 *Vanderbilt Law Review* 675 (2010).

Crawford, Susan. *Captive Audience: The Telecom Industry and Monopoly Power in the New Gilded Age.* New Haven: Yale University Press, 2013.

Crawford, Susan, and Stephen Goldsmith. *The Responsive City: Engaging Communities through Data-Smart.* San Francisco: Jossey-Bass, 2014.

boyd, danah. *It's Complicated: The Social Lives of Networked Teens.* New Haven: Yale University Press, 2014.

Danner, Richard, and Frank Houdeck, eds. ' "Legal Information and the Development of American Law' Further Thinking about the Thoughts of Robert C. Berring." 99 *Law Library Journal* 191 (2007).

Davis, William, and Helga Turku. "Access to Justice and Alternative Dispute Resolution." 2011 *Journal of Dispute Resolution* 47 (2011).

deBronkart, Dave, Eric J. Topol, and Danny Sands. *Let Patients Help!* CreateSpace Independent Publishing Platform, 2003.

Delgado, Richard, Chris Dunn, Pamela Brown, and Helena Lee. "Fairness and Formality: Minimizing the Risk of Prejudice in Alternative Dispute Resolution." *Wisconsin Law Review* 1359 (1985).

DeMars, Jo, Susan Nauss Exon, Kimberlee K. Kovach, and Colin Rule. "Virtual Virtues: Ethical Considerations for an Online Dispute Resolution (ODR) Practice." 17 *Dispute Resolution Magazine* 6 (2010).

De Sola, Pool Ithiel. *Technologies of Freedom.* Cambridge, MA: Harvard University Press, 1983.

Dibbell, Julian. *Play Money: Or, How I Quit My Day Job and Made Millions Trading Virtual Loot.* New York: Basic Books, 2006.

Dibbell, Julian. "A Rape in Cyberspace." <http://www.juliandibbell.com/articles/a-rape-in-cyberspace/>.

Donath, Judith. *The Social Machine.* Cambridge: MA: MIT Press, 2014.

Dorf, Michael C., and Jeffrey A. Fagan. "Problem-Solving Courts: From Innovation to Institutionalization." 40 *American Criminal Law Review* 1501 (2003).

Dorf, Michael C., and Charles F. Sabel. "Drug Treatment Courts and the Experimentalist Government." 53 *Vanderbilt Law Review* 831 (2000).

Dullabh, Prashila Norman Sondheimer, and Ethan Katsh. "Is There an App for That? Electronic Health Records (EHRs) and a New Environment of Conflict Prevention and Resolution." 74 *Law and Contemporary Problems* 31 (2011).

Dullabh, Prashila Norman Sondheimer, and Ethan Katsh, and Michael A. Evans. "How Patients Can Improve the Accuracy of their Medical Records." EGEMS (2014). < http://repository.edm-forum.org/cgi/viewcontent.cgi?article=1080&context=egems>.

Edelman, Lauren B., Howard S. Erlanger, and John Lande. "Internal Dispute Resolution: The Transformation of Civil Rights in the Workplace." 27 *Law & Society Review* 497 (1993).

Effy, Vayena, and Urs Gasser. "Strictly Biomedical? Sketching the Ethics of the Big Data Ecosystem in Biomedicine." In *The Ethics of Biomedical Big Data*, edited by Brent Daniel Mittelstadt and Luciano Floridi. New York: Springer-Verlag, 2016.

Eisenstein, Elizabeth. *The Printing Press As An Agent of Change* (New York: Cambridge University Press, 1979.

Ellickson, Robert. *Order without Law.* Cambridge: MA: Harvard University Press, 1994.

Fallers Lloyd L. *Law without Precedent.* Chicago: University of Chicago Press, 1969.

Febvre, Lucien, and Henri-Jean Martin. *The Coming of the Book.* London: NLB, 1976.

Felstiner, William L. F., Richard L. Abel, and Austin Sarat. "The Emergence and Transformation of Disputes: Naming, Blaming, Claiming . . ." 15 *Law & Society Review* 631 (1980).

Fisher, Roger, and William Ury. *Getting to Yes.* Boston: Houghton Mifflin, 1981.

Fiss, Owen M. "Against Settlement." 93 *Yale Law Journal* 1073 (May 1984).

Fleming, Chris. "New Era of Patient Engagement." 32 *Health Affairs* (2013).

Friedman, Lawrence M. "Access to Justice: Some Historical Comments." 37 *Fordham Urban Law Journal* 115 (2010).

Froomkin, A. Michael. "Wrong Turn in Cyberspace: Using ICANN to Route around the APA and the Constitution." 50 *Duke Law Journal* 17 (2000).

Fulda, K. G., and K. Lykens. "Ethical Issues in Predictive Genetic Testing: A Public Health Perspective." 32 *Journal of Medical Ethics* 143 (March 2006).

Galanter, Marc. "Access to Justice in a World of Expanding Social Capability." 37 *Fordham Urban Law Journal* 115 (2010).

Galanter, Marc. "Justice in Many Rooms: Courts, Private Ordering, and Indigenous Law." 13 *The Journal of Legal Pluralism and Unofficial Law* 1 (January 1981).

Galanter, Marc. "The Legal Malaise: Or, Justice Observed." 19 *Law & Society Review* 537 (1985).

Galanter, Marc. "Reading the Landscape of Disputes: What We Know and Don't Know (and Think We Know) about Our Allegedly Contentious and Litigious Society." 31 *UCLA Law Review* 4 (December 1983).

Galanter, Marc. "The Vanishing Trial: An Examination of Trials and Related Matters in Federal and State Courts." 1 *Journal of Empirical Legal Studies* 459 (November 2004).

Galanter, Marc. "Why the 'Haves' Come out Ahead: Speculations on the Limits of Legal Change." 9 *Law & Society Review* 95 (1974).

Galanter, Marc, and Angela M. Frozena. "A Grin without a Cat: The Continuing Decline & Displacement of Trials in American Courts." 143 *Daedalus* 115 (July 2014).

Garber, Marilyn, and Jerold S. Auerbach. "Justice without Law?" 71 *The Journal of American History* 104 (1984).

Gardner, Howard, and Katie Davis. *The App Generation*. New Haven, CT: Yale University Press, 2013.

Geiger, R. Stuart. "The Lives of Bots." In *Critical Point of View: A Wikipedia Reader*, edited by Geert Lovnik and Nathaniel Tkacz. Amsterdam: Institute of Network Cultures, 2011.

Geist, Michael. "Fair.com? An Examination of the Allegations of Systemic Unfairness in the ICANN UDRP." 27 *Brooklyn Journal of International Law* 903 (2002).

Gelms, Jeremy. "High-Tech Harassment: Employer Liability under Title VII for Employee Social Media Misconduct." 87 *Washington Law Review* 249 (2012).

Ghoshray, Saby. "Employer Surveillance versus Employee Privacy: The New Reality of Social Media and Workplace Privacy." 40 *Northern Kentucky Law Review* 593 (2013).

Gleick, James. *Faster*. New York: Vintage, 2000.

Gleick, James. *The Information: A History, a Theory, a Flood*. New York: Vintage, 2012.

Gleick, James. *What Just Happened: A Chronicle from the Information Frontier*. Pantheon Books, 2002.

Goldberg, Stephen B., Eric D. Green, and Frank E. A. Sander. *Dispute Resolution*. Boston: Little, Brown, 1985.

Goldman, Eric. "Unregulating Online Harassment." 87 *Denver University Law Review* 59 (2010).

Goldsmith, Jack, and Tim Wu. *Who Controls the Internet?: Illusions of a Borderless World*. New York: Oxford University Press, 2008.

Grabau, Charles M., and Llewellyn Joseph Gibbons. "Protecting the Rights of Linguistic Minorities: Challenges to Court Interpretation." 30 *New England Law Review* 60 (1996).

Greenstein, Shane. *How the Internet Became Commercial: Innovation, Privatization, and the Birth of a New Network*. Princeton: Princeton University Press, 2016.

Grillo, Trina. "The Mediation Alternative: Process Dangers for Women." 100 *The Yale Law Journal* 1545 (1991).

Grimmelmann, James. "The Virtues of Moderation." 17 *Yale Journal of Law and Technology* 42 (2015).

Grossman, Daniel, Kate Grindlay, Todd Buchacker, Kathleen Lane, and Kelly Blanchard. "Effectiveness and Acceptability of Medical Abortion Provided through Telemedicine." 118 *Obstetrics & Gynecology* 296 (August 2011).

Hadfield, Gillian K. "Innovating to Improve Access: Changing the Way Courts Regulate Legal Markets." 143 *Daedalus* 83 (July 2014).

Hensler, Deborah R. "Our Courts, Ourselves: How the Alternative Dispute Resolution Movement Is Re-Shaping Our Legal System." 108 *Penn State Law Review* 165 (2003).

Hill, E. Jeffrey, Joseph G. Grzywacz, Sarah Allen, Victoria L. Blanchard, Christina Matz-Costac, Sandee Shulkin, and Marcie Pitt-Catsouphes. "Defining and Conceptualizing Workplace Flexibility." 11 *Community, Work and Family* 149 (May 2008).

Hirsch, Jeffrey M. "Worker Collective Action in the Digital Age." 117 *West Virginia Law Review* 921 (2015).

Hobbs, Steven H. "Shout from Taller Rooftops: A Response to Deborah L. Rhode's Access to Justice." 73 *Fordham Law Review* 935 (2004).

Hodges, Christopher, Iris Benohr, and Naomi Creutzfeldt-Banda. *Consumer ADR in Europe*. Oxford: Hart Publishing, 2012.

Hoffman, David A., and Salil K. Mehra. "Wikitruth through Wikiorder." 59 *Emory Law Journal* 151 (2010).

Hoffman, Sharona, and Andy Podgurski. "E-Health Hazards: Provider Liability and Electronic Health Record Systems." 24 *Berkeley Technology Law Journal* 1523 (2009).

Hoffman, Sharona, and Andy Podgurski. "Finding a Cure: The Case for Regulation for Oversight of Electronic Health Record Systems." 22 *Harvard Journal of Law & Technology* 103 (2008).

Homeyman, Christopher, James Coben and Giuseppe De Palo. Rethinking Negotiation Teaching. St. Paul: DRI Press, 2009.

Hornle, Julia. *Cross-Border Internet Dispute Resolution*. Cambridge University Press, 2009.

Hornle, Julia. "Legal Controls on the Use of Arbitration Clause in B2C E-Commerce Contracts." 2 *Masaryk University Journal of Law and Technology* 23 (2008).

Huckabee, Gregory M., and Cherry Kolb. "Privacy in the Workplace, Fact or Fiction, and the Value of an Authorized Use Policy (AUP)." 59 *South Dakota Law Review* 35 (2014).

Hultmark, Christina. *Internet Marketplaces: The Law of Auctions and Exchanges Online*. Oxford: Oxford University Press, 2003.

Hung, Shin-Yuan, Chia-Ming Chang, and Shao-Rong Kuo. "User Acceptance of Mobile E-Government Services: An Empirical Study." 30 *Government Information Quarterly* 33 (January 2013).

Hunter, Dan, and Greg Lastowka. "The Laws of the Virtual Worlds." 92 *California Law Review* 1 (2003).

Huws, Ursula. *Labor in the Global Digital Economy: The Cybertariat Comes of Age* New York: Monthly Review Press, 2014.

Hyman, Jonathan M., and Lela P. Love. "If Portia Were a Mediator: An Inquiry into Justice in Mediation." 9 *Clinical Law Review* 157 (2002).

James, John T. "A New, Evidence-Based Estimate of Patient Harms Associated with Hospital Care." 9 *Journal of Patient Safety* 122 (2013).

Jeong, Sarah. *The Internet of Garbage*. Amazon Digital Services, 2015.

Johnson, David R., and David G. Post. "Law and Borders: The Rise of Law in Cyberspace." 48 *Stanford Law Review* 1367 (1996).

Johnson, David R. *Building and Using Hypertext Systems in the Practice of Law*. Washington: Wilmer, Cutler and Pickering, 1989.

Kaboli, Peter J., Brad J. McClimon, Angela B. Hoth, and Mitchell J. Barnett. "Assessing the Accuracy of Computerized Medication Histories." 10 *The American Journal of Managed Care* 872 (November 2004).

Kahin, Brian and Chrales Nesson (eds.). *Borders in Cyberspace: Information Policy and the Global Information Infrastructure*. Ccambridge, MA: MIT Press, 1997.

Kaplan, Robert and David Norton. *Strategy Maps*. Boston: Harvard University Press, 2004.

Katsh, Ethan. *The Electronic Media and the Transformation of Law*. New York: Oxford University Press, 1989.

Katsh, Ethan. *Law in a Digital World*. New York: Oxford University Press, 1995.

Katsh, Ethan, and Janet Rifkin. *Online Dispute Resolution: Resolving Conflicts in Cyberspace*. San Francisco: Jossey-Bass Inc., 2001.

Katsh, Ethan, and Colin Rule. "What We Know and Need to Know about Online Dispute Resolution." 67 *South Carolina Law Review* 329 (2016).

Katsh, Ethan and Janet Rifkin. "The New Media and a New Model of Conflict Resolution: Copying, Copyright, and Creating," 6 *Notre Dame J.L. Ethics & Pub. Pol'y* 49 (1992).

Katsh, Ethan, and Leah Wing. "Ten Years of Online Dispute Resolution: Looking at the Past and Constructing the Future." 38 *Toledo Law Review* 101 (2006).

Katsh, Ethan, Janet Rifkin, and Alan Gaitenby. "E-Commerce, E-Disputes, and E-Dispute Resolution: In the Shadow of 'eBay Law.'" 15 *Ohio State Journal of Dispute Resolution* 705 (2000).

Khan, Fazal. "The 'Uberization' of Healthcare: The Forthcoming Legal Storm over Mobile Health Technology's Impact on the Medical Profession." 26 *Journal of Law-Medicine* 123 (2016).

Kim, Nancy. *Wrap Contracts: Foundations and Ramifications*. New York: Oxford University Press, 2013.

Kirkpatrick, David. *The Facebook Effect: The Inside Story of the Company That Is Connecting the World*. New York: Simon & Schuster, 2010.

Kirstein, Peter T. "The Early Days of the Arpanet." 31 *IEEE Annals of the History of Computing* 67 (2009).

Kolb, Deborah M., and Susan S. Silbey. "Enhancing the Capacity of Organizations to Deal with Disputes." 6 *Negotiation Journal* 297 (October 1990).

Koppel, Ross, and David Kreda. "Health Care Information Technology Vendors' 'Hold Harmless' Clause." 301 *Journal of the American Medical Association* 1276 (March 25, 2009).

Koščík, Michal. "'Sucks Cases' in WIPO Domain Name Decisions." 1 *Masaryk University Journal of Law and Technology* 229 (2007).

Kossek, Ellen Ernst, and Jesse S. Michel. "Flexible Work Schedules." In *APA Handbook of Industrial and Organizational Psychology*, by Ellen Ernst Kossek and Jesse S. Michel, 535, edited by Sheldon Zedeck. Washington, D.C.: American Psychological Association, 2010.

Kuhn, Thomas. *The Structure of Scientific Revolutions*. Chicago: University of Chicago Press, 1970.

Kulp, Heather Scheiwe, and Amanda L Kool. "You Help Me, He Helps You: Dispute Systems Design in the Sharing Economy." 48 *Washington University Journal of Law & Policy* 179 (2015).

Lanier, Jaron. *You Are Not a Gadget: A Manifesto*. New York: Vintage, 2011.

Larson, David A. "Access to Justice for Persons with Disabilities: An Emerging Strategy." 3 *Laws* 220 (May 27, 2014).

Larson, David A. "Technology Mediated Dispute Resolution (TMDR): A New Paradigm for ADR." 38 *University of Toledo Law Review* 213 (November 16, 2006).

Lessig, Lawrence. *Code: And Other Laws of Cyberspace*. New York: Basic Books, 1999.

Lessig, Lawrence. *Code: And Other Laws of Cyberspace, Version 2.0*. New York: Basic Books, 2006.

Lessig, Lawrence. *The Future of Ideas: The Fate of the Commons in a Connected World*. New York: Random House, 2002.

Levine, Rick, Christopher Locke, Doc Searls, and David Weinberger. *The Cluetrain Manifesto*. New York: Basic Books, 2001.

Levy, Nathaniel, Sandra Cortesi, Urs Gasser, Edward Crowley, Meredith Beaton, June Casey, and Caroline Nolan. "Bullying in a Networked Era: A Literature Review." *Berkman Center Research*, Publication No. 2012–17 (September 15, 2012).

Lewis, Ray. "Employee E-Mail Privacy Still Unemployed: What the United States Can Learn from the United Kingdom." 67 *Louisiana Law Review* 959 (2007).

Lim, Marion. "ADR of Patent Disputes: A Customized Prescription, Not an Over-the-Counter Remedy." 6 *Cadozo Journal of Conflict Resolution* 155 (2004).

Lipsky, David B., Ronald L. Seeber, and Richard D. Fincher. *Emerging Systems for Managing Workplace Conflict: Lessons from American Corporations for Managers and Dispute Resolution Professionals*. San Francisco, CA: Jossey-Bass Inc., 2003.

Llewellyn, Karl N. *The Bramble Bush*. 1st ed. New York: New York: Oceana, 1930.

Lobel, Orly. "The Law of the Platform." 101 *Minn. L. Rev.* (forthcoming, 2016).

Lodder, Arno R., and John Zeleznikow. "Developing an Online Dispute Resolution Environment: Dialogue Tools and Negotiation Support Systems in a Three-Step Model." 10 *Harvard Negotiation Law Review* 287 (2005).

Lodder, Arno R., and John Zeleznikow. *Enhanced Dispute Resolution through the Use of Information Technology.* Cambridge: Cambridge University Press, 2010.

Lowndes, Benjamin. "'Join the Conversation': Why Twitter Should Market Itself as a Technology Mediated Dispute Resolution Tool." 2 *International Journal of Online Dispute Resolution* 128 (2015).

Luban, David. "Settlements and the Erosion of the Public Realm." 83 *Georgetown Law Journal* 2619 (1995).

Macduff, Ian. "Flames on the Wire: Mediating from an Electronic Cottage." 10 *Negotiation Journal* 5 (1994).

Mackay, Erin A. "Patients, Consumers, and Caregivers: The Original Data Stewards." 3 *eGEMs (Generating Evidence & Methods to Improve Patient Outcomes)* 1173 (March 23, 2015).

Maeda, John. *The Laws of Simplicity.* Cambridge, MA: MIT Press, 2006.

Makary, Martin. *Unaccountable: What Hospitals Won't Tell You and How Transparency Can Revolutionize Health Care.* New York: Bloomsbury Press, 2012.

Markoff, John. *What the Dormouse Said: How the 60's Counterculture Shaped the Personal Computer Industry.* New York: Penguin Books, 2006.

Maurer, Maureen, Pam Dardess, Kristin L. Carman, Karen Frazier, and Lauren Smeeding. *Guide to Patient and Family Engagement: Environmental Scan Report.* AHRQ Publication, 2012.

Mayer-Schonberger, Viktor, and Kenneth Cukier. *Big Data: A Revolution That Will Transform How We Live, Work, and Think.* Boston: Eamon Dolan/ Houghton Mifflin Harcourt, 2013.

McAdoo, Bobbi, and Nancy A. Welsh. "Look Before You Leap and Keep on Looking: Lessons from the Institutionalization of Court-Connected Mediation." 5 *Nevada Law Journal* 399 (2004).

McLuhan, Marshall. *Understanding Media.* New York: McGraw-Hill, 1964.

Menkel-Meadow, Carrie. "Pursuing Settlement in an Adversary Culture: A Tale of Innovation Co-Opted or The Law of ADR." 19 *Florida State University Law Review* 1 (1991).

Menkel-Meadow, Carrie. "Regulation of Dispute Resolution in the United States of America: From the Formal to the Informal to the 'Semi-Formal.'" In *Regulating Dispute Resolution: ADR and Access to Justice at the Crossroads,* edited by Felix Steffek, Hannes Unberath, Hazel Genn, Reinhard Greger, and Carrie Menkel-Meadow. Oxford: Hart Publishing, 2013.

Menkel-Meadow, Carrie. "Toward Another View of Legal Negotiation: The Structure of Problem Solving." 31 *UCLA Law Review* 754 (1984).

Menkel-Meadow, Carrie. "When Dispute Resolution Begets Disputes of Its Own: Conflicts among Dispute Professionals." 44 *UCLA Law Review* 1871 (1997).

Menkel-Meadow, Carrie. "When Litigation Is Not the Only Way: Consensus Building and Mediation as Public Interest Lawyering." 37 *Washington University Journal of Law & Policy* 42 (2002).

Merchant, Christina Sickles, and Cathy A. Costantino. *Designing Conflict Management Systems: A Guide to Creating Productive and Healthy Organizations*. San Francisco: Jossey-Bass Publishers, 1995.

Miller, Richard E., and Austin Sarat. "Grievances, Claims, and Disputes: Assessing the Adversary Culture." 17 *Law & Society Review* 52 (1983).

Mitchell, William J. *City of Bits: Space, Place, and the Infobahn*. Cambridge: MIT Press, 1996.

Mnookin, Jennifer L. Virtual(Ly) Law: The Emergence of Law in LambdaMOO, 2 Journal of Computer-Mediated Communication (June 1996).

Mnookin, Robert H., Scott R. Peppet, and Andrew S. Tulumello. *Beyond Winning: Negotiating to Create Value in Deals and Disputes*. Cambridge, MA: Harvard University Press, 2000.

Mnookin, Robert H., and Lewis Kornhauser. "Bargaining in the Shadow of the Law: The Case of Divorce." 88 *Yale Law Journal* 950 (1979).

Moffitt, Michael L. and Robert C. Bordone. *The Handbook of Dispute Resolution*. San Francisco: Jossey-Bass, 2005.

Moore, Christopher. *The Mediation Process*. San Francisco: Jossey-Bass, 1986.

Morozov, Evgeny. *The Net Delusion: The Dark Side of Internet Freedom*. New York: Public Affairs Press, 2011.

Morozov, Evgeny. *To Save Everything, Click Here: The Folly of Technological Solutionism*. New York: Public Affairs Press, 2014.

Murray, Andrew. *Information Technology Law: The Law and Society*. New York: Oxford University Press, 2010.

Nader, Laura, and Harry F. Todd. *The Disputing Process: Law in Ten Societies*. New York, 1978.

Nicholas, Carr. *The Glass Cage: How Our Computers Are Changing Us*. New York: W. W. Norton & Company, 2015.

Nicholas, Carr. *The Shallows: What the Internet Is Doing to Our Brains*. New York: W. W. Norton & Company, 2011.

Niemic, Robert and Donna Stienstra and Randall Ravitz. *Guide To Judicial Management of Cases in ADR*. Washingotn, DC: Federal Judicial Center.

Nolan-Haley, Jacqueline. "Court Mediation and the Search for Justice through Law." 74 *Washington University Law Review* 47 (1996).

Nolan-Haley, Jacqueline. "Mediation as the New Arbitration." 17 *Harvard Negotiation Law Review* 61 (2012).

Norman, Donald. *The Design of Everyday Things*. New York: Basic Books, rev. 2013.

Norman, Donald. *Living with Complexity*. Cambridge, MA: MIT Press, 2010.

Norman, Donald. *Things That Make Us Smart*. Cambridge, MA: Perseus Publishing 1994.

Norris, Donald F., and Christopher G. Reddick. "Local E-Government in the United States: Transformation or Incremental Change?" 73 *Public Administration Review* 165 (2012).

Noveck, Beth Simone. "The Future of Citizen Participation in the Electronic State: Modeling Communicative Action in E-Rulemaking Practice." 1 *A Journal of Law and Policy* 1 (2005).

Noveck, Beth Simone. *Wiki Government*. Washington, D.C.: Brookings Institution Press, 2009.

Nyman, Nicole J. "Risky Business: What Must Employers Do to Shield Against Liability for Employee Wrongdoings in the Internet Age?" 1 *Shidler Journal of Law, Commerce and Technology* 7 (February 2, 2005).

Palfrey, John, and Urs Gasser. *Born Digital: Understanding the First Generation of Digital Natives*. New York: Basic Books, 2010.

Palfrey, John and Urs Gasser. *Interop*. New York: Basic Books, 2012.

Panger, Galen. "Reassessing the Facebook Experiment: Critical Thinking about the Validity of Big Data Research." 19 *Information, Communication and Society* 1108 (October 19, 2016).

Pasquale, Frank. *The Black Box Society*. Cambridge, MA: Harvard University Press, 2015.

Pasquale, Frank, and Glyn Cashwell. "Four Futures of Legal Automation." 63 *UCLA Law Review Discourse* 26 (2015).

Perel (Filmar), Maayan, and Niva Elkin-Koren. "Accountability in Algorithmic Enforcement: Lessons from Copyright Enforcement by Online Intermediaries." *Stanford Technology Law Review* (2016).

Ponte, Lucille M., and Thomas D. Cavenagh. *Cyberjustice: Online Dispute Resolution (ODR) for E-Commerce*. Upper Saddle River, NJ: Prentice Hall, 2004.

Rabinovich-Einy, Orna. "Beyond Efficiency: The Transformation of Courts through Technology." 12 *UCLA Journal of Law and Technology* 1 (2008).

Rabinovich-Einy, Orna. "Deconstructing Dispute Classifications: Avoiding the Shadow of the Law in Dispute System Design in Healthcare." 12 *Cardozo Journal of Dispute Resolution* 55 (2010).

Rabinovich-Einy, Orna. "Technology's Impact: The Quest for a New Paradigm for Accountability in Mediation." 11 *Harvard Negotiation Law Review* 253 (2006).

Rabinovich-Einy, Orna, and Ethan Katsh. "Lessons from Online Dispute Resolution for Dispute Systems Design." In *Online Dispute Resolution: Theory and Practice: A Treatise on Technology and Dispute Resolution*, edited by M. S. Wahab, E. Katsh, and D. Rainey. The Hague: Eleven International Publishing, 2012.

Rabinovich-Einy, Orna, and Ethan Katsh. "Technology and the Future of Dispute Systems Design." 17 *Harvard Negotiation Law Review* 151 (2012).

Rabinovich-Einy, Orna, and Yair Sagy. "Courts as Organizations: The Drive for Efficiency and the Regulation of Class Actions." 4 *Stanford Journal of Complex Litigation* 1 (2016).

Radin, Margaret Jane. *Boilerplate: The Fine Print, Vanishing Rights, and the Rule of Law*. Princeton, NJ: Princeton University Press, 2013.

Raiffa, Howard. *The Art and Science of Negotiation*. Cambridge, MA: Harvard Unoiversity Press, 1982.

Rainey, Daniel, and Ethan Katsh. "ODR and Government." In *Online Dispute Resolution: Theory and Practice: A Treatise on Technology and Dispute Resolution*, edited by M. S. Wahab, E. Katsh, and D. Rainey, 248. The Hague: Eleven International Publishing, 2012.

Ramzan, Zulfikar. "Phishing Attacks and Countermeasures." In *Handbook of Information and Communication Security*, edited by Peter Stavroulakis and Mark Stamp, 433. Springer Science Business Media, 2010.

Raymond, Anjanette H. "Yeah, But Did You See the Gorilla? Creating and Protecting an Informed Consumer in Cross-Border Online Dispute Resolution." 19 *Harvard Negotiation Law Review* 129 (2014).

Raymond, Anjanette H., and Scott J. Shackelford. "Jury Glasses: Wearable Technology and Its Role in Crowdsourcing Justice." 17 *Cardozo Journal of Conflict Resolution* 115 (2015).

Raymond, Anjanette H., and Scott J. Shackelford. "Technology, Ethics and Access to Justice: Should an Algorithm Be Deciding Your Case?" 35 *Michigan Journal of International Law* 485 (2014).

Remus, Dana, and Frank S. Levy. "Can Robots Be Lawyers? Computers, Lawyers, and the Practice of Law." December 30, 2015. http://ssrn.com/abstract=2701092doi:10.2139/ssrn.2701092.

Resnik, Judith. "Diffusing Disputes: The Public in the Private of Arbitration, the Private in Courts, and the Erasure of Rights." 124 *Yale Law Journal* 2680 (2015).

Rhode, Deborah L. *Access to Justice*. New York: Oxford University Press, 2004.

Rhode, Deborah L. "Symposium the Constitution of Equal Citizenship for a Good Society: Access to Justice." 69 *Fordham Law Review* 1785 (2001).

Rich, Michael L. "Machine Learning, Automated Suspicion Algorithms and the Fourth Amendment." 164 *University of Pennsylvania Law Review* 871 (2015).

Rogers, Nancy H., Robert Bordone, Frank Sander, and Craig A. McEwen. *Designing Systems and Processes for Managing Disputes*. New York: Aspen Publishers, 2013.

Rosenberg, Arnold S. "Better than Cash? Global Proliferation of Payment Cards and Consumer Protection Policy." 44 *Columbia Journal of Transnational Law* 520 (2006).

Ross, Richard J. "Communications Revolutions and Legal Culture: An Elusive Relationship." 27 *Law and Social Inquiry* 637 (2002).

Ross, Sara. "Your Day in 'Wiki-Court': ADR, Fairness, and Justice in Wikipedia's Global Community." 10 *Osgoode Legal Studies Research Paper No. 56* (2014).

Rowe, Mary P. "The Ombudsman's Role in a Dispute Resolution System." 7 *Negotiation Journal* 353 (October 1991).

Rule, Colin. *Online Dispute Resolution for Business: B2B, E-Commerce, Consumer Employment, Insurance and Other Commercial Conflicts.* San Francisco: Jossey-Bass, 2002.

Rule, Colin. "Quantifying the Economic Benefits of Effective Redress: Large E-Commerce Data Sets and the Cost-Benefit Case for Investing in Dispute Resolution." 34 *University of Arkansas at Little Rock Law Review* 767 (2012).

Rule, Colin, and Mark Wilson. "Online Resolution and Citizen Empowerment: Property Tax Appeals in North America." In *Revolutionizing the Interaction between State and Citizens through Digital Communications,* edited by Sam B. Edwards III and Diogo Santos, 185. Information Resources Management Association, 2015.

Sandefur, Rebecca L. "The Fulcrum Point of Equal Access to Justice: Legal and Non-Legal Institutions of Remedy." 42 *Loyola of Los Angeles Law Review* 949 (2009).

Sander, Frank E. A. "Varieties of Dispute Processing." In *The Pound Conference: Perspectives on Justice in the Future,* edited by A. Levin and R. Wheelers. West, 1979.

Sander, Frank E. A., and Stephen B. Goldberg. "Fitting the Forum to the Fuss: A User-Friendly Guide to Selecting an ADR Procedure." 10 *Negotiation Journal* 49 (1994).

Scaturo, Tenesa S. "The Anti-Cybersquatting Consumer Protection Act and the Uniform Domain Name Dispute Resolution Policy, The First Decade: Looking Back and Adapting Forward." 11 *Nevada Law Journal* 877 (2011).

Schmitz, Amy J. "American Exceptionalism in Consumer Arbitration." 10 *Loyola University Chicago International Law Review* 81 (2016).

Schmitz, Amy J. "Legislating in the Light: Considering Empirical Data in Crafting Arbitration Reforms." 15 *Harvard Negotiation Law Review* 115 (2010).

Schmitz, Amy J. "Secret Consumer Scores and Segmentations: Separating 'Haves' from 'Have-Nots.'" 2014 *Michigan State Law Review* 1411 (2014).

Schmitz, Amy J., and Colin Rule. *The New Handshake: Online Dispute Resolution and the Future of Consumer Protection.* (2017).

Schneider, Andrea K. "Building a Pedagogy of Problem-Solving: Learning to Choose among ADR Processes." 5 *Harvard Negotiation Law Review* 113 (2000).

Schneier, Bruce. *Data and Goliath: The Hidden Battles to Collect Your Data and Control Your World.* New York: W. W. Norton & Company, 2015.

Schneier, Bruce. *Liars and Outliers: Enabling the Trust that Society Needs to Thrive.* New York: John Wiley, 2012.

Schuck, Peter. *The Limits of the Law.* Boulder, CO: Westview Press, 2000.

Schwab, Klaus. *The Fourth Industrial Revolution.* World Economic Forum, 2016.

Searls, Doc. *The Intention Economy: When Customers Take Charge.* Cambridge, MA: Harvard Business Review Press, 2012.

Searls, Doc, and David Weinberger. *New Clues.* 2015.

Senger, Jeffrey. *Federal Dispute Resolution Using ADR with the United States Government.* San Francisco: Jossey-Bass, 2003.

Shah, Rajiv C., and Jay P. Kesan. "Fool Us Once Shame on You—Fool Us Twice Shame on Us: What We Can Learn from the Privatizations of the Internet Backbone Network and the Domain Name System." 79 *Washington University Law Quarterly* 89 (2001).

Shirky, Clay. *Cognitive Surplus: How Technology Makes Consumers into Collaborators* New York: Penguin Books, 2009.

Shirky, Clay. *Here Comes Everybody: The Power of Organizing without Organizations.* New York: Penguin Books, 2008.

Simshaw, Drew, Nicolas Terry, Kris Hauser and M.L. Cummings, "Regulating Healthcare Robots: Maximizing Opportunities While Minimizing Risks." 22 *Richmond Journal of Law and Technology* 3 (2016).

Silbey, Susan S., and Sally E. Merry. "Mediator Settlement Strategies." 8 *Law and Policy* 7 (1986).

Slaikeu, Karl A. "Designing Dispute Resolution Systems in the Health Care Industry." 5 *Negotiation Journal* 395 (1989).

Slee, Tom. *What's Yours Is Mine* New York: OR Books, 2015.

Sourdin, Tania, and Archie Zariski. *The Multi-Tasking Judge Comparative Judicial Dispute Resolution.* Thomson Reuters Australia, 2013.

Starfield, Barbara. "Is US Health Really the Best in the World?" 284 *Journal of the American Medical Association* 483 (July 26, 2000).

Staroselsky, Maria, Lynn A. Volk, Ruslana Tsurikova, Lisa P. Newmark, Margaret Lippincott, Irina Litvak, Anne Kittler, Tiffany Wang, Jonathan Wald, and David W. Bates. "An Effort to Improve Electronic Health Record Medication List Accuracy between Visits: Patients' and Physicians' Response." 77 *International Journal of Medical Informatics* 153 (March 2008).

Starr, Paul. *The Social Transformation of American Medicine.* New York: Basic Books, 1983.

Staudt, Ronald W. "All the Wild Possibilities: Technology That Attacks Barriers to Access to Justice." 42 *Loyola Law Review* 1117 (2009).

Stoll, Clifford. *The Cuckoo's Egg: Inside the World of Computer Espionage.* New York: Simon and Schuster, 1989.

Sundararajan, Arun. *The Sharing Economy: The End of Employment and the Rise of Crowd-Based Capitalism.* Cambridge, MA: MIT Press, 2016.

Susskind, Richard E. *The Future of Law.* New York: Oxford University Press, 2008.

Susskind, Richard E. *Tomorrow's Lawyers: An Introduction to Your Future.* Oxford: Oxford University Press, 2013.

Susskind, Richard E., and Daniel Susskind. *The Future of the Professions: How Technology Will Transform the Work of Human Experts.* Oxford: Oxford University Press, 2015.

Swan, Melanie. *Blockchain: Blueprint for a New Economy.* Cambridge, MA: O'Reilly Media, 2015.

Tapscott, Don, and Alex Tapscott. *Blockchain Revolution: How the Technology Behind Bitcoin Is Changing Money, Business, and the World.* Portfolio, 2016.

Terrell, Timothy P. "Flatlaw: An Essay on the Dimensions of Legal Reasoning and the Development of Fundamental Normative Principles," 72 *Cal. L. Rev.* 288 (1984).

Terry, Nicolas. "Will the Internet of Things Disrupt Healthcare?" Indiana University Robert H. McKinney School of Law Research Paper No. 2016-21 (2016).

Thiessen, Ernest M., and Joseph P. McMahon. "Beyond Win-Win in Cyberspace." 15 *Ohio State Journal on Dispute Resolution* 643 (2000).

Thomas, Jude A. "Fifteen Years of Fame: The Declining Relevance of Domain Names in the Enduring Conflict between Trademark and Free Speech Rights." 11 *John Marshall Review of Intellectual Property Law* 1 (2011).

Thompson, Darin. "Dispute Prevention and Management in Online Dispute Resolution Systems" (2016) (on file with authors).

Topol, Eric. *The Patient Will See You Now: The Future of Medicine Is in Your Hands.* New York: Basic Books, 2015.

Tufte, Edward. *Envisioning Information.* Chester, CT: Graphics Press, 1990.

Turkle, Sherry. *Alone Together: Why We Expect More from Technology and Less from Each Other.* New York: Basic Books, 2012.

Turkle, Sherry. *Life on the Screen: Identity in the Age of the Internet.* New York: Simon & Schuster, 1995.

Turkle, Sherry. *Reclaiming Conversation: The Power of Talk in a Digital Age.* New York: Penguin Press, 2015.

Tyler, Tom R. *Psychology and the Design of Legal Institutions.* United States: Wolf Legal Publishers, 2007.

Ury, William L., Jeanne M. Brett, and Stephen B. Goldberg. *Getting Disputes Resolved: Designing Systems to Cut the Costs of Conflict.* San Francisco: Jossey-Bass Inc., 1988.

Varkey, P., Cunningham, J., and Bisping, S. "National Patient Safety Goals. Improving Medication Reconciliation in the Outpatient Setting." 33 *Joint Commission Journal on Quality and Patient Safety* 286 (May 2007).

Vermeys, Nicolas W., and Karim Benyekhlef. "ODR and the Courts." In *Online Dispute Resolution: Theory and Practice* edited by M. S. Wahab, E. Katsh, and D. Rainey. The Hague: Eleven International Publishing, 2012.

Vickrey, William C., Joseph L. Dunn, and Clark Kelso. "Access to Justice: A Broader Perspective." 42 *Loyola of Los Angeles Law Review* 1147 (2009).

Vigna, Paul, and Michael Casey. *The Age of Cryptocurrency: How Bitcoin and Digital Money Are Challenging the Global Economic Order.* New York: St. Martin's Press, 2015.

Wahab, Mohamed, Ethan Katsh, and Daniel Rainey. *Online Dispute Resolution: Theory and Practice.* The Hague: Eleven International Publishing, 2012.

Warren, Rossalyn. *Targeted and Trolled: The Reality of Being a Woman Online.* Amazon Digital Services, 2013.

Weinberger, David. *Everything Is Miscellaneous: The Power of the New Digital Disorder.* New York: Times Books, 2007.

Weingart, S. N., A. Cleary, A. Seger, T. K. Eng, M. Saadeh, A. Gross, and L. N. Shulman. "Medication Reconciliation in Ambulatory Oncology." 33 *Joint Commission Journal on Quality and Patient Safety* 750 (December 2007).

Welsh, Nancy A. "The Current Transitional State of Court-Connected ADR." 95 *Marquette Law Review* 873 (2012).

Welsh, Nancy, Donna Stienestra, and Bobby McAdoo. "The Application of Procedural Justice Research to Judicial Actions and Techniques in Settlement Sessions." In *The Multi-Tasking Judge Comparative Judicial Dispute Resolution*, edited by Tania Sourdin and Archie Zariski. Thomson Reuters Australia, 2013.

White, Lu Ann E., Marie A. Krousel-Wood, and Fran Mather. "Technology Meets Healthcare: Distance Learning and Telehealth." 3 *The Ochsner Journal* 22 (January 2001).

Wilborn, S. Elizabeth. "Revisiting the Public/Private Distinction: Employee Monitoring in the Workplace." 32 *Georgia Law Review* 825 (1997).

Winick, Bruce J. "Therapeutic Jurisprudence and Problem-Solving Courts." 30 *Fordham Urban Law Journal* 1055 (2003).

Wu, Tim. *The Master Switch: The Rise and Fall of Information Empires.* New York: Knopf, 2010.

Yeazell, Stephen C. "Courting Ignorance: Why We Know So Little about Our Most Important Courts." 143 *Daedalus* 129 (July 2014).

Zarsky, Tal Z. "Automated Prediction: Perception, Law, and Policy." 55 *Communications of the ACM* 33 (2012).

Zarsky, Tal. "Understanding Discrimination in the Scored Society." *Washington Law Review* 89, no. 4 (2014).

Zarsky, Tal Z. "The Trouble with Algorithmic Decisions: An Analytic Road Map to Examine Efficiency and Fairness in Automated and Opaque Decision Making." 41 *Science, Technology & Human Values* 118 (2016).

Zarsky, Tal Z. "Correlation vs. Causation in Health-Related Big Data Analysis: The Role of Reason and Regulation" (2016) (on file with the authors)

Zielinski, Krzysztof, Mariusz Duplaga, and David Ingram. *Information Technology Solutions for Healthcare.* New York: Springer-Verlag, 2006.

Zittrain, Jonathan. "Apple's Emoji Gun Control." *New York Times* (August 16, 2016). <http://www.nytimes.com/2016/08/16/opinion/get-out-of-gun-control-apple.html>.

Zittrain, Jonathan. *The Future of the Internet and What We Can Do about It.* New Haven: Yale University Press, 2008.

Zittrain, Jonathan. "A History of Online Gatekeeping." 19 *Harvard Journal of Law & Technology* 253 (2006).

Zittrain, Jonathan. "The Rise and Fall of Sysopdom." 10 *Harvard Journal of Law & Technology* 495 (1997).

Zuboff, Shoshana. *The Age of the Smart Machine.* New York: Basic Books, 1989.

Zuckerman, Ethan. *Digital Cosmopolitans: Why We Think the Internet Connects Us, Why It Doesn't, and How to Rewire It.* New York: W. W. Norton & Company, 2014.

INDEX

CPSIA information can be obtained
at www.ICGtesting.com
Printed in the USA
BVOW09s2313241017
498599BV00003B/10/P